Moral Theory

Elements of Philosophy
Series Editor: Robert Audi, University of Nebraska, Lincoln

The Elements of Philosophy series aims to produce core introductory texts and readers in the major areas of philosophy, among them metaphysics, epistemology, ethics and moral theory, philosophy of religion, philosophy of mind, feminist philosophy, and social and political philosophy. Books in the series are written for an undergraduate audience of second- through fourth-year students and serve as the perfect cornerstone for understanding the various elements of philosophy.

Moral Theory: An Introduction (2002) by Mark Timmons

Forthcoming books in the series:

Epistemology by Laurence BonJour
Philosophy of the Mind by Louise Antony and Joseph Levine

Moral Theory

An Introduction

MARK TIMMONS

ROWMAN & LITTLEFIELD PUBLISHERS, INC.
Lanham • Boulder • New York • Toronto • Oxford

ROWMAN & LITTLEFIELD PUBLISHERS, INC.

Published in the United States of America
by Rowman & Littlefield Publishers, Inc.
A wholly owned subsidiary of The Rowman & Littlefield Publishing Group, Inc.
4501 Forbes Boulevard, Suite 200, Lanham, Maryland 20706
www.rowmanlittlefield.com

PO Box 317
Oxford
OX2 9RU, UK

British Library Cataloguing in Publication Information Available

Library of Congress Cataloging-in-Publication Data

Timmons, Mark, 1951–
    Moral theory : an introduction / Mark Timmons
        p.   cm.—(Elements in philosophy)
    Includes bibliographical references and index.
    ISBN-13: 978-0-8476-9768-7 (alk. paper)
    ISBN-10: 0-8476-9768-1 (alk. paper)
    ISBN-13: 978-0-8476-9769-4 (pbk. : alk. paper)
    ISBN-10: 0-8476-9769-X (pbk. : alk. paper)
        1. Ethics.   I. Title   II. Series.

BJ1012.T56   2002
171—dc21   2001049239

1006332284

Printed in the United States of America

∞™The paper used in this publication meets the minimum requirements of American
National Standard for Information Sciences—Permanence of Paper for Printed Library
Materials, ANSI/NISO Z39.48–1992.

To my students over the years

Contents

Preface

This book is essentially a survey of various moral theories including the divine command theory, moral relativism, natural law theory, utilitarianism, Kant's moral theory, moral pluralism, virtue ethics, and moral particularism. The nine chapters that discuss these theories are preceded by an introduction whose purpose is to expose readers to some basic concepts and ideas common to all or most of the theories featured in the rest of the book. The conclusion ties together certain general themes that emerge from the study of the various theories.

My main goal in writing this book is to provide an intermediate-level introduction to moral theory. I have tried to go beyond many introductory ethics texts by delving into some of the complexity involved in debates within and about moral theories. But I have also tried to refrain from too much complexity, as is evident from the many places throughout the text where I cut off discussion of some issue by leaving it for readers to ponder on their own. This text, then, is written for those individuals who are ready for something more challenging than an elementary treatment of the questions and issues that come up in moral theory but who are not yet ready to tackle advanced research in ethics.

For the most part, the contents of the chapters are based on my lectures delivered over a number of years in upper-level undergraduate courses in ethics. My presentation of the ideas and arguments in the chapters to follow has been "classroom tested," so to speak. Over the years, and mainly as a result of student input, I have made many adjustments and changes to my course lectures, resulting in many improvements. I wish to thank those many students I have taught at Illinois State University, the University of Memphis, and the Katholischen Universität Eichstätt for their comments and questions that helped me improve my course on moral theory.

I received a Professional Development Assignment from the University of Memphis that released me from teaching responsibilities during fall semester 2000 and enabled me to make substantial progress on this book.

While writing this book, I received useful written comments on various chapters from Paul Bloomfield, Josh Glasgow, Mitch Haney, Nelson Potter, and David Shoemaker. I benefited greatly from e-mail discussions with Brad Hooker about various topics in moral theory as well as his comments on the chapters I sent him. In writing chapter 10, I benefited from weekly meetings of the fall semester 2000 moral particularism reading group, which included Jenny Case, David Henderson, Terry Horgan, Matjaž Potrč, John Tienson, and Debbie Zeller. I also had many useful conversations with my colleagues Terry Horgan, Tim Roche, and John Tienson about various topics covered in the pages to follow. My deepest thanks to all these philosophers for their help.

I am especially grateful to Robert Audi, the series editor for the Rowman & Littlefield series in which this book appears, for his encouragement and support and for his comments on certain parts of the book.

I wish to thank Eve DeVaro, associate editor at Rowman & Littlefield, for her help in guiding this book through the production process. And I wish to thank Cheryl Hoffman for her fine editorial advice.

1

An Introduction to Moral Theory

What makes an act right or wrong? What is it about individuals that makes them morally good or bad? How can we come to correct conclusions about the morality of what we ought to do and what sorts of persons we ought to be? Moral theory attempts to provide systematic answers to these very general moral questions about what to do and how to be. Because moral theorists have given different answers to these questions, we find a variety of competing moral theories. This book contains a survey of some of the most important moral theories—theories that are of both historical and contemporary interest.

But what is a moral theory? What does such a theory attempt to accomplish? What are the central concepts that such theories make use of? Furthermore, how can a moral theory be evaluated?

This chapter is an introduction to moral theory; it will address these and related questions and thus prepare readers for the chapters that follow. The kinds of general moral questions that are of concern in moral theory, and the apparent need for such theory, are easily raised by reflecting on disputed moral questions including, for example, questions about the morality of suicide.

1. A Sample Moral Controversy: Suicide

In 1997, the state of Oregon's Death with Dignity Act took effect, allowing physicians to assist patients in ending their own lives. From 1997 to 2000, forty-three people made use of the act in committing suicide. This unprecedented statute permitting physician–assisted suicide provoked highly charged debates about the legality and morality of this practice. The most significant legal response to Oregon's act came in 1999 when the U.S. House of Representatives passed the Pain Relief Promotion Act, intended

to promote pain control in patients but also prohibiting the use of con-
trolled substances for purposes of causing death or assisting another person
in causing death. This act effectively overturned the Oregon statute. There
are many other interesting legal issues that these two acts raise, but our concern is with the moral controversy that the Oregon act stirred.[1]

The moral debate over physician-assisted suicide concerns the larger
issue of the morality of suicide, and moral arguments both for and against
the Death with Dignity Act often depend on moral claims about suicide.
Those who think that there is nothing necessarily wrong with suicide often
argue that deciding to end one's own life is consistent with the dignity that
is inherent in every individual. Thus, according to this line of reasoning,
choosing to end one's life when continued existence threatens one's dignity is morally permissible. Those opposed to suicide on moral grounds
sometimes argue that God has dominion over our bodies and so the choice
between life and death belongs to him.[2] Another commonly voiced argument against suicide is that this kind of act is wrong because allowing it
would inevitably lead to bad consequences such as the killing of terminally ill patients against their will.

The moral controversy over suicide generally, and physician-assisted suicide in particular, is but one of a number of moral controversies including
abortion, treatment of animals, capital punishment, sexuality, privacy, gun
control, drugs, and discrimination. Debate about these issues focuses on
reasons for holding one or another moral viewpoint about them. As just
noted, appeal to the idea of human dignity has sometimes been offered as
a reason in support of the claim that suicide is not necessarily morally
wrong, while we find that appeals to the will of God and to the alleged bad
consequences of allowing suicide are sometimes used to argue that suicide
is morally wrong. Giving reasons like this for some claim that one wants to
establish is what philosophers call giving an argument for the claim. So
moral debates like the one over the morality of suicide feature arguments
on both sides of the issue.

To understand and evaluate such arguments, three main tasks must be
undertaken. First, there is the *conceptual* task of clarifying important concepts such as that of human dignity. What are we talking about when we
make claims about human dignity? In what does one's dignity consist? Unless we have an answer to this question, we will not really understand moral
arguments that make use of this concept.

A second main task in understanding moral arguments requires that we
evaluate various claims being made in the sorts of arguments mentioned
above. Is it true that suicide is against God's will? Is it true that allowing suicide would lead to bad social consequences? Is it true that suicide is consistent with human dignity? These claims are controversial and require examination.

A third main task concerning moral arguments involves *evaluating basic moral assumptions* that are often unstated in the giving of such arguments. For instance, when someone argues that suicide is wrong because it is contrary to God's will, the unstated assumption is that if an action is contrary to God's will, then it is wrong. Is this assumption correct? Again, the claim that suicide is wrong because it would have bad consequences assumes that if an action would have bad consequences, then it is wrong. Is this assumption correct?

Such moral assumptions often express ideas about what makes an action right or wrong, and hence about the nature of such actions. And questions about the nature of right and wrong, as well as about the nature of good and bad, are central in the study of moral theory. And in this way, reflection on ordinary moral debate and discussion, featuring moral arguments, leads us to the kinds of questions that a moral theory attempts to answer.

In order to explain more fully the project of moral theory, we need to consider (1) the main aims of moral theory, (2) the role of moral principles within a moral theory, (3) the main categories of moral evaluation, (4) the structure of such theories, and finally (5) questions about the evaluation of moral theories. These topics will occupy us in the next five sections of this chapter.

2. The Aims of Moral Theory

It will help in trying to understand what a moral theory is all about if we consider the main aims of moral theory—what such a theory is out to accomplish. There are two fundamental aims of moral theory: one practical, the other theoretical.

The practical aim of moral theory has to do with the desire to have some method to follow when, for example, we reason about what is right or wrong. Scientists employ scientific methodology in arriving at scientific conclusions about various phenomena under investigation, and such methodology provides a means of resolving scientific disputes. Similarly, we might hope to discover a proper moral methodology—a *decision procedure*, as it is often referred to by moral philosophers—that could be employed in moral thinking and debate and which would help to resolve moral conflicts.

We can summarize the practical aim this way:

Practical aim. The main practical aim of a moral theory is to discover a decision procedure that can be used to guide correct moral reasoning about matters of moral concern.

The theoretical aim of moral theory has to do with coming to understand the underlying nature of right and wrong, good and bad. When someone claims that an action is morally wrong, it makes sense to ask them why they think the action in question is wrong. We thus assume that when an action is morally right or wrong, there is something about the action that makes it right or wrong. (A similar point can be made in relation to claims about the goodness and badness of persons. But for simplicity's sake, let us just focus for the moment on questions about the rightness and wrongness of actions.)

To explain further, consider an analogy. What makes a liquid *water* (as opposed to ammonia or some other liquid) is its chemical composition. Underlying all bodies of water—big and small—is the fact that the liquid in question is composed of an appropriate number of molecules of hydrogen and oxygen. The fact that some liquid is H_2O is what makes it water. Something analogous might well be true about morality. We assume that when an action is right or wrong, there is something about the action that makes it right or wrong. Moreover, it is natural to wonder whether there might be some fixed set of underlying features of actions that make them right or wrong. Perhaps there is one such underlying feature, but perhaps there is more than one. Then again, we may find that although the rightness or wrongness of actions depends on certain underlying features of actions, such features vary so much from case to case that there is no fixed set of underlying features to be discovered.

The theoretical aim of moral theory, then, is to explore the underlying nature of right and wrong action in order to be able to explain what it is about an action that makes it right or wrong. If we suppose that there is some fixed set of underlying features that make an action right or wrong, they will function as standards, or *moral criteria*, of right and wrong action. Similar remarks apply to matters of good and bad: part of the theoretical aim of a moral theory is to discover what it is about persons that makes them good or bad.

We can express the main theoretical aim this way:

Theoretical aim. The main theoretical aim of moral theory is to discover those underlying features of actions, persons, and other items of moral evaluation that make them right or wrong, good or bad.

The practical and theoretical aims of moral theory are commonly thought to be related to one another in that satisfying one is either required for, or at least the best way of, satisfying the other. To explain this point and to deepen our understanding of the main aims of moral theory, let us consider the role of moral principles in moral theory.

3. Moral Principles and Their Role in Moral Theory

In the field of ethics, *moral principles* are to be understood as very general moral statements that purport to set forth conditions under which an action is right or wrong or something is good or bad.[3]

Here is a sample moral principle:

> An action is right if and only if the action does not interfere with the well-being of those individuals who are likely to be affected by the action.

For present purposes, we need not worry about what counts as interfering with the well-being of individuals, or whether the principle is true. The thing to notice about this principle is that it asserts a connection between an action's being right and its not interfering with the well-being of certain individuals. We were just noting that a moral theory has both a practical and a theoretical aim. Moral principles have traditionally played a central role in attempts by moral philosophers to accomplish both of these aims. Let us see how.

In attempting to satisfy the practical aim of providing a decision procedure for correct moral reasoning, moral philosophers have often been guided by the idea that such reasoning must be based on moral principles. Here is a simple example.

Suppose Brittany claims that it would be wrong for her to lie about her job experience on a job application, even when she is reasonably certain that a lie about this matter would not be found out. Suppose further that she is asked to give her reasons for thinking this, and, being a reflective person, she responds by pointing out that her lying in these circumstances might well negatively affect the chances of other applicants' getting the job and thereby interfere with the well-being of others. And so we imagine her attempting to justify the claim that her lying would be wrong by appealing to the sample moral principle stated above. Brittany's line of reasoning could be set out as follows.

> *Moral principle:* An action is right if and only if the action does not interfere with the well-being of those individuals who are likely to be affected by the action.

> *Factual claim:* The act of lying on a job application would interfere with the well-being of those individuals who will be affected by the action.

> *Conclusion:* The act of lying on a job application is not right (and hence is wrong).

The point I am making with this example is simply that the practical aim of providing a decision procedure for arriving at justified moral verdicts about actions (and other items of moral concern) has often been supposed to be a matter of reasoning from moral principles to conclusions about actions (and other items of moral concern). Understood as a decision procedure, then, a moral principle guides proper moral reasoning by indicating those features of actions whose recognition can guide one to well-reasoned verdicts about the morality of actions.

Of course, not any old moral principles will serve to satisfy this practical aim. In order to provide a decision procedure to guide *correct* moral reasoning, the moral principles used must themselves be correct. And this brings us to the theoretical aim of moral theory and the role of principles in achieving this aim.

In attempting to satisfy the theoretical aim of explaining what makes an action right or wrong or what makes something good or bad, moral philosophers have typically sought to formulate moral principles that express this information. In fulfilling this theoretical aim, then, a moral principle concerned with right and wrong action can be understood as indicating those most basic features of actions that make them right or wrong. According to our example principle, it is facts about how an action would affect the well-being of a certain group of individuals that are supposed to explain what makes an action right or wrong.

Moreover, moral principles that serve to explain what makes actions right or wrong will thus *unify* morality by revealing those basic features that determine in general an action's rightness or wrongness. (Similar remarks apply to principles of goodness and badness.) Finding the underlying unity behind the diversity of moral phenomena has thus been an aim of traditional moral theory—an aim that can supposedly be achieved by discovering moral principles that satisfy the main theoretical aim of moral theory.[4]

So moral principles are often cast by moral theorists in a dual role. In light of the theoretical aim of moral theory, these principles purport to express those underlying features in virtue of which an action, person, or other item of moral evaluation has the moral quality it has. In this way, moral principles aim to *unify* morality—revealing to us the underlying nature of right and wrong, good and bad. In light of the practical aim of moral theory, such principles are also supposed to provide a decision procedure for engaging in correct moral reasoning.

Let us return for a moment to the issue of the morality of suicide. A correct set of moral principles functioning as moral criteria would enable us to understand what makes an action of suicide right or wrong, thus giving us insight into the moral nature of such action. A correct set of moral principles functioning as a decision procedure would provide us the means for reasoning our way to correct moral verdicts about the morality of suicide.

As we shall see in later chapters, some philosophers deny the claim that a moral principle that satisfies the theoretical aim must also satisfy the practical aim. Moreover, some moral philosophers deny altogether the idea that there can be moral principles of the sort featured in most moral theories and thus deny that morality can be unified in the manner just explained. (The reader should therefore keep in mind that my introductory remarks are meant to capture traditional assumptions about moral theory and the roles of principles in any such theory, but that such assumptions have been challenged.)

Earlier, we noted that moral theory concerns questions about the morality of actions (what to do) as well as the morality of persons (how to be). And I have been saying that traditional moral theories are primarily in the business of formulating and defending principles about the morality of actions and of persons. Having explained the two main aims of moral theory and the role of principles in satisfying those aims, let us take a closer look at some of the basic categories of moral evaluation.

4. Some Basic Moral Categories

The concepts of right and wrong and good and bad are central in moral thinking; thus in theorizing about morality it will be useful to consider some of these concepts and the categories that they pick out. Since a concept picks out a category of things, let us consider the categories that are picked out by basic moral concepts. There are two main divisions of moral categories to consider: the deontic categories and the value categories.

The Categories of Deontic Evaluation

The term "deontic" is from the Greek word *deon*, which means duty. The categories of deontic evaluation are used primarily to evaluate the morality of actions—their rightness and wrongness. There are three basic deontic categories (which I will also call categories of right action): the *obligatory*, the *wrong*, and the *optional*. Let us briefly consider each one in turn.

> *Obligatory actions.* An obligatory action is one that one morally ought to do. Typically, we refer to actions that are obligatory as *duties*. Other terms used for this category include "required" and "right." (Use of the term "right" requires special comment. See below.)

> *Wrong actions.* A wrong action is one that morally ought not to be done. Other terms often used for this category include "forbidden," "impermissible," and "contrary to duty."

Optional actions. An action is morally optional when it is neither obligatory nor wrong—one is morally permitted to perform the action, but
need not. Sometimes actions in this category are referred to as "merely
permissible" ("merely," because unlike obligatory actions, which are permitted, they are not also required).

These characterizations are not meant to be illuminating definitions
that would help someone come to understand them. To be told that an
obligatory action is one that *ought* to be done is hardly illuminating. However, the brief remarks made about each category are, I think, still useful
for conveying an intuitive sense of the main categories of deontic evaluation.

What about the category of the right? Talk of right action has both a
narrow and a broad meaning. When it is used narrowly, it refers to the category of the obligatory, as when we say she did *the* right act (meaning she
did what she morally ought to have done). When the term is used broadly,
right action is the opposite of wrong action: an action is right, in the broad
sense of the term, when it is not wrong. For instance, to say of someone
that what she did was right often conveys the idea that her act was morally in the clear—that it was all right for her to do, that what she did was not
wrong. Since actions that are not wrong include the categories of both the
obligatory and the optional, talk of right action (in the broad sense) covers
both of these categories.

Figure 1.1 summarizes what I have been saying, where "right" is used in
its broad sense to mean simply "not wrong." In the chapters that follow,
when I want to refer to the species of moral evaluation that we are now
considering, I will speak indifferently about the *deontic status* of an action
and of the *rightness* or *wrongness* of an action. These expressions are to be
understood as shorthand for referring to an action's being either obligatory, optional, or wrong.

The Categories of Value

To speak of the value of something is to speak of its being either good
or bad, or neither good nor bad (some things have no value, positive or
negative). I have already mentioned that one concern of moral theory is
with answering the question of what makes an individual a good or bad
person. Goodness or badness of persons is not the only kind of value that
is of concern to moral theory, as I will explain shortly. But let us begin to
clarify the categories of the good and the bad by distinguishing between
things with intrinsic value and things with extrinsic value.

To say that something has intrinsic value—that it is intrinsically
good—is to say that there is something about *it* that makes it good in itself. In other words, its goodness is grounded on something that is inter-

Figure 1.1 Basic Deontic Categories

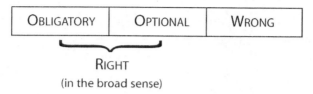

nal to that thing. By contrast, to say that something is extrinsically good is to say that it possesses goodness because of how it is related to something else that is good. Here is an example. Many people would agree that money is a good thing. But what is the source of its goodness? It seems pretty clear that the goodness of money is not somehow internal to the pieces of paper and bits of metal that compose it. Rather, what makes money good has to do with how it is related to other things that have value. Money's goodness has to do with its enabling its possessor to purchase things and services that are themselves good. So, its goodness is borrowed, so to speak, from being related to other things that are good. Its goodness, we say, is *extrinsic*.

Obviously, for something to be extrinsically good, there must be something else to which that thing is related and which is good. But if this other thing is only extrinsically good, its goodness is also borrowed. Since not all goodness can be borrowed in this way, it would seem that there must be some things whose goodness is intrinsic. In short, for something A to be extrinsically good in some way, there must be something B (to which it is related) such that B is intrinsically good and is the ultimate source of the goodness that is possessed by A. So the concept of intrinsic goodness is more basic than the concept of extrinsic goodness, and the same goes for the concepts of intrinsic and extrinsic badness.

Theories about the nature of value are, therefore, theories about the nature of intrinsic value. And here again we find that there are three basic categories (see fig. 1.2). In addition to the categories of the intrinsically good (or valuable) and the intrinsically bad (or disvaluable), there is the category of what we may call the *intrinsically value-neutral*. This third category comprises all those things that are neither intrinsically good nor intrinsically bad (though such things may have either positive or negative extrinsic value).

Figure 1.2 Basic Categories of Value

INTRINSICALLY GOOD	INTRINSICALLY VALUE-NEUTRAL	INTRINSICALLY BAD

Moral Value and Nonmoral Value

When philosophers speak of something having *moral value* or *moral worth* (these expressions are used interchangeably), they are typically referring to persons. This is because talk of moral value or worth is used in connection with objects of evaluation regarding which it makes sense to morally praise or blame them for how they are and what they do. The sorts of things regarding which such praise and blame are appropriate are things that are responsible for who they are and what they do. Hence, persons are the sorts of things that qualify for being either morally good or morally bad because they can be held responsible for who they are and what they do.

But many moral theories, in explaining what makes an action right or wrong, appeal to things, experiences, and states of affairs that are taken to have intrinsic value. For instance, according to the classical utilitarian moral theory (which we examine in chapter 5), the deontic status of an action (its rightness or wrongness) depends on how much intrinsic value the action would produce, where what is intrinsically valuable or good on this theory is happiness. Happiness is something that persons may (or may not) possess, but the state of being happy and the pleasant experiences that happiness involves are not themselves responsible agents. And so when it is said that happiness is intrinsically good (as some philosophers hold), the sort of goodness being ascribed to happiness is appropriately called "nonmoral" goodness. It has this label, not because the goodness of happiness is morally irrelevant—it is morally relevant in determining the deontic status of actions, at least according to some moral theories—but, as I hope I have made clear, because things other than persons that are intrinsically good are not responsible agents, and it is only responsible agents that are candidates for being *morally* good or bad.

For the time being, the essential thing to understand here is simply that we evaluate persons as being morally good or bad, and we also evaluate things other than persons as being good or bad. *Moral* value (positive and negative) is something only agents can possess; other things (including experiences and states of affairs in the world) may have *nonmoral* value (positive and negative).

5. Moral Theory and Its Structure

What I wish to do in this section is fill out a bit my introduction to moral theory by explaining what is meant by referring to the "structure" of a moral theory. In doing so, I will make use of some of the distinctions we have been noting.

In light of the fact that a moral theory aims to answer very general questions about what makes actions right or wrong and what makes persons (as

Figure 1.3 Components of Moral Theory

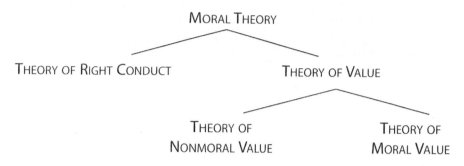

well as items of nonmoral value) good or bad, we may divide such a theory into two main branches. Let us say that in giving an account of the nature of right and wrong action, a moral theory is giving us a *theory of right conduct.* And let us say that in giving an account of the nature of intrinsic value, a moral theory is giving us a *theory of value.* Since we have distinguished between moral value and nonmoral value, we have two branches relating to theory of value generally. Figure 1.3 shows the various subtheories that compose a moral theory.

One question for moral theory is how it is internally organized. How are considerations of right conduct related to considerations of value? Answers to such questions concern the *structure* of a moral theory—how the various subtheories within a moral theory are related.

In giving accounts of the nature of right action and of value (both moral and nonmoral), moral theories organize and relate the various categories of moral appraisal. For instance, in some moral theories, the concepts (and related categories) of value are more basic than the deontic concepts (and related categories). In such theories, the principles of right conduct define or characterize right and wrong action in terms of what has value. The classical utilitarian moral theory, for example, begins with an account of intrinsic value according to which it is happiness that has such value. Then, the theory specifies that an action is right if and only if it produces the greatest amount of what has intrinsic value, namely, happiness. Thus the utilitarian theory attempts to explain the nature of right and wrong action in terms of what has intrinsic value. Considerations of intrinsic value, for this theory, are most basic, and an account of the nature of right and wrong action rests on such considerations. In connection with such theories the idea of a structure becomes clear: facts about what has intrinsic value are the basis, or foundation, and the rest of the theory is built up from this foundation.

Other moral theories differ in structure from those that make value most basic. This is not the place to examine possible structures for a moral theory; these structures will be explained as needed in the chapters to come.

Before going further, let us pause a moment to review some of what we have learned about moral theory. The main points are these:

- The moral evaluation of actions concerns their deontic status—their rightness and wrongness. One task of moral theory is to investigate the nature of right and wrong action.

- The moral evaluation of persons concerns their moral goodness and badness—their moral value or worth. And so another task of moral theory is to investigate the nature of moral value.

- Because some moral theories make the deontic status of actions depend on considerations having to do with the value of things other than persons, an additional task for such theories is to investigate the nature of nonmoral value.

- The structure of moral theory is determined by how it relates the various branches of moral theory (and the categories these branches contain).

- In giving accounts of the nature of right and wrong, good and bad, a moral theory aims to discover principles of right and wrong and good and bad that will provide (if possible) both a unified theoretical account of the nature of such things and a decision procedure that can be used to reason correctly about matters of morality.

This concludes my introductory remarks about moral theory. Readers who are encountering moral theory for the first time may find some of what has been presented a bit much to absorb completely in one reading. However, as the book proceeds, the points I have been making will be illustrated by the theories we examine; this should help deepen the reader's understanding of the elements of a moral theory.

In the remainder of this chapter, I will briefly explain how to evaluate a moral theory and then make some general remarks about the field of ethics. I will conclude with a brief summary of the chapters to come.

6. Evaluating Moral Theories

In this section, I wish to convey some idea of how one is to go about evaluating a moral theory. I recommend using this section for reference when, toward the end of each chapter, we turn to an evaluation of the theory being featured in the chapter. (I will prompt the reader to do so at relevant places in the text, and for quick reference, I have listed in the appendix the standards for evaluating a moral theory.)

Since a moral theory has the practical aim of providing a decision procedure for making correct moral judgments as well as the theoretical aim of providing moral criteria that explain the underlying nature of morality, it makes sense to evaluate a moral theory according to how well it satisfies these two aims. Here, then, is a list of six desiderata—six characteristics that it is ideally desirable for a moral theory to possess if it is to accomplish the practical and theoretical aims just mentioned.

Consistency

A moral theory should specify principles whose application yields consistent moral verdicts about whatever is being morally evaluated. One blatant way in which a moral theory might fail to be consistent is when its principles (together with relevant factual information) imply that some particular concrete action is both right and wrong. For example, if the principles of some theory were to imply that a particular instance of lying is both obligatory and not obligatory, it would fail the consistency standard.[5]

So, according to the *consistency standard*:

> A moral theory should be consistent in the sense that its principles, together with relevant factual information, yield consistent moral verdicts about the morality of actions, persons, and other objects of moral evaluation.

The rationale for this standard can be easily explained by reference to the practical and theoretical aims of moral theory. Any moral theory that fails to yield consistent moral verdicts in a range of cases will fail (at least in those cases) to supply a decision procedure of the sort desired. To be told that some action is both obligatory and not obligatory is of no use in deciding what to do. Furthermore, if a theory of right conduct implies, for instance, inconsistent claims about the morality of certain actions, then the theory itself must be mistaken; it cannot be giving us a correct theoretical account of the nature of morality.

Determinacy

To say that a moral theory is determinate is to say that its principles, when applied to concrete cases, yield definite moral verdicts about the morality of whatever is being evaluated. One way in which a moral theory might fail to be determinate is when its basic principles are excessively vague and so fail to imply, in a wide range of cases, any specific moral verdicts. Suppose, for instance, that a moral theory tells us that an action is morally right if and only if it is respectful of persons. Unless the theory also defines fairly explicitly what it means to be respectful of persons, the theory will not yield definite moral conclusions about the morality of actions in a wide range of cases. For instance, does capital punishment respect persons? What about lying to save a life? And so on.

So, according to the *determinacy standard*,

A moral theory should feature principles that, together with relevant factual information, yield determinate moral verdicts about the morality of actions, persons, and other objects of evaluation in a wide range of cases.

A moral theory that is grossly indeterminate will fail to provide a useful decision procedure, since in being indeterminate it will simply provide no guidance about what to do and what to believe regarding a wide range of cases. Again, if a theory is indeterminate, this may indicate that it is failing to explain properly the underlying nature of right and wrong or good and bad. Supposing that there is some feature of actions that makes them right or wrong, a theory that is indeterminate because it is vague has apparently failed to pinpoint exactly what it is about such actions that makes them right or wrong. So, again, the determinacy standard is appropriate for evaluating moral theories in light of both the practical and the theoretical aims of such theories.

The remaining standards for evaluating a moral theory all have to do with wanting our moral theory in general and the principles they feature in particular to be appropriately related to (1) our beliefs about morality, (2) our considered moral beliefs, and (3) our nonmoral beliefs and assumptions.

Intuitive Appeal

In addition to moral beliefs (beliefs about what is right or wrong, good or bad) we have beliefs *about morality*. Beliefs of the latter sort include such ideas as morality concerns the well-being of individuals; morality is rooted in facts about human nature; and morality represents an impartial standpoint for evaluating actions, people, and institutions. These ideas are vague, but as we shall see, moral theories often begin with intuitively appealing beliefs about morality and then go on to develop such ideas in a systematic way. So one kind of consideration that counts in favor of a moral theory is what I will call its appeal. The corresponding *standard of intuitive appeal* claims:

A moral theory should develop and make sense of various intuitively appealing beliefs and ideas about morality.

Internal Support

Despite the fact that people disagree about the morality of actions like abortion, animal experimentation, suicide, euthanasia, and other matters of moral controversy, most people do agree about the morality of a wide range of actions. We agree that rape is wrong, that killing innocent human beings is wrong, that torture is wrong, and so forth. That is, there are many moral beliefs we have that are deeply held and widely shared and which we would continue to hold were we to reflect carefully on their correctness. Call these our considered moral beliefs.

One way to check the correctness of a moral principle is to test it against our considered moral beliefs about specific cases. When a principle, together with relevant information, logically implies one of our considered moral beliefs, we can think of the principle as having a correct moral implication. And having correct implications is one way a moral principle receives support, support that comes from moral beliefs—beliefs internal to morality.

On the other hand, a moral theory whose principles have implications that conflict with some of our considered moral beliefs are (according to this standard) mistaken. So according to the standard of *internal support,*

> A moral theory whose principles, together with relevant factual information, logically imply our considered moral beliefs, receives support—internal support—from those beliefs. On the other hand, if the principles of a theory have implications that conflict with our considered moral beliefs, this is evidence against the correctness of the theory.[6]

Obviously, the rationale behind this standard has mainly to do with the theoretical aim of discovering moral criteria underlying our moral evaluations.

Explanatory Power

A moral theory attempts to discover not only moral principles that logically imply our considered moral beliefs but also principles that *explain* what it is about actions that *makes* them right or wrong (or something good or bad). Clearly this is something we want in a moral theory that intends to satisfy the theoretical aim of providing moral criteria.

We can express the *standard of explanatory power* this way:

> A moral theory should feature principles that explain our more specific considered moral beliefs, thus helping us understand *why* actions, persons, and other objects of moral evaluation are right or wrong, good or bad.

Moral principles of right conduct that satisfy this standard are said to *unify* morality because, in effect, they reveal the underlying nature of the various actions that are right (or wrong). Discovering principles that explain and thereby unify morality directly reflects the theoretical aim of a moral theory.

External Support

The main idea behind the standard of external support was expressed by J. L. Mackie (1912–82), who noted that "Moral principles and ethical theories do not stand alone: they affect and are affected by beliefs and assumptions which belong to other fields, and not least to psychology, metaphysics, and religion" (Mackie 1977, 203). Whereas the standard of internal support has to do with the support a moral principle may receive from those considered moral beliefs it implies, the standard of external support has to do with the support a moral theory in general, and its principles in particular, may receive from nonmoral views and assumptions, including those from the specific fields of inquiry, such as the ones Mackie mentions. The idea behind this standard is that a moral theory is more likely to represent a correct theory about the nature of morality (and thus satisfy the relevant theoretical aim of such theories) if its principles enjoy corroborative support from well-established beliefs and theories from other areas of thought.

As we shall see in the chapters to come, proponents of various moral theories attempt to defend their favored theory by appealing to nonmoral theories and assumptions. For instance, defenders of the divine command theory often appeal to religious theories and assumptions in support of their favored moral theory. Defenders of moral relativism are fond of appealing to certain findings from the field of anthropology in arguing that a relativist moral theory is correct. And other theories look to various other nonmoral views for support.

But just as the fact that a moral theory is supported by some nonmoral theory is some evidence in its favor, so also the fact that a moral theory conflicts with certain well-established nonmoral views is evidence against it. I will not elaborate further; there will be plenty of examples in what is to come of how the standard of external support plays an important role in the overall evaluation of moral theories.

So, according to the standard of *external support*,

The fact that the principles of a moral theory are supported by nonmoral beliefs and assumptions, including well-established beliefs and assumptions from various areas of nonmoral inquiry, is some evidence in its favor. On the other hand, the fact that the principles conflict with established nonmoral beliefs and assumptions is evidence against the theory.

This list is not complete; there are other desiderata (and associated standards) that philosophers invoke in evaluating moral theories. But the ones I have listed are among the most common that we find being used, and in the chapters to come they will figure prominently in our evaluation of the theories.

Let me close this section by making a few comments about these standards and their use. First, satisfying these standards is a matter of degree. For instance, a theory can be more or less determinate in its implications about the morality of actions. Again, the moral principles of a theory can vary in the extent to which they logically imply our considered moral beliefs, and so forth for the other standards on our list.

Second, it is worth keeping in mind that in addition to determining how well any one theory does according to these standards, part of evaluating moral theories involves comparing them with one another to see how well they do in satisfying the relevant standards. Since we are looking for several desirable characteristics in a moral theory, we may find that some theories possess some but not all of these characteristics to varying degrees. This means that evaluating a theory can be a very complex matter.

Finally, some of these standards are controversial, others are not. The standards of intuitive appeal and consistency are fairly uncontroversial, but others, such as the principle of internal support, are questioned by some moral philosophers. Questions about the proper standards for evaluating moral theories belong to a subfield of ethics called metaethics, which I will briefly describe in the next section.

7. Some Remarks about the Field of Ethics

Ethics (often called moral philosophy) is the area of philosophy that inquires into morality. There are two main branches of ethics: *normative ethics* and *metaethics*. Normative ethics investigates *moral* questions, and it is common to distinguish between questions of theory and questions of application. *Normative moral theory* is what this book is all about; as we have seen, it attempts to answer very general moral questions about what to do and how to be. *Applied moral theory* investigates the morality of specific actions and practices, particularly those that are controversial. Books on applied ethics typically deal with such moral issues as abortion, the death penalty, euthanasia, and others, many of which we have already mentioned.

The relation between moral theory and applied ethics is somewhat like the relation between pure science (like physics) and engineering. Just as issues in engineering are matters of applying scientific principles to real-world projects and problems, so issues in applied ethics are often thought of as matters requiring the application of the principles of a moral theory to real-world moral problems.

This way of conceiving the relation between the sorts of general moral questions raised in moral theory and the more specific moral questions raised in applied ethics suggests a natural order of inquiry, illustrated earlier by the controversy over suicide. Confronted with moral disputes about a variety of moral issues, a reflective person will be led to ask questions about the nature of right and wrong, good and bad, and thus will be led to raise the sorts of questions dealt with in moral theory. The hope is that by answering these more general, theoretical questions, one will then be able to use the results in correctly answering more specific moral questions about the morality of suicide, capital punishment, abortion, and other such issues.

However, as we shall see in the chapters to follow, competing moral theories give competing answers to the general questions raised in moral theory. This naturally raises questions about how one might come to know which moral theory is correct. Questions about knowledge belong to the area of philosophical inquiry called *epistemology,* from the Greek term *episteme,* or knowledge. So one important philosophical question concerns how one can come to know moral statements generally and moral principles in particular. The branch of epistemology that deals with such questions is called *moral epistemology.*

Of course, epistemological questions about knowledge in turn raise further philosophical questions about the meaning and truth of moral statements. To really come to know a moral principle, one must be justified in accepting the principle in question. But in order to be justified in accepting some claim, one must understand what the claim means, and this in turn requires that one know something about what makes the claim true or false. Questions about meaning are *semantic* questions, and thus in addition to epistemological questions about morality there are semantic questions about the meaning of moral statements. For instance, when someone says that abortion is wrong, what does such a claim mean? The branch of semantics that deals with such questions about moral thought and language is called *moral semantics.*

Questions about meaning are related to *metaphysical* questions. Metaphysics is that branch of philosophy that inquires into the nature of reality—into what exists (what is real) and its ultimate nature. Questions about the existence and nature of space and time, about causation, about substance, and about events are all matters of metaphysical inquiry.

There are also metaphysical questions concerning morality. For instance, are there moral facts whose existence is what makes a true moral statement true? If so, what kind of fact is a moral fact? Is it the kind of fact that can be scientifically investigated? If so, what kind of scientific fact is it? Biological? Sociological? Anthropological? Perhaps a combination of these? Are moral facts (supposing that such facts exist) instead some sort of nonscientific fact? Perhaps moral facts are facts about the will of a deity. Some

Figure 1.4 Main Divisions of Ethics

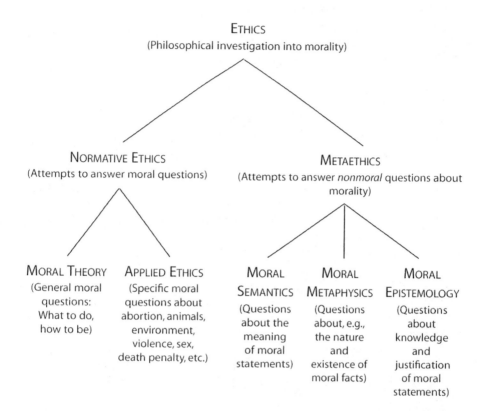

philosophers have been skeptical of the existence of moral facts, denying that there really are any. The branch of metaphysics dealing with such questions is called *moral metaphysics.*

These epistemological, semantic, and metaphysical questions *about* morality are typically referred to as metaethical questions. And the branch of ethics called *metaethics* ("meta" meaning "about") attempts to answer them. Figure 1.4 summarizes the main divisions of ethics.

I wish to make one final but very important comment about the distinction between normative ethics and metaethics. The description I have just given suggests a neat and tidy division between them. But, as we shall see, no such neat and tidy division really exists. A moral theory not only attempts to discover true or correct moral principles but is also concerned to justify or prove such principles. Thus questions about the proper way to justify or prove moral principles in particular, and moral claims in general, are necessarily involved in giving a normative moral theory. That is, epistemological questions about justification (as well as the sorts of semantic and metaphysical metaethical questions that naturally arise in connection with epistemological questions) are just beneath the surface when engaging in moral theory. Since the focus of this book is on moral theory, I have kept metaethical discussions to a minimum. However, as the reader will discover, metaethical questions arise throughout this book.[7]

8. Sneak Preview

In the chapters to follow, we shall examine representative versions of the following moral theories: divine command theory, moral relativism, natural law theory, utilitarianism, Kant's moral theory, moral pluralism, virtue ethics, and moral particularism. Each chapter is devoted to one of these theories, though utilitarianism is covered in two chapters, owing to the many varieties of this general type of view.

In each chapter I introduce readers to the main concepts involved in the theory being featured and then proceed to develop a version of the theory (sometimes I present both a classical and a more contemporary version), followed by a critical evaluation of the theory. The critical evaluation will typically involve an appeal to one or more of the six basic desiderata explained above.

In presenting each theory, one main focus will be its theory of right conduct. And for some, but not all, moral theories we will also have to examine the theory of nonmoral value that is being proposed as a basis for understanding right action. (Recall that some moral theories make the deontic status of an action depend on considerations of nonmoral value.) Theories of moral value, as we shall see, do not play a prominent role in many of the moral theories we shall examine (or at least they will not receive nearly as much attention in such theories). So in my treatment of some theories, moral value is not mentioned, while in connection with others, it is mentioned only briefly.

A final comment: The moral theories featured in the following chapters all build on widely recognized ideas that will be familiar to most readers. (Recall the standard of intuitive appeal.) The idea that morality is based on God's commands is familiar and at the heart of the divine command theory. The idea that morality is simply relative to culture is likewise familiar and is the key idea in versions of moral relativism. The idea that morality requires that we not go against nature or do anything unnatural is related to the natural law theory. The utilitarian moral theory works with the idea that the morality of an action depends on how it affects human happiness, while the idea that morality involves respecting persons is central to Kant's moral theory. One might think of these various theories, then, as attempts to develop these familiar ideas in a rigorous philosophical manner.

So although the study of these moral theories may be a new experience for many readers, many of the core ideas featured in them are familiar. This book is an invitation to explore ideas that are often taken for granted and often only vaguely understood.

Notes

1. For instance, in 1997, the U.S. Supreme Court ruled that although individuals do not have a right to physician–assisted suicide, states are free to permit such a practice.

2. Throughout, and merely for convenience, I use the masculine pronoun in referring to God.

3. Moral principles are often contrasted with *moral rules.* A moral rule (concerning right conduct) is less general than a principle and states that some specific type of action is right or wrong. Each of the Ten Commandments, for instance, expresses a moral rule. The role of moral rules in moral theory will be explored in later chapters.

4. In chap. 10, we will explore in more detail the relationship between moral principles and assumptions about the underlying unity of moral phenomena.

5. Note that a moral theory does not violate the consistency standard merely if its principles imply, for example, that *in general* lying is wrong and at the same time yields the verdict *in some specific case* that a particular instance of lying is not wrong (so long as the theory can account for the difference between lies that are wrong and those that are not).

6. In later chapters, it will be useful to distinguish between a strong sense and a weak sense of internal support. A moral principle receives strong internal support from considered moral beliefs when the principle (together with relevant factual information) logically implies the beliefs in question. A moral principle receives weak internal support when the principle is merely consistent with considered moral beliefs.

7. For a more detailed overview of the field of metaethics, see Timmons 1999, chap. 1.

2

Divine Command Theory

In the minds of many people, there is a deep connection between morality and religion. Historically, of course, religious worldviews contain a moral outlook as part of an overall vision of the place and purpose of human beings in the world. People brought up in a religious community thus come to associate morality with religion. In addition to the historical connection between morality and religion, there are other possible connections between them. For instance, one might claim that moral knowledge requires revelation. However, in this chapter we are mainly interested in a particular way in which morality has been thought to depend on religion, or more precisely, on the commands of God. The thought, central to the divine command moral theory, is that morality itself—what is right and wrong, good and bad—depends on God's commands. It is God's act of commanding that we avoid certain types of action that *makes* those actions wrong, and similarly for other moral concepts.

1. The Theory

Let us focus for the time being on the theory of right action—that branch of moral theory that concerns the nature of right and wrong action. The main idea is that what makes an action right or wrong depends on (and thus can be expressed in terms of) God's commands. Theologian Robert C. Mortimer explains the view this way:

> From the doctrine of God as Creator and source of all that is, it follows that a thing is not right simply because we think it is, still less because it seems expedient. It is right because God commands it. This means that there is a real distinction between right and wrong that is independent of what we happen to think. It is rooted in the nature and will of God. (Mortimer 1950, 8)

23

Mortimer mentions the rightness of actions being based on God's commands (by which he means an action's being obligatory), but all the other moral categories can be similarly characterized. In order to focus on the divine command theory, it will help if we express the essentials of the theory in terms of a set of basic principles.

Theory of Right Conduct

An action A is *obligatory* if and only if God commands that we A.

An action A is *forbidden* (wrong) if and only if God commands that we not A.

An action A is *optional* if and only if it is not the case that God commands that we A (thus, not obligatory), and it is not the case that God commands that we not A (thus, not forbidden). Less cumbersomely: An action A is optional if and only if God neither commands that we A nor that we not A.

If we turn for a moment to the divine command theory's account of value—the goodness and badness of persons, things, experiences, and states of affairs—it is, again, facts about God's will that make certain things good and others bad (or evil). Typically, in presenting a theory of value we are concerned with the nature of *intrinsic* goodness and badness. However, in connection with the divine command theory, it would be misleading at best to talk about what is intrinsically good—good in itself—since the very idea here is that nothing is intrinsically good or bad. Rather, on this theory it is something extrinsic to whatever is good or bad that confers upon it the value it has, namely, God's commands.[1] With this in mind, we can set forth the divine command theory of value:

Theory of Nonmoral Value

Something S is *good* if and only if God commands that we bring about or preserve S.[2]

Something S is *bad* if and only if God commands that we refrain from bringing about or preserving S.

Something S is *value-neutral* if and only if God neither commands that we bring about or preserve S nor that we refrain from bringing about or preserving S.

What is crucial for understanding the divine command theory is the idea that what makes an action right or wrong, good or bad, is nothing but brute facts about God's commands. The fact that he commands that we not kill, rape, torture, and so forth is what makes such actions wrong; their wrongness consists entirely in the fact that he commands that we not do such actions.[3] We will come back to this point in section 3.

How might the theory be used? One obvious way involves appealing to some source, such as the Bible, that purports to contain evidence of God's commands. According to Mortimer, for example, the Bible provides moral guidance in three principal ways. First, "it recalls and restates in simple and even violent language fundamental moral judgments which men are always in danger of forgetting or explaining away. It thus provides a norm and standard of human behavior in the broadest and simplest outline" (1950, 15). For instance, the Ten Commandments of the Old Testament and Christ's teachings regarding love for fellow human beings in the New Testament provide general moral rules for all human beings.

Second, in addition to moral rules—which we might call the letter of the moral law as commanded by God—we find evidence of the proper spirit for following God's commands. Ideally, humans are to strive toward holiness by following God's commands, not out of fear or self-interest, but out of love for God. Because the moral goodness of persons has to do with their motives, this point about the spirit of morality presumably reveals the divine command theory's account of moral goodness: the moral goodness (and hence moral virtue) of individuals is measured by how closely they come to fulfilling God's commands out of the motive of love for God.

Finally, according to Mortimer, biblical revelation "suggests new emphases and new precepts, a new scale of human values which could not at all, or could not easily, have been [otherwise] perceived" (1950, 16). As an example Mortimer notes that the Incarnation, signifying the restoration of fallen human nature, instructs us that God has equal concern for all human beings, including the outcast, downtrodden, and despised. This equal concern means that all human beings have a special dignity and that consequently all humans are to be treated as ends in themselves. The idea of human dignity is a moral idea that might otherwise be obscure to human beings except for revelation.

2. Defending the Theory

Let us now consider why anyone might accept the divine command theory—or at least anyone who is already a theist. There are three arguments worth considering.

According to what I will call the *linguistic argument*, the divine command theory is true simply because "obligatory," when used in its moral sense, just means "commanded by God" (and so on for the other moral concepts).

Consider someone who would deny the truth of any of the theory's moral principles. According to the linguistic argument, such a denial would be like denying the general claim that all bachelors are unmarried. If one denies this latter claim, while also intending to use the term "'bachelor" as it is ordinarily used, then one shows a lack of understanding of the concept of a bachelor. Similarly, so it might be claimed, if one denies the principles of the divine command theory, one thereby shows that one does not understand basic moral concepts like 'obligatory', 'good', and so on.

However, this appeal to meaning is implausible. Indeed, its implausibility is easily revealed by comparing the bachelor example with any of the divine command theory's principles. It certainly would show a lack of understanding on the part of someone to deny that all bachelors are unmarried, for it is manifestly clear that part of what we mean by the term "bachelor" is "someone who is unmarried." If we know that someone is a bachelor, the question of whether he is also unmarried is settled. Or to put it another way: if one claims that someone is a bachelor but then goes on to claim that he is married, one can be accused of contradicting oneself. But similar points cannot be made about moral concepts. If one claims that some action is obligatory but that the action is not commanded by God (perhaps because the speaker does not believe there is a God), one is not guilty of self-contradiction. So, the linguistic argument under consideration is not persuasive.[4]

Religious arguments for the theory appeal to theistic premises, for example, premises about the nature of God. Such arguments, then, attempt to provide support for this moral theory by appealing to nonmoral views, and thus represent an appeal to the standard of external support for evaluating moral theories that was explained in section 6 of chapter 1. We have already encountered one such argument in the first quote from Mortimer. He infers the truth of the divine command theory from the theistic claim that God is creator of all. We can elaborate Mortimer's line of thought as follows. God must be the creative source of morality and hence the divine command theory must be true, because if he were not the source of morality, then there would be some moral standards or principles independent of God. And if there are moral standards and principles independent of God, it follows that he would not be creator of all things. So, if God is creator of absolutely everything (except himself), then we are committed to the divine command theory.

I will pass over this argument for now since we return to it in the next section, where I will argue that the theist has good reason to question one of its basic assumptions.

We come finally to what I will call the *argument from moral objectivity*. This argument claims that the only moral theory that provides an objective basis for a single true morality is the divine command theory. According to monotheism there is a single God, who issues a set of commands to all human beings, regardless of culture and historical setting. This means that, contrary to moral relativism, there is a single set of objectively true moral principles, and hence the kinds of problems that infect moral relativism do not apply to the divine command theory.[5]

The problem with this argument is that it is premature. The other theories presented in this book (excluding, of course, moral relativism) can each be understood as attempts to articulate and defend nonrelativist conceptions of morality according to which what is right or wrong, good or bad is an objective matter. Thus, in order for the argument from moral objectivity to have any real force, it would have to be true that these other various nonrelativist moral theories somehow fail. This remains to be seen, hence (at least in terms of where we are in our examination of various types of moral theory) the argument is premature. Furthermore, there are serious problems with the divine command theory to which we now turn.

3. The Euthyphro Dilemma

Many thinkers (both theists and nontheists) have claimed that the divine command theory should be rejected owing to a dilemma that takes it name from the title of one of Plato's dialogues, the *Euthyphro*. In this dialogue Euthyphro professes to know what piety is, and Socrates questions him about it. After Euthyphro gives examples of what he takes to be pious actions, the dialogue continues:

> *Socr:* Remember, then, that I did not ask you to tell me one or two of all the many pious actions that there are; I want to know what is characteristic of piety which makes all pious action pious. You said, I think, that there is one characteristic which makes all pious actions pious, and another characteristic which makes all impious actions impious. Do you remember? (Plato 1976, 7)[6]

After some discussion, we get Euthyphro's answer:

> *Euth:* Well, I should say that piety is what all the gods love, and that impiety is what they all hate. (11)

Socrates then poses the crucial question:

> *Socr:* Now consider this question. Do the gods love piety because it is pious, or is it pious because they love it? (11)

Here, Socrates is asking about the relation between piety and the love of the gods. But the same question can be raised in connection with the relation between morality generally and the commands of God: does God command that we do obligatory actions because they *are* obligatory, or is some action obligatory *because* God commands that we do it? To fully appreciate the dilemma that results from having to choose between these two options, it will be useful to pause for a moment and review a few of the key tenets of traditional theistic belief.

According to many versions of theism, there is a single personal God who is an all-perfect being, possessing every perfection to the highest degree. God's perfections include omniscience (all-knowingness) and omnipotence (all-powerfulness). In addition:

G1 *Creator:* God is creator of everything (other than himself). God's omnipotence ensures that he can bring about anything possible, and his being creator is a matter of his realizing his omnipotence in bringing about this particular world from among the possible worlds he might have created instead.

G2 *Full rationality:* There is a sufficient reason for all of God's actions— everything he does, he does for a reason and with complete wisdom.

G3 *Perfect moral goodness:* God, as a being, is morally good in the fullest possible sense: he possesses every moral perfection to the highest possible degree. If we were to make a list of these perfections, we could begin by saying that he is all-just, omnibenevolent (all-loving), all-merciful, and so forth.

I won't pause to elaborate these tenets, hoping that my readers will find them clear enough for present purposes.

The Euthyphro dilemma is a dilemma for the theist who accepts these claims about the nature of God. And, as noted above, it arises in connection with the question: How is morality related to God's commands? There are two possibilities. Either morality depends on God's commands, or it does not. To be more precise, the two options are these. Either:

1. What is right and wrong depends on God's commands in the sense that his commands alone are what *make* actions right or wrong. (Similarly for goodness and badness);

or

2. God commands us to perform certain actions and refrain from performing others because certain actions are right and others are wrong, and being fully rational he knows what is right and wrong, and being completely good he issues commands to humanity that

conform to his moral knowledge. (Similarly for goodness and bad-ness).

The first option represents the divine command theory; the second option represents the rejection of the divine command theory because it presup-poses that, independently of God's commands, certain actions are right and others wrong.

The dilemma can now be easily explained. In response to the question about how God and morality are related, either the theist accepts the di-vine command theory (option 1) or not (option 2). Whichever option one takes, one runs afoul of one or more of the basic theistic tenets mentioned above. Let us see why.

First, if one embraces the divine command theory, one is forced to give up G2, the claim that everything God does, he does for a reason. To grasp this point is to grasp the very idea of the divine command theory. As I have been saying, according to the divine command theory, what makes an ac-tion obligatory is the mere fact that God commands that we do it. This means that God's commands are arbitrary—he has no reason for com-manding that we keep our promises and avoid hurting others; he might just as well have commanded us to ignore our promises and ignore how our ac-tions affect others.

We can perhaps bring out this point more clearly if we suppose that God does have reasons for his commands. For example, suppose he has some rea-son for commanding that we help others in need. What sort of reason might that be? Apparently, it would be some fact about the action—some fact that makes that action an action we ought to do. But then if God is basing his commands on reasons of this sort, we are committed to saying that God commands what he does because certain actions are right or wrong and, given God's nature, he conforms his commands to what is (in-dependently of his commands) right or wrong. So in supposing that God has reasons for his commands, we are in effect rejecting the divine com-mand theory. Thus, implied by the divine command theory is the idea that God's commands are arbitrary.

Furthermore, if we accept the divine command theory, we cannot make sense of God's goodness, which means that we are forced to abandon G3. Consider the claim that God is good. According to the divine command theory something S is good if and only if God commands that we bring about or preserve S. Accordingly, God is good if and only if God commands that we bring about or preserve him. Surely this is not correct, and not just because it is nonsense to talk about human beings bringing about or pre-serving an all-sufficient being. God is good in virtue of possessing certain characteristics, not as a result of commands he issues.

Since the divine command theory forces the theist to give up G2 and G3, the theist has reason to reject this theory.

What about the other option that involves rejecting the divine command theory? Notice first of all that it does not represent some alternative moral theory. Rather, all it says in effect is that God conforms his commands to what is right and wrong, but it does not tell us what it is that makes actions right or wrong. It leaves that open. However, this option also seems to be at odds with theism because it seems to conflict with G1, the idea that God is creator. After all, if we admit that right and wrong, good and bad are not a matter of God's commands, aren't we saying that there exists a moral code or standard independent of God? Thus, he is not creator of everything, contrary to G1. Mortimer's religious argument, recall, was to the effect that we have to accept the divine command theory in light of the idea of God as creator.

Whether the theist accepts the divine command theory (option 1) or rejects it (option 2), it looks as if she must give up some of the important tenets of theistic belief about God. Hence, the dilemma.

4. A Way Out

What are the theist's options at this point? It would be too much for the theist to give up the claims expressed in G2 and G3 to the effect that God is fully rational and is perfectly good. In particular, the theist cannot give up the claim about God's goodness, since it is the basis for devotion and worship. If this is correct, the theist must reject the divine command theory.

But what about the other option? If we give up the divine command theory, must we compromise the idea of God as creator? Many philosophers and theologians do not think so. Let us see why.

The gist of the solution to the dilemma that I shall propose involves two main claims: (1) The theist should recognize that there is an important sense in which what is right and wrong, good and bad depends on God's creative choices, and so there is a sense in which morality depends on God. (2) However, the theist should accept the idea that there are basic facts about what is right and wrong, good and bad that are independent of God's commands. Maintaining both of these claims requires that we refine our understanding of God as creator; but (so I shall maintain) the theist need not give up anything essential to her theism in doing so. Let us take this one step at a time.

Given God's omnipotence, there are many possible worlds he might have created, much different from the actual world he did create. In particular, not only might he have created a planet in place of Earth with a very different environment, he might have created intelligent beings whose natures are different in important ways from human nature. However, as a matter of fact (and for good reason) God created human beings—beings that are mortal, whose bodies are such that they can be harmed in various ways, who must work to develop certain talents and capacities, and so forth. Moreover, he placed humans in a certain kind of natural environment in which they must toil for food and shelter and which, because of limited resources, leads to competition among such beings. For a theist, all of this depends on God's will; it might have been different.

Now because humans are of a certain nature and find themselves in a certain environment, there are certain actions that, for example, it would be wrong to do owing to their effects on human well-being. Moral rules against murder and theft thus apply to human beings, but notice that part of the reason they apply has to do with the fact that God created humans with a certain nature and put them in a certain environment. Had he created another type of being who was, for instance, unharmable and in an environment where there was no need of property, rules against murder and theft would not apply. Thus, in a sense, God has control over what moral rules correctly apply to human beings. Hence, in a sense, God has control over morality—over what is right and wrong for us to do.

Still, *given* that human beings are the way they are, there are certain moral principles or rules that are true or correct, and their truth or correctness is independent of God's commands. For creatures who can be harmed in all the ways humans can be harmed, certain actions are morally wrong, perhaps because of how such actions adversely affect human well-being, or perhaps for some other reason. (It is the task of moral theory to discover what the reason is.) What God does in creating human beings is make it the case that a certain set of moral principles or rules are the ones that correctly apply to human beings.

At this point, an analogy might help. Suppose that I want to build a machine of some sort but that there are various ways in which I might design the machine's motor. I might construct it so that it runs on gasoline, or I might make it so that it runs on vegetable oil, or on beer, or whatever. The worth of the machine is its running well. If I make the one that runs on gasoline, I should fill its tank with gas, but if I make the one that runs on vegetable oil, I should fill its tank accordingly. The idea is that whether I should fill the machine with one fluid or another depends on two factors: (1) facts about various sorts of motors and (2) my decision about what sort of motor to create.

The suggestion, then, is that for various sorts of possible creatures subject to moral requirements, there are basic moral principles whose truth or correctness does not depend on God's commands (just as facts about various motors and what they will run on is not up to me). However, since God has control over the kind of creature he will create, he does exert control over which set of principles is to be followed (just as it is up to me to decide what kind of motor to build).

Can a theist be happy with this solution? After all, although it grants that God has a kind of control over morality, it still maintains that basic moral

principles are independent of God's commands. It is not God's commanding that we refrain from murder that makes murder wrong; rather murder
is wrong because of how it affects the interests and lives of human beings.
But should we understand the claim that God is creator to mean that in addition to the physical universe, which theists believe he created, he also created moral standards and such abstract things as mathematical truths and the
principles of logic?

Many philosophers hold that such standards, truths, and principles are
not only true, but *necessarily* true. A truth is necessary when it is not possible for it to be false. Consider the mathematical proposition that $2 + 2 = 4$.
This is not only true, but necessarily so: it is not possible for the equation
to be otherwise. God couldn't make $2 + 2$ turn out to be 5 given the quan-
tities designated by 2 and by 5 and given what "+" and "=" mean. But so
what? As many theologians have argued, the fact that God cannot do or
bring about what is impossible represents no genuine limit on God's omnipotence. So if we understand basic moral principles to be necessarily true,
we can likewise point out that it is no real limit on God's omnipotence that
the truth of those principles does not depend on God's will. If we reconsider the claim about God as creator (as expressed in G1), we should reformulate it to say that, as omnipotent, God has power over everything that is
not a matter of necessity. In particular, God is creator of the entire physical
universe including human beings, whose existence is certainly not a necessary fact.

Some theists might be reluctant to embrace this solution. But embracing the divine command theory is going to force the theist to reject or
modify G2 and G3, and I've already mentioned why doing so is unattrac-
tive. Moreover, the reluctant theist should reflect on the fact that many theologians and philosophers embrace a solution like the one I have offered.[7]

5. Evaluation of the Divine Command Theory

In evaluating the divine command theory, let us consider what can be said
both for and against the theory, making use of the standards for evaluating
moral theories introduced in section 6 of chapter 1.

First, if we assume that God's commands are consistent and that he has
revealed enough detail about his commands to guide our moral decisions,
then we may conclude that the theory satisfies the standards of consistency and determinacy.

Second, according to the standard of intuitive appeal, a moral theory
should develop and make sense of plausible beliefs about morality. One
such belief (held by many) is that there is a deep connection between
morality and religion. And, of course, this idea is what guides the development of the divine command theory.

Third, the attempt by Mortimer and others to argue from religious claims about God to the truth of this theory represents an appeal to the standard of external support.

However, we have found reason to reject the divine command theory. Indeed, reflection on the Euthyphro dilemma reveals why, despite initial appearances, the theory is at odds with some basic tenets of theism, giving the theist reason to reject this theory. Ironically, then, this theory conflicts with certain religious tenets that, according to the standard of external support, count against it.

Finally, let us suppose that the principles of right conduct and value can be used (together with facts about what God commands) to derive our considered moral beliefs. The theory will thereby satisfy the standard of internal support. But again, the Euthyphro dilemma helps us see that it is not God's commands that make something right or wrong, good or bad, and so the divine command theory fails to plausibly explain what *makes* something right or wrong, good or bad; it fails to satisfy the standard of explanatory power. This means that it fails to satisfy the main theoretical aim of a moral theory of providing moral criteria for the right and the good.

6. Conclusion

Rejecting the divine command theory does not mean that religion generally, and God's commands in particular, are of no importance for morality. Certainly, assuming there is a God of the sort believed in by many theists, one can look to revelation for some moral guidance. Moreover, one can look to revelation for some indication of what makes an action right or wrong or some state of affairs good or bad. Christ's teachings concerning love might be construed as advocating an ethic of universal benevolence—the idea behind the utilitarian moral theory that we will consider in chapters 5 and 6. Mortimer, recall, claims that the Bible contains the idea that all humans possess a kind of dignity—an idea that is central in the moral philosophy of Immanuel Kant, which we take up in chapter 7. The idea that human beings are created by God and designed to fulfill certain purposes is, of course, an idea to be found in the Bible; this idea is featured in Thomas Aquinas's moral theory, which we examine in chapter 4.

Whereas the divine command theory attempts to ground morality on the will of God—his commands—the theory known as moral relativism attempts to ground morality on the will of society. Both views share the idea that morality is ultimately a matter of the dictates of some authority, but they are otherwise quite different. Moral relativism is the subject of the next chapter.

Further Reading

Adams, Robert M. 1973. "A Modified Divine Command Theory of Ethical Wrongness." In *Religion and Morality: A Collection of Essays*, ed. Gene Outka and John P. Reeder. New York: Doubleday. Reprinted in Helm 1981. A sophisticated defense of the divine command theory.

Berg, Jonathan. 1993. "How Can Morality Depend on Religion?" In *A Companion to Ethics*, ed. Peter Singer. Cambridge: Blackwell. Covers much the same ground as this chapter. Includes a select bibliography.

Helm, Paul, ed. 1981. *Divine Commands and Morality.* New York: Oxford University Press. Twelve essays (many of them on an advanced level) by leading philosophers debating the divine command theory. Includes a useful introductory essay by the editor plus a bibliography.

Quinn, Philip. 1978. *Divine Commands and Moral Requirements.* Oxford: Oxford University Press. A sophisticated defense of the divine command theory.

Notes

1. We might attempt to capture something of the contrast between things with intrinsic value and things having extrinsic value by distinguishing those things with regard to which God issues commands—things having what we might call *fundamental goodness* or *badness*—from those things that, because they are instrumental in bringing about what is fundamentally good or bad, can be said to have derivative value. But since this complication does not matter for our purposes, I will ignore it.

2. Strictly speaking, this characterization of nonmoral goodness makes everything that is nonmorally good something that human beings are in a position to do something about. But surely there could be things or states of affairs that are nonmorally good but which are beyond the range of what humans can either bring about or preserve (perhaps because they are in some remote corner of the universe that we will never experience). (I thank Robert Audi for calling my attention to this problem.) To fix this defect, either we can restrict these characterizations to only those things, experiences, and states of affairs that humans can do something about, or we could replace reference to what God does and does not command with reference to what God does and does not *approve* of. (God may approve of all sorts of things that simply do not relate to human existence.) Since it is the divine *command* theory, I have chosen to express both the principles of right conduct and the principles of nonmoral value in terms of God's commands. So we are to understand the principles of nonmoral value as restricted in the manner just explained.

3. Throughout, and merely for convenience, I use the masculine pronoun to refer to God.

4. This does not mean that all possible versions of the linguistic argument are as easily refuted. Sophisticated linguistic arguments that cannot be considered here are to be found in, e.g., Adams 1973, 1979.

5. We study moral relativism and its problems in the next chapter.

6. All references to Plato's *Euthyphro* are from Plato 1976.
7. See, e.g., Swinburne 1974.

3

Moral Relativism

Studies of the moral beliefs and practices of various cultures reveal that different cultures often have very different moral beliefs and attitudes about the same sort of action. Consider a few examples.

- *Honor killings.* Members of some groups think that if an unwed woman becomes pregnant, it is the obligation of her family to kill her to restore family honor.

- *Parricide.* Anthropologists report that many cultures practice parricide—killing one's parents—once the parents become aged. It is a practice that members of the community, including the parents, take to be morally permissible and perhaps even morally required.

- *Premarital sex and wife sharing.* Some cultures do not think that there is anything wrong with premarital sex; indeed, it is condoned as an important and normal part of courtship. Moreover, in some cultures, it is considered a great honor if one's wife engages in sexual relations with other men.

- *Cannibalism.* There are numerous documented cases of cultures that engage in the eating of human flesh. Members of such cultures think the practice not only morally permissible but in some cases obligatory.

- *Treatment of animals.* Again, anthropologists report that many cultures are indifferent to the suffering of animals. For instance, in recent times there have been some groups who pluck live chickens in the belief that their meat will be particularly succulent. Other cultures condone "games" that involve inflicting intense pain on animals.

This short list is but a sampling of practices that are either permitted or required in certain cultures but are condemned as immoral in many others.

The practices of infanticide, abortion, homosexuality, female circumcision, usury, and public nudity also meet with different moral reactions among different cultures; this list could be extended. Such examples make clear not only that there are some intercultural differences in moral belief but also that many such differences are about matters of fundamental moral importance.

Reflection on such intercultural diversity in moral belief has led many anthropologists and some philosophers to embrace a moral theory typically called moral relativism. What is moral relativism? How exactly do cases of cultural diversity in moral belief lead to relativism? Is moral relativism plausible? Such questions are the main focus of this chapter. Let us begin our study of moral relativism with an explanation of this type of moral theory.

1. What Is Moral Relativism?

Unfortunately, in ethics the term "relativism" is used as a label for quite a variety of views and ideas that differ in important ways. We shall consider some of these views and ideas as we proceed, but for the time being we are concerned with a normative moral theory that is appropriately called *moral relativism* (also referred to as ethical relativism). Again, there are different versions of moral relativism, but we shall be concerned with the version according to which the rightness or wrongness of actions ultimately depends on the moral code of the culture to which one belongs. According to this view, then, the moral code of one's culture is the touchstone of moral truth and falsity when it comes to questions of right and wrong. And this implies that if two cultures differ in their moral codes, actions that are right for members of one of the two cultures may be wrong for members of the other.[1] In order to clarify moral relativism as a moral theory, let us begin by explaining some of its central concepts.

Moral relativism makes right and wrong depend ultimately on the moral code of a culture. What is meant by talk of a culture's moral code? Since cultures are made up of individuals, consider first the moral code of an individual.

The very idea of having a *code* of some sort involves accepting a system of rules or norms. Most adults accept various codes for behavior, codes of etiquette and moral codes being the most obvious examples. We can understand an individual's moral code in the following way.

Individuals have moral beliefs about the rightness and wrongness of actions that vary in their generality. Some moral beliefs are about specific, concrete actions; others are more general beliefs about types of actions. Let us say that to have a general moral belief about the morality of a type of action is to accept a moral norm regarding such actions.[2] Typical moral norms might include *lying is wrong (unless one has a good reason), intentionally killing a person is wrong (except in self-defense)*, and *one ought to help those in need of assistance when one can do so at little or no cost to oneself.*

Of the moral norms an individual accepts, we can plausibly suppose that some are more basic than others in the sense that some are (or can be) derived from others, while some are underived and represent an individual's basic moral commitments. For instance, one might accept a norm prohibiting embezzlement because one recognizes that embezzlement is a form of stealing and one accepts a moral norm to the effect that stealing is wrong. In this case, the norm about embezzlement is (for the individual in question) a nonbasic moral norm that can be derived from the more general norm about stealing. If the moral norm about stealing is not itself based on any other, more basic norm the individual accepts, it is basic for that individual.

Since, as noted above, a code for behavior is basically a set of rules or norms governing behavior, let us simply define an individual's moral code (that he or she possesses at some particular time) as the set of those moral norms that the individual accepts (at the time in question).

There is much more to having a moral code than simply accepting a bunch of norms. In addition, having a moral code involves being disposed to act in certain ways and to feel a certain range of emotions. For instance, if someone sincerely accepts a moral norm prohibiting gossip, then that person is disposed to avoid engaging in gossip. Moreover, such a person who knowingly violates the norm in question is likely to experience feelings of guilt or perhaps shame as a proper response to the violation. Such remarks only hint at a very complex phenomenon that we need not investigate here. Although having a moral code is not simply a matter of having general moral beliefs about types of actions, the norms that are the objects of such beliefs will be our main focus in what follows.

We can now define the notion of a culture's moral code by specifying how this code is a function of the moral codes of the individuals who are members of the culture. For each individual, we make a list that includes the types of actions morally prohibited and the types of actions morally required by that individual's moral code. We then compare these lists, looking for those moral norms that are widely accepted among the members of the culture in question. Having collected the widely shared moral norms of a culture, we select that subset of moral norms that represents the widely shared *basic* moral norms of individuals who are members of the culture. The set of basic moral norms represents the ultimate touchstone of rightness and wrongness for the culture in question, and so it is in terms of this set of norms that we can characterize moral relativism. So if we let C refer to a culture, we can spell out the principles of right conduct for moral relativism this way:

Theory of Right Conduct

An action A, performed by a member of C, is *obligatory* if and only if, according to the basic moral norms of C, A is required.

An action A, performed by a member of C, is *wrong* if and only if, according to the basic moral norms of C, A is prohibited.

An action A, performed by a member of C, is *optional* if and only if A is neither required nor prohibited by the basic moral norms of C.

In what follows, it will be useful to express the central idea of moral relativism as economically as possible; we can do this as follows:

MR What is right and what is wrong for the members of a culture depends on (is ultimately determined by) the basic moral norms of their culture.

In understanding what moral relativism is all about, it is important to note that the above moral principles are intended as moral criteria—as specifying what it is that *makes* an action right or wrong. The relativist makes parallel claims about goodness and badness. What *makes* something good or bad (for an individual who is a member of some culture) is the basic norms of goodness and badness that are part of the moral code of the individual's culture.

William G. Sumner (1840–1910), an anthropologist, nicely summarizes the basic idea of moral relativism when he writes:

> It is most important to notice that, for the people of a time and place, their own mores are always good, or rather that for them there can be no question of the goodness or badness of their mores. The reason is because the standards of good and right are in the mores. (Sumner [1906] 1959, 58)[3]

Notice that Sumner begins this passage with a remark that he immediately qualifies—in fact, corrects. It would be inconsistent for the moral relativist to say of a culture's basic moral norms (its basic mores) that they are good, because this would imply that there are norms of goodness that are independent of the mores in question and that can be used to evaluate those mores. But this is precisely what the relativist denies and what Sumner goes on to make explicit. With regard to the basic moral norms of the culture, one cannot sensibly raise questions about their goodness or badness (or their rightness or wrongness) *since they represent the very standards of good and bad, right and wrong applicable in the culture that accepts them.*

Thus, moral relativism is a moral theory that presents a positive account of the nature of right and wrong, good and bad. But there is more to the relativist's stance in ethics than is expressed in its theory of right conduct. Moral relativism is opposed to the *universality thesis:*

> UT There are moral norms whose correctness or validity is indepen-
> dent of the moral norms a culture does or might accept, and thus
> they express universally valid moral standards that apply to all cul-
> tures.[4]

It is the denial of this thesis that prompts the relativist's account of right and wrong. After all, if there are no universally valid moral norms that apply to all cultures, then apparently the only standards available for determining what is right and wrong, good and bad are represented by the moral norms that individual cultures happen to accept. As we shall see, the denial of the universality thesis plays a crucial role in the main argument for moral relativism.

However, before we consider this argument, let us sharpen our understanding of moral relativism by contrasting it with what I will call the context sensitivity thesis.

2. The Context Sensitivity Thesis

It is uncontroversial that what is right or wrong for someone to do can often depend on one's circumstances, including facts about one's culture. I am going to call such dependence the context sensitivity thesis. The important point about this thesis is that it is not equivalent to moral relativism, nor does it imply relativism. Since failure to understand this point leads to confusion, it is well worth our time to examine this thesis and compare it to moral relativism. Let us begin with some illustrations of the thesis in question.

What is right or wrong to do in a situation depends on certain facts about the situation in question. Suppose that you are an expert swimmer and one day while walking along a deserted beach, you see a young child flailing away in the water some twenty yards from shore, struggling for air, and obviously in immediate danger of drowning. You surely have a moral obligation to rescue the child. But suppose it is I who am walking along the same deserted beach—someone who can't swim. Since I would almost certainly drown if I tried to rescue the child, I do not have an obligation to go into the water to save the child (though I have an obligation to run or call for help). So here the action that you ought to do is not the same sort of action that I ought to do.

Of course, the reason our specific obligations differ in this case is that there is a difference between us that in this case is morally significant: you can swim, I can't. And it is this fact about our situation that helps explain why you have an obligation to perform a certain specific action while I do not. So sometimes differences in facts about agents can affect what it is morally right or wrong to do in a particular context. But the fact that what is right or wrong depends in this way on facts about agents has nothing to do with moral relativism.

The point I am making is often explained by pointing out that moral norms or principles have different implications depending on differences in situation or context. The following is a plausible moral principle of aid:

> One ought to help those who are in need of help when one is in a position to do so and can avoid serious risk of life and limb to oneself.

Suppose for the moment that this principle is universally valid—valid independently of the moral code of any culture. Still, this principle, when applied to the two cases just described, yields different moral conclusions about what each of us ought to do. In short, the application of moral principles will yield different moral verdicts in different contexts depending on the morally relevant details of the context. This is uncontroversial and something that is compatible with the denial of moral relativism.

For another example of this type of context sensitivity, consider the morality of insults.[5] It is plausible to suppose that it is morally wrong to insult someone. Let us suppose that this is true independently of the moral code of any culture. However, notice that what counts as an insult will vary from culture to culture. In some places, for a student to address a professor by her or his first name would be insulting to the professor. In other places, with different cultural norms for what counts as an insult, such address may not be considered an insult. This is yet another illustration of the thesis of context sensitivity and is compatible, like the previous example, with supposing that morality is not relative, that there are moral principles that are transculturally correct.

The point being made here is simple. The rightness or wrongness of particular actions performed in some specific context depends in part on certain nonmoral facts that obtain in the context in question. The same point can be made in connection with the application of moral principles. When we apply moral principles to particular cases, nonmoral facts about agents and their environment (including their culture) can be relevant in determining the morality of actions. For clarity's sake, let us formulate what I am calling the *context sensitivity thesis* as follows:

CS   The rightness or wrongness of an action (performed in some particular context) partly depends on nonmoral facts that hold in the context in question—facts concerning agents and their circumstances.

This thesis goes by other names, including *situational relativism, environmental relativism, application relativism*, and *circumstantial relativism*. I prefer to avoid using such terminology since using the term "relativism" invites confusion of this thesis with moral relativism.

In addition to the labels, what sometimes leads to confusion are such remarks as "What is right for me may not be what is right for someone else," and "What is right in one culture may not be right in another culture." These remarks are ambiguous—they can be interpreted in more than one way. Interpreted as saying something uncontroversial, they are most likely referring to CS: what is right in one culture may not be right in some other culture since, for example, specific actions or remarks that count as insulting and hence wrong for the members of one culture may not count as insults for the members of another culture. Again, we might interpret these remarks as referring to the facts of intercultural differences in moral belief: what is *believed* right in one culture may not be *believed* right in another. Again, this claim is uncontroversial.

But sometimes such remarks are intended to express moral relativism. The danger to be avoided, then, is sliding from the thought that the remarks in question express something uncontroversial and even enlightened about morality to the thought that moral relativism is true.

What about the truth of moral relativism?

3. The Moral Diversity Thesis

As already noted, diversity in moral belief across cultures is responsible for leading some thinkers to accept moral relativism. In the following three sections, we will examine the attempt to infer relativism from such diversity, but let us first consider more closely the issue of intercultural diversity in moral belief.

The thesis that some cultures accept moral beliefs that conflict with the moral beliefs of other cultures is often called *descriptive relativism* because it purports to state an anthropological fact about cultures that can be scientifically investigated and described. What is of particular interest here is the thesis that there are sometimes *deep-going, fundamental conflicts* in moral belief across cultures—conflicts at the level of basic moral norms.[6] This idea can be expressed by what I will call the *moral diversity thesis:*

MD The moral codes of some cultures include basic moral norms that conflict with the basic moral norms that are part of the moral codes of other cultures.

One main argument for moral relativism is based on this thesis. Before considering this argument, however, let us consider the idea of moral norms in conflict.

In order to represent moral conflicts as conflicts between conflicting moral norms, we need to impute to a culture's moral code norms of permission. Let me explain. Moral norms are typically of two sorts: (1) norms of prohibition, which are concerned with actions that are wrong or forbidden, and (2) norms of requirement, which specify obligatory actions. For actions that are neither wrong nor obligatory—for actions that are morally optional—we normally don't formulate what might be called norms of permission. Actions that we are permitted but not required to perform are simply all of those actions not mentioned in either norms of prohibition or norms of requirement.

Now whenever the moral code of one culture includes a norm requiring that actions of certain sorts be performed (e.g., the eating of human flesh under certain circumstances) while the moral code of some other culture includes a norm forbidding such actions, we have a conflict of moral norms. But there are also cases in which the norms of one culture include either a norm of prohibition or a norm of requirement regarding some type of action while another culture simply lacks a moral norm regarding such an action. To be able to represent such cases as involving a conflict of moral norms, I am suggesting that we impute to the second culture a norm of permission.

Thus, when it comes to intercultural conflicts of moral norms, there are three types of cases to consider. First, it may be that with regard to some type of action, one culture accepts a norm of prohibition while the other culture accepts a conflicting norm of requirement. For example, one culture may prohibit the eating of human flesh, while another culture may (under certain circumstances) require such an action. Second, there are cases in which, with regard to some type of action, one culture may accept a norm of requirement (e.g., that its members render aid to strangers in need) while the other culture may only (implicitly) accept a norm of permission regarding such action. Finally, there may be cases in which, with respect to some type of action, one culture accepts a norm of prohibition (e.g., regarding homosexuality) while the other culture accepts a conflicting norm of permission.

Having explained the idea of moral norms in conflict featured in the moral diversity thesis, let us now begin to explore how the moral diversity thesis and moral relativism are related. In the next three sections, we will consider whether the moral diversity thesis, if true, provides good, or perhaps conclusive, evidence for the truth of moral relativism. But to help sharpen our understanding of moral relativism, let us consider whether the truth of moral relativism commits one to the moral diversity thesis.

Our first question is: If moral relativism is true, does it follow that the moral diversity thesis must also be true? One might initially think so, but strictly speaking, moral relativism is compatible with widespread agreement in the basic moral norms accepted by different cultures. Moral relativism, as I have explained, makes a dependency claim: it says that what makes some action right or wrong depends ultimately on the moral code (in particular, the basic moral norms) of the agent's culture. Whether or not different cultures accept different and conflicting basic moral norms is an empirical matter and does not affect the truth of relativism. Thus, even if it turns out (now or sometime in the future) that all cultures accept the same set of basic moral norms, moral relativism might still be true.

To see this more clearly, let us consider an analogy. We all know that when it comes to driving a vehicle, different countries have different rules, and that these different rules are equally valid. According to the rules that govern driving a vehicle in the United States, one is supposed to drive on the right side of the road. In England, the corresponding rule requires that one drive on the left side of the road. It would be silly to ask which rule expresses the truly correct way to drive on roads, as though one of these rules must be mistaken. Rather, the rules in question are purely conventional. Now if, in the future, England were to change its rule about driving and accept the same rule as the United States, and indeed, if every country were to adopt the same rule about driving on the right side of the road, the universal acceptance of such a rule would not count against such a rule being purely conventional.

The same point applies to moral relativism. If we find out that all cultures accept the same basic moral code (or if in the future, this comes to pass), this would not show that relativism is false. What the moral relativist would say in light of this possibility is that even though as a matter of fact all cultures at the present time happen to embrace the same moral code, it is possible for there to be a culture whose moral code differs from the one enjoying widespread currency. And, adds the relativist, for any such culture, what is right and wrong, good and bad would depend on its moral code.

But even though it is possible for moral relativism to be true when MD is false, the most powerful reason for accepting relativism is the belief that MD is true. Reasons for supposing that MD is true come from the field of anthropology, so let us consider the connection between anthropology and moral relativism.

4. Anthropology and Moral Relativism

The bearing of work in anthropology on moral theory in general, and moral relativism in particular, is more complex than one might initially suppose. My plan is to begin with a rather simple argument for moral relativism based on anthropology that, despite its appeal and popularity, is flawed. Since I think the flawed argument in question does not adequately express the real motivation leading from work in anthropology to moral relativism, I want to consider how the relativist might best express the core idea that prompts relativism. Doing so will lead us, in the following section, to clarify the sorts of intercultural moral disagreements that are offered in support of moral relativism; then in section 6 I will present what I take to be the strongest version of the anthropologist's argument.

The work of anthropologists makes clear that moral beliefs and attitudes vary across cultures and, in some cases, the differences are quite striking. We began the chapter with some examples of intercultural differences in moral belief and attitude, and reflection on such differences may prompt the following line of reasoning.

The Anthropologist's Argument (version 1)

1. Different cultures have different moral codes; in particular, the moral codes of some cultures include basic moral norms that conflict with the basic moral norms of other cultures (= MD).

2. If MD is true, then there are no universally valid moral norms applying to all cultures (= denial of UT).

3. If there are no universally valid moral norms applying to all cultures (= denial of UT), then what is right and what is wrong for the members of a culture depends on the basic moral norms of their culture (= MR).

Thus,

4. Moral relativism (MR) is true.

Because this argument attempts to support moral relativism by appeal to nonmoral claims from anthropology—factual claims about moral diversity—it represents an appeal to the standard of external support (explained in section 6 of chapter 1). Is the argument a good one?[7]

One source of difficulty is premise 2, which asserts that intercultural disagreement or conflict about some matter of fundamental moral importance entails that there is no single truth about the matter in question. But why should mere difference in belief over some issue entail that there is no single correct belief about that issue? Different cultures have had (and may still have) different beliefs about the shape of the earth, some believing that it is flat, others believing that it is spherical, others perhaps believing something else. But from the fact that there are differences in belief about the shape of the earth, we do not first conclude that there is no single truth about its shape and then (as in the above argument) go on to conclude that the truth about the shape of the earth is relative—that it is literally flat for those who believe it is flat, spherical for those who have this belief, and so on. In other words, in general we do not suppose that mere difference in belief about a subject means that there is no single truth about that subject. So unless we are given some reason why we should suppose that a disagreement in moral belief is a legitimate basis for thinking that there is no single truth about morality, we should deny the second premise of this argument.

Some critics also raise questions about the truth of the first premise. It is clear that there are cross-cultural differences in moral belief about certain actions. Some cultures, for example, find nothing wrong in the practice of wife sharing; others do. But the thesis of moral diversity claims not merely that there are differences across cultures in their moral beliefs about various types of action but also that we find differences in the *basic* moral norms accepted by different cultures. To understand the significance of the thesis of moral diversity and why, despite the fact that cultures may disagree about the morality of certain types of actions, they may not really disagree in their basic moral norms, we need to consider the phenomenon of moral disagreement in more detail.

5. Understanding Moral Disagreements

The thesis of moral diversity asserts that there is some intercultural conflict at the level of basic moral norms. The extent of such intercultural disagreement is perhaps controversial. But one might suppose that the work of anthropologists in describing different moral beliefs, attitudes, and practices of different cultures easily and plainly establishes the moral diversity thesis. However, this issue is more complicated, and hence more controversial, than it may at first appear. To see why, we need to distinguish what may be called *fundamental moral disagreement* from *nonfundamental moral disagreement*.

Nonfundamental Moral Disagreements

Imagine that you and I disagree about the morality of capital punishment: I think it is morally wrong, and you do not. Our disagreement may stem from the fact that we disagree about certain nonmoral factual matters. Suppose, then, that I believe that capital punishment has no positive social benefits and, in particular, that it is not an effective crime deterrent. And suppose that I accept as a basic moral norm the following:

1. In response to violations of its laws, a society ought to employ only those punishments that have overall beneficial consequences for society (= P).

This norm, together with my nonmoral belief about the effects of capital punishment,

2. Capital punishment does not have overall beneficial consequences for society.

leads me to conclude that

3. Capital punishment ought to be abolished.

Now like me, you accept the above basic moral norm P, but you disagree with me about the deterrent effects of capital punishment, so you reason as follows:

1. In response to violations of its laws, a society ought to employ only those punishments that have overall beneficial consequences for society (= P).

2. Capital punishment, because it is an effective crime deterrent, does have overall beneficial consequences for society.

Thus,

3. It is not the case that capital punishment ought to be abolished.

This simple example is supposed to illustrate a *nonfundamental* moral disagreement. You and I agree in our basic convictions about the morality of punishment; our disagreement about the morality of capital punishment is due to differences in nonmoral beliefs about this kind of punishment. The thing to notice about this disagreement is that were one of us to change our mind about the overall social benefits of capital punishment—were you to become convinced by relevant empirical research that this practice is not an effective crime deterrent and that it possesses no other social benefits— then you should come to agree with me about the morality of capital punishment. Because our disagreement here is rooted in a disagreement about a nonmoral factual matter that is suitable for scientific investigation, it is one that is rationally resolvable. It gets resolved once we find out the truth about the social effects of capital punishment.

Fundamental Moral Disagreements

A fundamental moral disagreement between two parties is one rooted in the basic moral norms of the parties in question. It is thus a disagreement that would persist even if both parties agreed about all of the relevant nonmoral facts about the disputed issue. Again, consider a moral disagreement over capital punishment. Only this time suppose that you and I agree about the social consequences of this practice; we agree, let us suppose, that it has no significant deterrent effect on crime. Still, we disagree about the morality of capital punishment because we accept different moral norms concerning punishment. To see this more clearly, suppose that instead of P, you accept the following norm:

P* Punishments for crimes ought to involve, whenever possible, inflicting harm on the wrongdoer that is equivalent to the harm that the wrongdoer inflicted on his or her victim(s).

This principle, together with the belief that in cases of murder the death of the murderer is the only penalty equivalent to the crime, leads to the conclusion that capital punishment is obligatory in such cases and hence not morally wrong. Now if the moral conclusion I reach about capital punishment is based on P and the conclusion you reach is based on P*, then our disagreement results from a disagreement in our basic moral norms. And when a moral disagreement stems from a disagreement over basic moral norms, the moral disagreement is *fundamental*.

Is the Moral Diversity Thesis True?

Having illustrated and explained the difference between a nonfundamental and a fundamental moral disagreement between individuals, let us now consider moral disagreements across cultures. The main thing to notice is that the fact that two cultures disagree about some moral issue does not automatically mean that the disagreement stems from a disagreement over basic moral norms. Consider the practice of putting one's parents to death once they reach a certain age. Suppose that most, if not all, of the members of some culture believe that this practice is morally obligatory. Our own culture does not hold such a moral belief and, in fact, holds that it is morally wrong to engage in such killing. Because this intercultural disagreement is rather striking, one might be tempted to conclude that our culture accepts as a basic moral norm something like the following:

One ought to treat one's elders with respect, no matter their age.

Furthermore, it may seem that the other culture in question rejects this moral norm and that this is what explains the intercultural difference in moral belief about killing one's parents. It may seem that we have here an example of a fundamental moral disagreement, indicating a conflict of basic moral norms.

However, this diagnosis of the disagreement is too hasty. To see this, suppose that the culture in question believes in an afterlife full of activities like hunting and playing and that one has the body in the afterlife that one last had in this life. This nonmoral belief about the afterlife, together with the above norm of respect, would lead one to conclude that one ought to kill one's parents once they get to be a certain age, before their bodies become too decrepit to enjoy the afterlife. Thus, what may at first appear to be a case of fundamental moral disagreement between two cultures may turn out to be nonfundamental.[8]

With this in mind, let us now briefly reconsider the thesis of moral diversity. It says that the *basic* moral norms of some cultures often conflict with those of other cultures. If there are such differences, the cultures in question will disagree fundamentally about the morality of certain actions. Now clearly different cultures do sometimes disagree over the morality of actions, but the crucial question is: How many such disagreements are fundamental, thus indicating intercultural conflicts in basic moral norms?

Perhaps intercultural moral disagreements can all be explained in terms of intercultural differences in the relevant nonmoral beliefs, as in the case of the treatment of one's parents. The thesis of moral diversity does not specify the extent of intercultural conflict over basic moral norms. If most or all intercultural disagreement is nonfundamental, and so can be traced to differences in nonmoral factual beliefs, then the thesis of moral diversity, if not false, would certainly be less tempting as a basis for inferring moral relativism. After all, perhaps if there are very few fundamental moral conflicts across cultures, they can be explained as being about moral issues that are extremely difficult to resolve, even though there is a single moral truth about these few disputed issues. It is the belief that there is *widespread* intercultural conflict in basic moral norms that leads some anthropologists and philosophers to embrace moral relativism. Is there such widespread conflict in basic moral norms across cultures?

The issue is an empirical one, to be decided by available evidence. Although some anthropologists, particularly those who embrace moral relativism, have stressed intercultural differences and conflicts in moral norms, other anthropologists have wanted to stress intercultural similarities. So, for example, anthropologist Clyde Kluckhohn (1905–60) noted that

> Every culture has a concept of murder, distinguishing this from execution, killing in war, and other 'justifiable homicides'. The notions of incest and other regulations upon sexual behavior, of prohibitions upon untruth under defined circumstances, of restitution and reciprocity, of mutual obligations between parents and children—these and many other moral concepts are altogether universal. (Kluckhohn 1955, 672)

Writing in 1959, philosopher Richard Brandt (1910–97), having examined the anthropological evidence for the thesis of moral diversity as well as for the thesis, expressed by Kluckhohn, that there is widespread intercultural agreement over basic moral norms, concluded that

> no anthropologist has offered what we should regard as really an adequate account of a single case, clearly showing there is ultimate disagreement in moral

principle. Of course, we must remember that this lack of information is just as serious for any claim that there is world-wide agreement on some principle. (Brandt 1959, 102)

More recently, Michele Moody-Adams has argued that there are deep methodological problems that stand in the way of establishing the moral diversity thesis (what she refers to as "descriptive relativism"). She writes:

The most serious obstacles to formulating contrastive judgments about the moral practices of particular human groups, and to establishing the truth of descriptive relativism, reflect a difficulty peculiar to the study of cultures: that of deciding who—if anyone—has the "authority" to represent the defining principles, especially the basic moral principles, of a given culture. (Moody-Adams 1997, 43)

Moody-Adams goes on to argue that because of the complexity of cultures and the problem of determining a moral authority for a culture, it is extremely difficult, if not impossible, to gather the kind of empirical evidence that would be needed to support the moral diversity thesis. Whether or not one shares her pessimism, I think we must conclude that the moral diversity thesis has not been established. And so, lacking the needed evidence to support premise 1, the anthropologist's argument collapses.

6. The Anthropologist's Argument Reconsidered

But let us suppose that the thesis of moral diversity is true and there is significant intercultural conflict in the basic moral norms across many cultures. We noted in section 4 that there is a problem going from the thesis of moral diversity (MD) to the denial of the universality thesis (UT). Just because different cultures accept different and conflicting basic moral norms, and so work with different basic moral assumptions, the claim that there are no universally valid moral norms does not logically follow. After all, as we pointed out earlier, differences in belief about the shape of the earth or about the movements of the planets do not tempt us to conclude that there is no single truth about such matters and that it is all just a matter of what your culture believes. So why accept this kind of inference in the case of morals?

Now if the advocate of the anthropologist's argument were simply attempting to infer the denial of the universality thesis from MD (as represented in the second premise of version 1 of the argument), this point would be decisive against the argument. However, there seems to be more to the argument than is expressed in the formulation from section 4. Let me explain.

Those who are impressed with what they take to be deep-going, fundamental moral disagreements across cultures are also likely to hold the view that such disagreements cannot be resolved in the way in which disagreements about, say, the shape of the earth or the movement of the planets can be resolved. With respect to differences in belief about the shape of the earth, we have ways of explaining why one party to the disagreement is mistaken. Prescientific cultures lacked the kind of evidence we now possess about the earth's shape and so came to accept a false belief based on limited evidence. This kind of mistake—inference based on limited evidence—can be corrected in principle by rational means. Thus, disagreements between two cultures over the shape of the earth, and many other such scientific matters, are capable of being resolved by rational means. In the case of scientific disputes, rational means include the various methods and procedures characteristic of good science. Furthermore, the fact that such disagreements are rationally resolvable is to be expected given two further assumptions. First, we assume that with regard to matters like the shape of the earth, the movements of the planets, and many more such matters about the universe, there is some single set of facts or truths about our universe out there waiting to be discovered. And, second, we assume that we are capable of getting at the truth. These assumptions would explain why, over time at least, there is convergence in scientific belief about our universe.

The moral relativist will now insist that there is a crucial difference between disagreements over scientific matters, on the one hand, and moral disagreements, on the other. As just explained, the former are in principle resolvable by rational methods and procedures, but (so the relativist claims) this is not so in the case of many moral disagreements—in particular those involving a conflict between basic moral norms. So, it is not merely the fact that there are fundamental moral disagreements between cultures but that such disagreements are (unlike disputes in science) *rationally irresolvable*. Moreover, what this indicates, according to the relativist, is that when it comes to such disputes, there is no single moral truth about the matter being disputed, for if there were, we would expect more intercultural moral agreement at the level of basic moral norms than the anthropological evidence suggests. Thus, moral truth is plausibly relativized to the basic norms of individual cultures. In short, the irresolvability by rational means of certain moral disagreements indicates that there are no culture-independent moral norms to be discovered.

So, based on these reflections, here is an improved version of the anthropologist's argument that captures this idea about irresolvability.

The Anthropologist's Argument (version 2)

1. Different cultures have different moral codes; in particular, the moral codes of some cultures include basic moral norms that conflict with

the basic moral norms of other cultures (= MD).

2.   Such conflicts cannot be resolved by rational means.

Thus,

3.   There are rationally irresolvable intercultural conflicts over basic moral norms.

4.   The best explanation for such irresolvable conflicts is: there are no universally valid moral norms applying to all cultures (= denial of UT).

5.   If there are no universally valid moral norms applying to all cultures (= denial of UT), then what is right and what is wrong for the members of a culture depends on the basic moral norms of their culture. (= MR).

Thus,

6.   What is right or wrong depends on the basic moral norms of the culture in which the action is performed (MR).

This version of the anthropologist's argument is an improvement over the first version. In the first version, premise 2 just claims, without explanation, that the denial of the universality thesis follows immediately from the moral diversity thesis, which, as we have seen, is problematic. In the new version, the denial of the universality thesis is being proposed in premise 4 as the best explanation of the apparent irresolvability of the sort of deep-going conflict mentioned in the moral diversity thesis. This way of arguing for the denial of the universality thesis allows the relativist to plausibly explain why moral disagreements differ importantly from scientific disagreements. So, if we grant the thesis of moral diversity, the case for moral relativism (based on anthropological evidence) depends on whether or not such disagreements in basic moral norms can be rationally resolved.

A Nonrelativist Response

In responding to this argument, then, the nonrelativist who accepts the universality thesis is going to question premise 2. In doing so, she will have to explain how such disagreements about moral issues can be rationally resolved, at least in principle. What means of rational resolution might be available in ethics?

The topic is a large and complex one; indeed, attempts by philosophers to elaborate and defend nonrelativist moral theories of right conduct and value can be viewed as attempts to answer this question. For instance, you may recall from the last chapter that according to the divine command theory, rational resolution of moral disagreement involves appealing to facts about God's commands. According to the natural law theory (which we take up in the next chapter), fundamental moral disagreements can in principle be resolved by appeal to facts about the nature of human beings. Other theories to be considered, including utilitarianism, Kant's moral theory, and virtue ethics, make other proposals regarding the rational resolution of moral conflicts. Thus, a full answer to this question would involve an examination of the sorts of moral theories featured in this book.

However, for the time being, we can indicate, if only very briefly, how a nonrelativist might attempt to respond to the above argument. To focus our thinking about this matter, let us ask how an individual's basic moral norms might be rationally criticized. Suppose we encounter someone who does not think it is morally wrong for people to engage in activities that inflict pain on lower animals and condones "games" like "chicken pull," described by Richard Brandt.

> In this "game," a chicken is buried in the sand, up to its neck. The contestants ride by on horseback, trying to grab the chicken by the neck and yank it from the sand. When someone succeeds in this, the idea is then for the other contestants to take away from him as much of the chicken as they can. The "winner" is the one who ends up with the most chicken. (Brandt 1959, 102)

Let us suppose further that the individual who finds nothing morally objectionable about this game and other such treatment of animals does not have nonmoral beliefs about animals that differ from ours. For example, the individual does not believe that chickens and other animals are just nonconscious automata, cleverly designed to emulate genuine pain behavior. Nor does the individual believe that such activities are necessary to please the gods and thus ensure a good harvest. Rather, this individual shares all of our nonmoral beliefs about animals, it is just that his moral code does not include a norm prohibiting such treatment of animals; the individual in question sees nothing wrong with games like chicken pull.

The question is: Can we make sense of the suggestion that this individual is mistaken in thinking that there is nothing morally wrong with painful treatment of animals? Here is one way of doing so. We might begin by noting that proper moral thinking about some issue may require that one have the capacity for thinking sympathetically about the effects of one's actions on creatures that are affected by them and that one engage this capacity in contemplating various courses of action. So, although the person who does not see anything wrong with games like chicken pull may have correct beliefs about the pain caused to animals, he might not properly appreciate such facts owing to a lack of proper sympathy. If exercise of sympathy is involved in properly reasoning about matters of morality, then failing to engage sympathetically with the victims of chicken pull will lead one to mistaken moral convictions about such treatment.

This is but a sketch of how a nonrelativist might attempt to show that individuals can be mistaken in their basic moral convictions. Much more would have to be done in elaborating and defending any such view about proper moral methodology. But the important point here is that we should not assume that the relativist is correct in claiming that in ethics there is no method for rationally resolving moral disagreements, even fundamental ones.

On the basis of what has been said thus far, I think we must conclude that the final verdict is still out on the cogency of the anthropologist's argument.

7. The Price of Moral Relativism

What about the plausibility of moral relativism? Although I do not think there is a decisive refutation of this type of moral theory, I do think that in accepting moral relativism, one must pay a heavy price. Here, I want to focus on three challenges facing the moral relativist: (1) problems having to do with formulating the theory that affect the theory's consistency and determinacy; (2) problems having to do with what I shall call our critical practices concerning moral issues that bear on the standard of intuitive appeal; and, finally, (3) problems having to do with the standard of internal support. Let us take these up in order.

Problems of Formulation

According to moral relativism, the rightness or wrongness of actions depends on the moral code of the culture to which the agent belongs. (Similar remarks apply to what is good or bad.) But what counts as one's culture? This question is perhaps not difficult when it comes to small groups that exhibit a high degree of social cohesion. But what counts as the culture of people living in the United States, a country exhibiting a great deal of nonuniformity in moral belief and practice? Should we suppose that all citizens of the United States are members of one, single culture—American culture? Or perhaps we should carve up cultures by smaller geographical regions of the United States, so that we would have midwestern culture, southern culture, northeastern culture, and so on. Or perhaps culture can be specified in terms of religious affiliation (at least for those who have such an affiliation) since religions involve moral codes. Again, political organizations, like the U.S. Democratic and Republican Parties, would seem to count as cultures. The point is that there is a plurality of ways in which we might conceive of a culture, and the relativist needs to provide a principled account of what counts as one's culture for purposes of moral evaluation.

Failure to do so means that the relativist has failed to specify what it is that makes an action (done by a particular person at a particular time) right or wrong and thus has failed to provide a determinate moral criterion. This means that the theory fails the standard of determinacy as explained in chapter 1.

There is another aspect of this problem worth bringing out. In our pluralistic society, there are many cultures (or subcultures, as they are often called) and at any given time most individuals are members of more than one of them. Unless the relativist specifies which culture is relevant for moral evaluation, it can turn out that moral relativism implies inconsistent moral evaluations of the same action. Suppose, for example, that Susan is a member of the Roman Catholic Church, which forbids almost all abortions, but that she is also a member of the Democratic Party, whose moral code does not forbid abortion and in fact condones it in a wide variety of cases. If one accepts moral relativism, it appears that one must conclude that for Susan, having an abortion (at least under certain conditions) would be both right and wrong! This means that the theory fails to satisfy the standard of consistency for moral theories explained in chapter 1. So the problem of specifying, in a nonarbitrary way, what is to count as one's culture for purposes of moral evaluation is not just some technical point that the relativist can push aside.

Unless the moral relativist can plausibly deal with these problems of formulation, the theory fails both the determinacy and consistency standards for evaluating moral theories.

Moral Relativism and Our Critical Practices

More serious problems for moral relativism concern our critical practices. We normally think that it makes sense to evaluate the moral codes of different cultures and claim that in some respects the moral code of some particular culture is mistaken. We also suppose that the moral code of our own culture (whatever that is) can improve or become worse. And we normally think that moral reformers are sometimes correct in their critical evaluations of the moral codes of the culture to which they belong. But, if moral relativism is correct, then none of these assumptions about our common critical practices is correct. Let us consider these problems in order.

The Problem of Intercultural Evaluation. Consider the case of critically evaluating the moral codes of different cultures. Notice first of all that it is possible, according to the version of moral relativism we have been examining, to sensibly raise objections to *nonbasic* moral norms of a culture. Suppose, for example, a culture accepts as basic a moral norm to the effect that killing sentient creatures—creatures with a developed capacity to experience pleasure and pain—is wrong. Suppose they also have the nonmoral belief that a certain species of plant is sentient and thereby come to accept the derived moral norm that killing this species of plant is morally wrong. If they are mistaken in their nonmoral belief, then we can say that their derived moral norm is (for them) mistaken. However, if moral relativism is true, the *basic* moral norms of a culture set the standard for right and wrong conduct for the members of the culture in question. And, if these norms set the very standard for right and wrong, then it makes no sense to question the correctness of those norms—they just are the ultimate standards for the relevant culture.

To really fix on this idea—which goes to the heart of relativism—consider the meter bar. The meter bar is a bar, located in France, that represents the standard for the meter. Suppose you and a friend are looking at the meter bar and your friend turns to you and asks, "How do we know that it's a meter long?" Now your friend might be wondering how we can be sure that the bar has remained the same length since the time it was first established as the standard for a meter. But suppose your friend is wondering whether the bar was ever a meter long. In wondering about this, your friend shows that he doesn't understand what the meter bar represents: it *is* the standard for something's being a meter in length, and questions about whether it—the very standard—is (or was originally) a meter long make no sense.

The parallel with moral relativism should be obvious. According to moral relativism, the basic moral norms of a culture represent the moral meter bar, so to speak, for the culture. Thus, questions about the correctness of those standards for the members of the relevant culture cannot be sensibly raised. But surely it makes sense to question the correctness of the basic norms of culture. Consider a culture some of whose basic norms are racist. Surely it makes sense to criticize such norms and claim that they are mistaken. But if we accept moral relativism, engaging in such criticism makes no sense.

Clearly, having to accept this implication is a high price to pay for being a moral relativist.

The Problem of Intracultural Evaluation. Consider now the practice of comparing the moral code of a culture at one time in its history with its code at another time. We have all heard preachers and politicians talk about how, with regard to some practices, morality has declined. It is sometimes said, for instance, that widespread acceptance of homosexuality marks a change for the worse in the morality (or moral code) of contemporary culture and so in this respect at least today's moral code is worse than the moral code accepted a generation ago.[9] Similarly, we have all heard claims to the effect that in some ways our moral code has improved over the course of time with respect to racial and gender equality, as well as the treatment of animals.

But can such comparative claims make sense for the moral relativist? Clearly not, since if at some time in our history, say 1950, it was part of our moral code that homosexuality is wrong, then it was wrong (for members of the culture at that time) to engage in such sexual activity. If we find that now our moral code has changed so that homosexuality is no longer condemned, then such activities are no longer morally wrong. For the moral relativist, one cannot make sense of the idea that the basic norms of a moral code of culture have gotten better or worse, that it has improved in some ways or degenerated in others. Rather, all the relativist can say is that over time what is right or wrong has changed for members of some culture.

The Moral Reformer Problem. Finally, consider the very idea of a moral reformer. A moral reformer is someone who attempts to change the moral beliefs and attitudes of a culture, possibly her own. So imagine someone who thinks that the practice of honor killing (mentioned earlier) is morally wrong and who, as a member of the culture in question, publicly opposes the practice as morally wrong. According to relativism, if this practice really is part of the moral code of the culture in question (it is required or permitted by its basic moral norms), then the moral reformer in question is necessarily saying something false when she says, "The practice of honor killing is wrong." But this implication of relativism just seems completely mistaken. We don't think that the claims of a moral reformer that go against the moral grain of her culture are necessarily mistaken. Indeed, we normally think that moral reformers are sometimes correct in their moral opposition to certain practices of their own culture.

These various critical practices reflect beliefs about morality to the effect that criticism of the moral norms of other cultures as well as one's own culture is possible. As we have seen, moral relativism implies that such intuitively appealing beliefs about morality are mistaken. Recall from chapter 1 that according to the standard of intuitive appeal, a moral theory should make sense of various intuitively appealing beliefs about morality. Thus, moral relativism (at least the version under consideration) can be criticized for not accommodating such beliefs.

Conflicts with Our Considered Moral Beliefs. If we accept moral relativism, then if a culture's basic moral norms either condone or require the torture and killing of certain human beings just because of their ethnic background or whatever, we have to conclude that such behavior really is right (perhaps even obligatory) for that culture. The example of Naziism is often brought up as an example. It was part of the Nazi value system that Jews should be exterminated. But no one should conclude that therefore the torture and killing of Jews was morally right for the dedicated Nazi. The reader can no doubt think of other examples where moral relativism conflicts with our considered moral beliefs. Thus, moral relativism fails to satisfy the standard of internal support for evaluating a moral theory.

Finally, the fact that moral relativism conflicts with various considered moral beliefs indicates that it also fails to provide a correct explanation of what makes an action right or wrong, or something good or bad, and thus that it fails the standard of explanatory power. Appealing to the moral code accepted by a culture may explain why many members of the culture have the moral beliefs they do in fact have. But we are interested in explaining what makes something have the moral quality it has, and mere facts about the moral norms accepted by cultures fail to give us the desired explanation.

As I mentioned earlier, these observations do not decisively refute moral relativism, if only because there are more sophisticated versions that we have not been able to consider and which perhaps avoid these problems.[10] However, the objections we have raised show that one common variety of moral relativism is deeply problematic. Certainly one will want to consider nonrelativist moral theories before embracing some form of moral relativism.

8. Relativism and Tolerance

Before concluding, let us consider the issue of relativism and tolerance. Some anthropologists who infer moral relativism from facts about intercultural differences in moral convictions have also apparently thought that a relativist stance in ethics commits one to a principle of tolerance. Ruth Benedict, for instance, claimed that on the basis of moral relativism,

> We shall arrive then at a more realistic social faith, accepting as grounds of hope and as new bases for tolerance the coexisting and equally valid patterns of life which mankind has created for itself from the raw materials of existence. (Benedict 1934, 278)

The suggestion seems to be that moral relativism commits one to tolerance regarding the moral beliefs and convictions of other cultures since, after all, what is right or wrong is simply a matter of the basic moral norms of one's society. So if a culture, on the basis of its moral code, engages in honor killing, parricide, or games like chicken pull that members of other cultures might find abhorrent, there is no basis for these outraged cultures to interfere with the practices of other cultures, at least if moral relativism is true. In engaging in honor killings, the culture that takes this practice to be morally right is engaging in actions that really are morally right for members of the culture in question. And if the members of a culture are engaged in practices that are morally right (at least for them), then there is no moral basis for interfering with such practices. Thus, according to this line of argument, moral relativism is committed to a principle of tolerance:

It is morally wrong for any culture to interfere with moral practices of another culture.

Perhaps this principle needs to be qualified to allow that under certain conditions interference in the practices of other cultures is permitted—particularly in cases where those practices threaten the welfare of members of one's own culture. However, the question to be considered here is whether moral relativism commits one to accepting this principle of tolerance.

It takes little reflection to see that moral relativism involves no such commitment. Notice that the above moral principle is intended to state a moral requirement that is valid for all cultures. It would in fact be inconsistent for a relativist to advocate the principle in question as a universally valid moral norm. After all, according to moral relativism, what is right or wrong depends on the moral code of one's culture. This implies that whether or not it is morally wrong for some culture C to interfere with the practices of another culture depends on the moral code of C. Clearly, if one accepts moral relativism, then the truth or validity of any principle of tolerance is relative: it is true or valid for those cultures whose basic moral norms include or imply this principle, false or invalid for those cultures that do not.

In addition, it should be noted that nonrelativist moral theories do not commit one to the denial of a principle of tolerance like the one above. It might be supposed that unless one accepts moral relativism, one will be committed to the idea that our culture ought to engage in a moral campaign to convert other cultures with different moral codes to our own moral outlook. But again, this inference is clearly mistaken. According to the divine command theory, the morality of interfering with the practices of other cultures depends on God's commands, and those commands may condemn all sorts of interference. A similar remark applies to the other nonrelativist moral theories featured throughout the rest of this book.

In summary, if we accept moral relativism, then whether or not we ought to be tolerant of the moral practices of other cultures depends on the moral code of our own culture. And, of course, whether members of other cultures ought to be tolerant in this way depends on the moral codes of their cultures. Moreover, tolerance may be required by the moral principles featured in nonrelativist moral theories.

9. Conclusion

The topic of relativism in ethics is complex and potentially very confusing. Our main focus has been on a normative moral theory that I have been calling moral relativism. Perhaps the most appealing feature of this theory (recall the standard of intuitive appeal from chapter 1, section 6) is the fact that it coheres nicely with idea that there are deep-going differences in the moral codes of different cultures, an idea that many people find appealing, especially given the work of anthropologists. However, the theory faces serious problems.

We have discovered that the main argument for this type of theory—the anthropologist's argument—faces certain challenges, so we have not been presented with a truly compelling case in its favor. More importantly, relativism encounters serious objections concerning its formulation and consequently has difficulty satisfying the standards of determinacy and consistency for evaluating moral theories. Furthermore, the theory is seriously at odds with the standards of intuitive appeal, internal support, and explanatory power. These problems should prompt us to consider competing non-relativist theories.

What are the prospects for a nonrelativist moral theory? Some anthropologists have suggested that facts about human nature may provide a basis for a universally valid set of moral norms. Consider what Kluckhohn says:

> While specific manifestations of human nature vary between cultures and between individuals in the same culture, human nature is universal. All value systems have to make some of the same concessions to the natural world of which human nature is a part. Some needs and motives are so deep and so generic that they are beyond the reach of argument. (Kluckhohn 1955, 676)

If, as Kluckhohn says, there is a universal human nature, then since morality has to do with what to do and how to be, it makes sense to consider grounding morality in facts about universal human nature. And this is exactly a guiding idea behind the natural law moral theory to which we now turn.

Further Reading

Benedict, Ruth. 1946. *Patterns of Culture.* New York: Pelican Books. A classic defense of moral relativism by a noted anthropologist.

Brandt, R. B. 1959. *Ethical Theory.* Englewood Cliffs, N.J.: Prentice-Hall. Chapters 5 and 11 are both notable for an informed discussion of relevant anthropological data bearing on relativism.

Cook, John W. 1999. *Morality and Cultural Differences.* New York: Oxford University Press. A useful attempt to examine the issue of moral relativism bringing together both philosophical and anthropological sources. Cook is critical of relativism.

Harman, Gilbert. 1975. "Moral Relativism Defended." *Philosophical Review* 84: 3–22. An important statement and defense of moral relativism.

Harman, G., and Judith Thomson. 1996. *Moral Relativism and Moral Objectivity.*

London: Blackwell. Harman defends relativism, and Thomson defends nonrelativism. Included also are lively responses by both authors to the views of the other.

Ladd, John. 1985. *Moral Relativism*. Lanham, Md.: University Press of America. A collection of writings from anthropologists and philosophers debating relativism.

Moody-Adams, Michele M. 1997. *Fieldwork in Familiar Places: Morality, Culture, and Philosophy*. Cambridge: Harvard University Press. A penetrating critique of moral relativism and a defense of the claim that morality is objective.

Moser, Paul, and Thomas L. Carson. 2001. *Moral Relativism: A Reader*. New York: Oxford University Press. A wide-ranging collection of essays with a useful introduction and bibliography by the editors.

Paul, Ellen F., Fred D. Miller, and Jeffrey Paul. 1994. *Cultural Pluralism and Moral Knowledge*. Cambridge: Cambridge University Press. Contains some important essays on moral relativism.

Stewart, Robert M., and Lynn L. Thomas. 1991. "Recent Work on Moral Relativism." *American Philosophical Quarterly* 28: 85–100. An overview of some work on moral relativism from the 1970s and 1980s. Includes a useful bibliography.

Westermark, Edward. 1960. *Moral Relativity*. New York: Humanities Press. Of particular interest is chapter 7, which contains a brief overview of the anthropological evidence for diversity in moral belief.

Wong, David. 1984. *Moral Relativity*. Berkeley and Los Angeles: University of California Press. A sophisticated defense of a version of moral relativism that differs importantly from the version examined in this chapter.

Notes

1. The moral relativist gives a similar account of goodness and badness in terms of the moral codes of cultures. Since the theory of value offered by the moral relativist is parallel to the relativist theory of right conduct, we shall focus almost exclusively on the theory of right conduct.

2. Moral norms, then, include moral principles and moral rules. I talk about norms to have a term to cover both principles and rules and because much of the literature on relativism uses this term.

3. In another place, Sumner writes: "The notion of right is in the folkways. It is not outside of them, of independent origin, and brought to them to test them" ([1906] 1959, 28).

4. This thesis is often called *moral absolutism*. But since the term "absolutism" is also commonly used to refer to the claim that certain moral rules like "Do not lie" do not admit of exceptions (an idea that we take up in the next chapter), I am avoiding that label here.

5. I thank Tom Nenon for this example.

6. The idea of a fundamental conflict or disagreement in moral belief will be explained in sec. 4.

7. In what follows, premises 1 and 2, but not 3, are subjected to critical scruti-

ny because they tend to be the premises that attract the most critical attention in the debate over moral relativism. However, premise 3 can also be challenged.

8. Notice that in this example, unlike the one about capital punishment used to illustrate nonfundamental moral disagreements, the disagreement may turn out to be rationally irresolvable if there are no rational procedures for deciding factual questions about the afterlife, including whether there is one.

9. Such claims about the erosion and decline of the moral codes of such countries as England and the United States are explored in Himmelfarb 1995.

10. Recent defenders include Wong (1984) and Harman (1975, 1996).

4

Natural Law Theory

On April 15, 1989, seventeen-year-old Tony Bland was attending a soccer match at Hillsborough Football Stadium in Sheffield, England. As thousands of fans were hurrying to enter the stadium, some of them were smashed against a barrier, leaving ninety-five people dead and many others seriously injured. Bland was injured in the incident, and although he did not die, his lungs were crushed by the pressure of the crowd, resulting in a loss of oxygen to his brain. The unhappy result was that the cortex of his brain was destroyed, causing permanent loss of consciousness, though his body was kept alive by machines and feeding tubes. Tony Bland's family and the attending physician, Dr. J. G. Howe, were prepared to withdraw life support, since his continued existence was (so they thought) pointless. To avoid the possibility of criminal charges, the hospital treating Bland applied to the Family Division of the High Court for permission to withdraw treatment. The case stirred moral and legal controversy and was eventually settled in the British courts in a decision that held that physicians are not under a legal obligation to continue treatment that does not benefit a patient. However, there were those who were morally and legally opposed to withdrawing life support from Bland. They argued that since withdrawing treatment would be the intentional killing of an innocent human being, such action would be wrong, even in tragic cases like Bland's.

The idea that there are certain types of actions that are morally wrong in all circumstances is characteristic of the natural law theory of ethics, a moral theory that represents the moral teachings of the Roman Catholic Church. Other types of action that, according to this theory, are always wrong include homosexuality, artificial means of birth control, suicide, abortion, and artificial insemination. Are such types of action always morally wrong? If so, what reason can be given for such restrictions? The natural law theory represents an attempt to work out a systematic answer to these questions and will be the focus of this chapter.

As we shall see, the natural law theory—at least the version of it that we will examine—involves some interesting complexity, and so it will be presented in stages. We begin, in the first section, with some general remarks about natural law ethics and then proceed in sections 2 through 11 to examine the version of natural law suggested in the writings of Saint Thomas Aquinas. In section 12 we consider various objections to this moral theory.

1. What Is Natural Law?

In many contexts, talk of natural law refers to laws of nature—the sorts of laws that are investigated by the sciences. Such laws are descriptive—they describe certain regularities in nature. Boyle's law, for example, states that the pressure and volume of a gas vary inversely at a given temperature. Of course, in English, the term "law" is also used to refer to the sorts of norms and rules that characterize a legal system. Such civil laws are prescriptive: they express norms and rules for how citizens are supposed to behave. In ethics, natural law refers to moral laws (or principles) that, like the laws of a legal system, prescribe how individuals ought to behave.

However, there is an important contrast between natural law in ethics and the laws of a legal system. The term "natural" in natural law ethics indicates that moral laws have a source and authority that distinguish them from the civil laws of any society. At the end of the last chapter, I quoted a passage from the work of anthropologist Clyde Kluckhohn in which he suggests that a possible basis for a nonrelativist, universally valid set of moral principles is our common human nature. The idea that there is an objective set of moral principles based in human nature is central to the natural law theory. Moral laws (or principles), according to this theory, are natural in the sense that they are grounded in human nature and thus represent universally valid norms for the behavior of all human beings. In this respect, natural law ethics contrasts sharply with moral relativism.

Thus, according to the natural law theory of ethics, there are moral laws (or principles) that express requirements on behavior that, because they are grounded in human nature (and because human nature is the same for all human beings), are valid and hence apply to all human beings, regardless of culture.

However, this characterization does not capture what is distinctive about natural law ethics. Other nonrelativist moral theories that we shall study in the following chapters set forth moral principles that are grounded at least partly in facts about human beings and that purport to be universally valid. Unfortunately, the theories representative of the natural law tradition, because they differ over what is and is not essential to natural law ethics, make it difficult to provide a definitive characterization of this type of moral theory. Perhaps the best way to proceed in examining natural law ethics is simply to consider the version we find in Aquinas—arguably the greatest proponent of this type of theory—and let this version be representative of the natural law tradition. In any case, there are elements of Aquinas's view that we do not find in rival moral theories and which therefore make his view worth studying.

Let us begin our study of natural law theory with some general remarks about some of its basic elements. We will then be ready to examine the version we find in Aquinas.

2. Three Components of Natural Law Moral Theory

As I will present the theory, it has three main components. First, there is what I will call the theory's core, which involves a *perfectionist theory of value* that is the basis for understanding right and wrong conduct. This is a *value-based* moral theory, since the value concepts are more basic than the deontic concepts. Aquinas grounds his perfectionist theory of value in facts about human nature: it is because we are creatures of a certain sort, sharing a common human nature, that certain kinds of states of affairs and activities are intrinsically valuable. It is also part of Aquinas's view that acting morally—doing the right thing—is a matter of acting rationally, and so moral principles of right action represent basic requirements of practical rationality.

The second component of this theory addresses the question of whether it is ever morally permissible to do what is bad or evil in order to promote what is good. The theory's answer to this question is expressed in the *principle of double effect,* which raises interesting issues about the moral importance of intention and foresight in action.

The third component of traditional natural law ethics is its commitment to *moral absolutism*—the idea that certain kinds of action are always morally wrong, regardless of whatever good might result from them. Such actions are featured in absolutist moral rules—rules that, for example, absolutely prohibit such acts as killing innocent human beings, lying, and homosexuality.

Let us now proceed to examine these three components in more detail. Following the thought of Aquinas, the next two sections outline the theory's core.

3. Aquinas's Perfectionism

The essential features of the moral theory of Thomas Aquinas (1224–74) are contained in a few short sections of his massive work, *Summa Theologiae (Summary of Theology).* This theory, like all of Aquinas's philosophical work, was strongly influenced by the ideas of the Greek philosopher Aristotle (384–322 B.C.). (The moral theory of Aristotle is featured in chapter 9.) Though there are important differences in the moral theories of Aquinas and Aristotle, they do share a certain conception of the connection between human nature and the good in relation to humans that is a natural starting point in coming to understand their moral theories. To understand this conception of the human good, it will be useful to begin with some general remarks about the relation between a thing's essential nature and the good of that thing.[1]

Purpose, Perfection, and Goodness

The essential nature, or essence, of a thing is what makes that thing what it is. According to Aquinas (following Aristotle), a thing's purpose, or end, is crucial for understanding its essence. (In this context, the terms "purpose," "end," "function," and "goal" all refer to the same thing.) This is easiest to understand in relation to human artifacts. Consider a knife. To understand what a knife is—to understand its essence—one must understand its purpose, or function, which is to cut.[2] Of course, a knife might or might not be useful for the purpose of cutting owing to such things as the sharpness of its blade, its size, and so forth. Knives with dull blades are difficult, if not impossible, to use for the purpose of cutting. This means that the state a knife is in with respect to its end or purpose can vary. A knife that can be used to perform its cutting function well is in a state of perfection or excellence (for that sort of knife). And it is the perfection of a knife that constitutes its goodness. The goodness of a knife, then, is its being in a state of perfection, and to be in a state of perfection is for it to be able to perform its function well. Since there are different types of knives, designed for different jobs—bread knives, paring knives, butcher knives, steak knives, and so on—a good knife of a certain type is one that cuts certain sorts of things well. A good bread knife, for example, is one that can be used to cut bread well.

According to a teleological worldview (from the Greek word *telos*, meaning end or goal), which Aquinas inherited from Aristotle, all things in nature have purposes, and thus to understand the essence of anything requires that one understand a thing's purpose (or purpose*s*, in the case of things with complex natures). So for instance, to understand a plant—its essence—one must understand its purposes, which include taking in nutrition, growth, and reproduction. The perfection, and hence the good, of a plant, then, is its taking in nutrition, growing, and reproducing well.

Again, nonhuman animals are to be understood in terms of their purposes, which, in addition to those characteristic of plants, also include (at least for many animals) such capacities as locomotion and sense perception. The perfection of an animal with such capacities is for it to be in a state in which its capacities are fully developed and engaged. In general, with regard to organisms, we can say that their good is a matter of their flourishing as the types of organisms they are.

Human Nature and the Good for Humans

The same general point about purpose, perfection, and goodness applies to humans: the perfection, and hence good, of a human being is a matter of its being in a state in which those purposes characteristic of human beings are fully developed and engaged. However, unlike plants and lower animals, human beings are rational agents with free will. This means, first of all, that it is up to humans (in a way that it is not up to plants and lower animals) to come to understand their essential nature and thus come to understand their good through the use of reason. It also means that humans are then to exercise free will in fully achieving their good or perfection based on their understanding of their good. In short, it is up to human beings to understand and develop those capacities whose development perfects human nature and hence represents the good for humans.

Value Perfectionism

We are now in a position to explain Aquinas's theory of intrinsic value for human beings. The basic idea, as just presented, is that the good of a thing is a matter of its fully developing those capacities that are essential to its nature, which, in turn, results in that thing's having or achieving its ends or purposes. For something to achieve such ends or purposes is for it to achieve a state of perfection.

In ethics, *value perfectionism* is the view that goodness in relation to some thing is a matter of its fully developing those capacities that are essential to it. Aquinas's theory of value is thus a version of perfectionism.

Moral perfectionism is the view that a perfectionistic account of value is central in understanding the nature of right and wrong action. Aquinas, as we shall see, is also a moral perfectionist.[3] We can now set forth the basic principles of Aquinas's theory of intrinsic value in relation to human beings as follows:

Theory of Nonmoral Value

Some state of affairs S is *intrinsically good* in relation to human beings if and only if the realization of S is part of what perfects human nature.

Some state of affairs S is *intrinsically bad* in relation to human beings if and only if S involves the hindrance or destruction of those states of affairs that perfect human nature.

Some state of affairs S is *intrinsically value-neutral* in relation to human beings if and only if S is neither part of what perfects human nature nor involves the hindrance or destruction of those states of affairs that perfect human nature.

The Four Basic Human Goods

This perfectionist account of the human good is hardly illuminating until we specify something about the essential nature of human beings. Doing so requires that we specify those ends or purposes characteristic of such beings. Which purposes or ends are essential to human beings? According to Aquinas, we can discover essential human purposes or ends by observing our natural inclinations:

> Since good has the nature of an end and evil its opposite, all the things to which man has a natural inclination are naturally apprehended by the reason as good and therefore as objects to be pursued, and their opposites as evil to be avoided. Therefore the order of the precepts of the natural law follows the order of our natural inclinations. (*ST,* 49)[4]

Furthermore, according to Aquinas, observation and reflection upon the natural inclinations of human beings reveal four basic human goods (basic values): *life, procreation, knowledge,* and *sociability.* The idea is that human beings have certain capacities and powers—capacities and powers that are part of the very essence of humanity. By nature, we are living creatures with powers of rationality, and these facts about us ground certain basic values.

As *living* creatures, we are naturally inclined to preserve our own lives as well as assure the continuation of the species through procreation. Thus, with respect to individual human life Aquinas writes:

> There is in man, first, an inclination to the good that he shares by nature with all substances, since every substance seeks to preserve itself according to its own nature. Corresponding to this inclination the natural law contains those things that preserve human life and prevent its destruction. (*ST,* 49–50)

In addition to human life, procreation is a basic good, as indicated by the fact that there are certain inclinations we share with nonhuman animals:

> Secondly, there is in man an inclination to certain more specific ends in accordance with the nature that he shares with other animals. In accordance with this, the natural law is said to contain what nature has taught all animals, such as the union of man and woman, the education of children, etc. (*ST,* 50)

As *rational* creatures we are inclined to seek knowledge about ourselves and the world in which we live as well as form various sorts of social bonds, and hence knowledge and sociability are basic goods.

> Thirdly, there is in man a natural inclination to the good of the rational nature which is his alone. Thus man has a natural inclination to know the truth about God and to live in society. Thus the things that pertain to inclinations of this kind belong to the natural law, such as that man should avoid ignorance, that he should not offend others with whom he must associate, and other related actions. (*ST,* 50)

We can summarize this discussion in three main points: (1) Aquinas embraces a perfectionist theory of value according to which the good in relation to human beings is a matter of their achieving a state of perfection by fully realizing those ends or purposes that are essential to being human. (2) Those ends or purposes that are essential to human beings are reflected in natural human inclinations and dispositions, and so we can consult such inclinations and dispositions in coming to a more precise understanding of what constitutes human perfection. (3) Upon investigation we find that life, procreation, knowledge, and sociability are the basic ends of human nature whose realization perfects human nature and thus count as the most basic goods for human beings.

4. Rationality and Right Conduct

I mentioned in section 2 that the natural law theory is value based in the sense that value concepts are more basic than the concepts of right and wrong. We now must consider how the concepts of right and wrong are related to the concepts of good and bad in the natural law theory in general and in Aquinas's thought in particular.

According to Aquinas, human beings are rational creatures, and there are two realms or spheres of rationality. Theoretical (speculative) reason has to do with knowledge of how things are, while practical reason has to do with how we ought to behave. Just as in our quest for understanding the world around us we need reason to properly guide our inquiries, so in our efforts to live our lives properly we need reason to determine what is good and hence worth pursuing and how we should go about pursuing such goods.

In both of these realms, there are very general propositions expressing truths that are the proper basis for inferring more specific propositions, forming a hierarchy of ordered propositions. With regard to knowledge about the world—about being—Aquinas tells us (again, following Aristotle) that the most basic proposition is the principle of contradiction: "something cannot be affirmed and denied at the same time" (*ST,* 49). Moreover, such basic propositions that guide the use of theoretical reason are self-evident in the sense that their truth can be grasped, and hence they can be known, on the basis of rational reflection upon the proposition in question. Such knowledge is knowledge on the basis of reason. So, one can come to know the principle of contradiction as a result of coming to understand the relation among the concepts mentioned in the principle. Knowledge on the basis of self-evidence contrasts with coming to know a proposition's truth as the result of learning it from direct sense experience or inferring it from some other proposition. The principle of contradiction and other general principles, then, represent the most basic first principles that can be grasped through the use of theoretical reason.

Moral propositions expressing truths about right conduct and value can be arranged in a hierarchy, with the most general propositions being the basis for deriving more specific ones. The most fundamental moral propositions are self-evident: their truth can be grasped, and hence they can be known, on the basis of rational reflection.

The most general such truth concerning right conduct is "Good is to be done and pursued, and evil is to be avoided" (*ST*, 49). This principle of right conduct, combined with Aquinas's account of the basic goods for humans, implies the following basic principle of right conduct:

NLT   Life, procreation, knowledge, and sociability are to be preserved
       and promoted; their hindrance and destruction are to be avoided.

As we shall see, this principle will have to be refined and qualified, but before going further, let us pause for a moment to see what this principle implies about various ethical issues. In order to use this principle to arrive at specific conclusions about the morality of actions, we need to say more about the four basic goods. Let us briefly consider them one by one.

- *Life.* Human life has intrinsic value and is to be preserved. Hence, we are obligated to protect and promote our own lives and the lives of others. For instance, since our lives require that we maintain our health, we have an obligation to promote our own health and the health of others. Since suicide and murder involve the intentional taking of human life, it follows that such actions are wrong.[5]

- *Procreation.* Procreation involves both the having and the rearing of children. Actions that are necessary or otherwise crucial for having and raising children are morally required. This includes, for example, providing for their education. According to Aquinas, actions that hinder or destroy this value include adultery, artificial means of birth control, and homosexuality.

- *Knowledge.* In the final passage quoted in the previous section, Aquinas mentions knowledge of God in particular as something to be promoted and maintained because, as a theist, he maintains that such knowledge is of the highest, most perfect kind. However, this value also includes the pursuit of knowledge about the world in which we live. Actions that would interfere with the pursuit of knowledge such as suppression of religious and scientific ideas are wrongs to be avoided.

- *Sociability.* This basic good concerns the ways in which human beings are inclined to live together and cooperate for mutual benefit. Thus, such bonds as friendship, marriage, and civil society are to be pursued. Activities that destroy such bonds, such as lying, slander, and treason, are wrong.

The types of actions mentioned in connection with each of these basic values represent but a few instances of some of the more specific moral requirements that allegedly follow from Aquinas's basic principle of right conduct (NLT). Obviously, the specific conclusions one can infer from NLT depend crucially on how one interprets the four basic values. For instance, since skydiving involves certain life-threatening risks, does it violate the value of human life? What about smoking? Can civil disobedience intended to challenge certain laws be justified, or do such actions violate the value of sociability? What about divorce and the value of procreation? If one answers such questions by claiming that in certain cases divorce, smoking, and the rest are not in violation of the basic values featured in natural law theory and hence not wrong, no doubt there can be legitimate disagreement over where to draw the line between permissible and impermissible instances of such actions.

These remarks are not meant as criticisms of the natural law theory, but they do serve to bring into focus Aquinas's view about the degree of certainty that attaches to moral claims of various sorts. According to Aquinas's vision of moral theory, the most general moral propositions of the theory—its fundamental principles—are self-evident and hence can be known with certainty. These principles, together with claims about human nature, yield conclusions about the morality of specific sorts of actions expressed by moral rules—rules against suicide, killing others, lying, and so forth. And again, these rules, because they are supposed to follow deductively from the basic principles, can be known with certainty.[6] However, in order to arrive at moral conclusions about specific concrete actions, one must apply the rules to oftentimes complex moral situations, and such applications will often involve uncertainties. I have mentioned a few such uncertainties in the previous paragraph. Figure 4.1 illustrates the levels and ordering of moral truths.

Thus far in this chapter I have been describing what I call the core of Aquinas's natural law theory—a core consisting of a perfectionist theory of value that is central in his account of what makes an action right or wrong.

Figure 4.1 Levels of Moral Truths

PARTICULAR MORAL VERDICTS
(about specific actions)

↑

MORAL RULES
(about suicide, lying, adultery, etc.)

↑

FUNDAMENTAL MORAL PRINCIPLES
(of nonmoral intrinsic value and right conduct)

But there is more to the theory than its core; indeed, there must be more if the theory is to deal with cases of moral conflict. In what follows, we shall complete our presentation of Aquinas's natural law theory by first explaining the problem of moral conflict that looms for the theory and then explaining how this problem is avoided.

5. The Problem of Moral Conflict

The basic principle of natural law ethics instructs us to do good and avoid evil, where human life, procreation, knowledge, and sociability represent the basic goods to be brought about and maintained, and the evil to be avoided is the hindrance or destruction of such goods. But there is an obvious problem with the theory as so far presented having to do with cases in which it is not possible both to do good and to avoid evil, and so it appears as if the fundamental principle of natural law theory sometimes yields contradictory moral evaluations of the same action.

To illustrate the problem, let us consider a few cases. Suppose that in order to preserve one's own life against an unjust aggressor, one must kill the assailant; there is just no other way. In this sort of kill-or-be-killed situation, may one kill in self-defense? The natural law theory requires that we promote and maintain the basic goods, one of which is human life. Since, in the situation imagined, the only way of protecting one's own life is by taking the life of another human being, the theory yields the conclusion that we ought to take the life in question. On the other hand, the natural law theory tells us that we are to avoid bringing about evil, and since intentionally taking the life of a human being is an evil, the theory apparently yields the conclusion that we ought not kill the assailant. So, the natural law theory, as so far explained, yields the contradictory moral conclusion that we ought to kill the assailant and that we ought not to kill the assailant.

Here is another case of moral conflict in which the natural law theory yields apparently contradictory moral judgments. Suppose a woman has cancer of the uterus and therefore needs to undergo a hysterectomy (an operation in which the uterus is removed) to safeguard her life. Suppose also that she is pregnant and that because she is in the early stages of pregnancy, the fetus cannot be removed without bringing about its death. If we assume that the fetus counts as a human being with full moral standing, we are led by the natural law theory (as so far presented) to contradictory moral judgments.[7] On the one hand, the woman ought to undergo the hysterectomy in order to preserve her life. But, on the other hand, this surgical procedure will inevitably bring about the death of her unborn child and hence violate the basic good of human life. So she ought not to have the operation. This case, like the previous case, involves the prospect of bringing about the death of a human being, though unlike the assailant in the previous case, the fetus is completely innocent.

While both the self-defense and hysterectomy cases involve a single basic value—human life—other problematic cases involve multiple basic values. Consider this example. Suppose that I am hiding an innocent person being hunted by a band of killers who are now asking me about the location of their intended victim. If I tell them the truth (or refuse to answer), they will find the person I'm hiding; if I lie to them, I can very likely save this innocent person (at least for the time being). Lying, recall, violates the value of sociability. So, it is only by engaging in the evil act of telling a lie that I can bring about the good result of preserving a human life. In this situation it looks as if I ought to do what I can to save an innocent human life (so I ought to lie), but since I am to avoid evil, I ought not to lie.

Because these situations of moral conflict that arise for the natural law theory (as so far presented) yield inconsistent moral verdicts, the theory fails to satisfy the consistency standard for evaluating moral theories (see section 6, chapter 1). Thus, we must either reject the theory (since a theory that yields inconsistent moral judgments cannot be correct), or we must find some way to qualify or revise the theory so that it avoids inconsistency.

One way (and apparently Aquinas's way) of qualifying the theory involves attaching moral importance to the difference between what one strictly intends in acting and what one merely foresees as a result of acting. This distinction and its moral importance are expressed in the principle of double effect that we consider in section 7. But before turning to such matters, it will be useful to consider one possible solution to the problem of moral conflict—a solution that natural law theorists reject—because it will help bring out another important feature of classical natural law thinking.

6. The Incommensurability of Basic Values

The natural law theory directs us to promote what is good and avoid evil. But in the cases of moral conflict just described, in order to promote what is good, the agent must do something that will bring about bad or evil effects. Now it would certainly appear that in these cases, it would not be wrong to kill in self-defense, have a hysterectomy, or lie to save an innocent life. So we can pose the question about moral conflict this way: According to natural law theory, is one ever morally permitted to do or bring about what is bad or evil in order to promote or bring about something good? One straightforward way of answering this question (rejected by the natural law theory) is to decide *how much* good and *how much* bad would result from some action and then perform the act if the amount of good that would result from the action outweighs the amount of bad that would result. To see how this works, let us revisit some of our examples.

In the self-defense case, then, the current proposal for resolving the conflict would be to calculate the amount of good and the amount of evil that would result from the act of killing in self-defense and compare the net value of killing with the net value of refraining from such an act. The option that has the highest net value is, on the current proposal, the morally right option. Granted, whether one refrains from killing the assailant and thereby allows one's life to be taken or kills in self-defense, a human life will be lost. But obviously such facts as that the assailant is an unjust aggressor and the would-be victim is innocent are morally relevant in this case, and one way this might be reflected in our moral thinking is to suppose that the innocent life is *worth more* than the life of the aggressor. We might, that is, compare the values of these different human lives on some sort of scale and then reason as follows. Since the life of an unjust aggressor is worth less than the life of someone who is innocent, the good to be preserved in an act of self-defense is greater than the bad or evil result of bringing about the death of the assailant. Hence, all things considered, one is permitted, and perhaps even morally obligated, to kill in self-defense.

Consider the case in which one must lie to save an innocent life. Isn't it clear that, in the situation as described, whatever evil is brought about by telling a lie to the would-be killers is far less of an evil than would be brought about by the murder of their intended victim? Granted, in the situation described, one cannot avoid performing an action that violates one of the basic values. Still, if we compare the value attached to an innocent life with the value attached to not telling a lie (and if we suppose that these are cases where no matter what we choose, some evil will result), shouldn't we act to minimize the *amount* of evil?

Hence, by calculating *degrees* of goodness and badness and then requiring that in cases of moral conflict we act to maximize the net value of what we do, don't we have a solution to cases of moral conflict?

However, natural law theory is opposed to any such solution for two reasons. First, this sort of solution presupposes that values can be compared on some common scale of value—that they are *commensurable*. But it is characteristic of natural law thinking that such values are *incommensurable*—that there is not a common scale of measurement by which we could balance and weigh the good and bad consequences of actions in order to determine *how much* goodness or badness some action would cause. Thus, according to natural law thinking, we cannot calculate how much badness is associated with the telling of some lie and how much goodness is associated with saving a life and compare amounts of goodness and badness. Were such calculations possible, we would be able to say that the evil involved in the death of one human being is equivalent in value to the evil brought about by a certain number of lies. But how, asks the natural law theorist, could there be some common unit for measuring values that would allow us to compare these seemingly very different kinds of evil?[8]

The second reason a natural law theorist is opposed to this solution is that, according to natural law thinking, the deontic status of an action is not just a matter of the goodness and badness of the consequences of actions. Rather, as we shall see, one's *intentions* are an important element in what makes an action right or wrong.

7. The Principle of Double Effect

The principle (or doctrine) of double effect provides a set of guidelines for dealing with cases of moral conflict of the sort we have been considering. It provides an answer to the question we have been asking: Is one ever morally permitted to do or bring about what is bad or evil in order to promote or bring about something good?

To explain adequately the principle of double effect (PDE) and how it figures into natural law thinking, it will be useful to explain some basic concepts and distinctions involved in it.

Some Preliminary Distinctions

The PDE makes use of the distinction between means and ends of our actions. Often, when we act, we act for some ultimate goal or end that we hope to bring about through what we do. The ultimate end shapes our subsequent choices. So, for instance, if one of my ends is to earn a skydiving certificate, then there are other, related ends that I must set for myself as means to my main end of earning the certificate. For instance, I must accumulate so many hours of instruction, I must pass a written test, and so forth. Of course, in setting myself these derivative ends, there may be other tasks I must complete and so other ends I must achieve. And in pursuing these derivative ends, I will have to engage in various actions. Clearly, the derivative ends and the actions I will perform in achieving them all count as *means* to my ultimate end of earning a skydiving certificate.

Another important distinction featured in PDE is between what we intend and what we merely foresee as resulting from our actions. That is, with regard to our efforts, we can distinguish between those effects of our actions that are intended and those that are not intended but merely foreseen. A few examples will help make the distinction clear. When I drive my car either for pleasure or to get to some destination, it is not part of my purpose to wear down my tires as I drive. I do, however, foresee that as a result of driving my car, I inevitably cause tire wear, but tire wear is not an integral part of my plan.[9] Here, we can say that my driving has the wearing down of my tires as one of its effects; but this effect, although foreseen, is not intended. Here is another example. I may know enough about one of my students to know that if she receives any grade in my course other than an A, this will cause her to be severely depressed. In giving her the B that she deserves, I can foresee her depression as an effect of my assigning this grade, but I do not thereby intend this effect. Since the tire wear and the student's depression are not an integral part of the plan of action and hence not intended, they are referred to as "side effects."

A Formulation of the Principle

Some actions bring about two (or more) effects, one good and one bad, which are both foreseen—hence a "double effect." The principle of double effect sets forth conditions under which it is morally permissible to perform such actions.

PDE   Whenever an action would produce at least one good effect and one bad or evil effect, then one is permitted to perform the act if and only if all of the following conditions are met:

1. The action in question, apart from its effects, must not be wrong.

2. The bad effect must not be intended by the agent. There are two principal ways in which an effect might be intended:

   a. Any effect that is a chosen end of action is intended.

   b. Any effect that is a means for bringing about some intended end is also intended.

3. The bad effect must not be "out of proportion" to the good effect. What counts as being in or out of proportion cannot be

precisely specified, and certainly it would be inconsistent with the thesis of incommensurability to suppose that it is possible to measure degrees of goodness and badness of effects according to some common scale of measurement. However, lack of commensurability does not mean that good and bad effects cannot be compared and judged in the way presupposed by this requirement.

To understand this complex principle, let us work with the previously mentioned example involving a hysterectomy. In that example, recall, a woman with cancer of the uterus is pregnant. Her choices are to have the uterus removed, which will unavoidably cause the death of the fetus, or to refuse the operation, in which case both she and her unborn child will die. Since the operation would have the good effect of saving the woman's life and the bad effect of bringing about the death of a human being, we can apply PDE to determine whether the operation is nevertheless permissible.

First, the operation—removal of cancerous tissue—is not itself morally wrong. Second, the bad effect is not the ultimate end of the operation; the ultimate end is to save the woman's life. Nor is the bad effect a means for bringing about the good effect. After all, it is not the fetus but the cancer that poses a threat to her life, and so the death of the unborn child is not part of the means for saving her life. She would have the operation even if she were not pregnant. It is worth noting that if there were some other medical procedure that would save the woman's life and yet not end the life of the child, then normally we would be justified in assuming that the death of the unborn child is part of the overall plan of action and is therefore intended. After all, if we have two available and (let us assume) affordable procedures that are equally effective in bringing about the good effect and yet we knowingly choose the one that involves a bad effect, what other reason could there be for our choice except the aim of bringing about the bad effect?

Third, since we are assuming that both woman and fetus are human beings with full moral standing, we may assume that the decision to engage in actions that would terminate one human life in order to save another (given that the other conditions are met) satisfies the requirement that the bad effect not be out of proportion to the good effect. Since all three conditions of the PDE are satisfied, we may conclude that the hysterectomy in question is morally permissible according to the natural law theory.

By applying the PDE to this case, we have thus resolved the problem of moral conflict involving the hysterectomy case. More generally, the PDE represents an answer to our question of whether, in ethics, it is ever morally permissible to do or bring about what is bad or evil in order to bring about a good result. As we have seen, the principle does allow that in some cases one may bring about a good effect in the knowledge that bad effects will result from what one does. However, the principle, in effect, accepts the directive of Saint Paul (Romans 3:8) that one may not do evil that good may come about, and so yields a negative answer to our question. Good ends do not justify using evil means to obtain them! So, although we are sometimes permitted to do what we can foresee will have bad or evil effects, we are never permitted to bring about such effects intentionally.

8. Moral Absolutism

In natural law thinking, there is a greater emphasis on avoiding wrong acts—acts that no moral person should do—than there is on promoting in a positive way what is good. The claim that there are certain very general types of actions that are always morally wrong to perform, even when performing them would bring about good results, is called *moral absolutism*. Such types of action are thus *absolutely* prohibited and are featured in *exceptionless moral* rules. Here are some examples:[10]

It is wrong to intentionally kill human beings (period).

It is wrong to lie (period).

It is wrong to engage in adultery (period).

It is wrong to engage in homosexual behavior (period).

Many versions of natural law ethics embrace moral absolutism. What is important to notice about such absolutist versions is that the PDE, by prohibiting the intentional bringing about of bad effects, makes it clear that what is absolutely prohibited is not just any action that, for example, kills a human being. After all, were there an absolute prohibition on actions that bring about the death of human beings, we would still be stuck with those cases of moral conflict illustrated earlier in section 5. Rather, the PDE helps the natural law absolutist make clear that it is the *intentional* taking of human life that is absolutely prohibited. Moral absolutism, then, represents the third main component in the natural law theory.[11]

9. The Theory of Right Conduct

In explaining some of the basic ideas in the moral theory of Aquinas, we began with his basic principle of right conduct (NLT), according to which we are required to do good and avoid evil, where good and evil have to do with the basic human goods of life, procreation, knowledge, and sociability. We then noted that, unless the theory is somehow qualified, there will be cases of moral conflict in which it yields inconsistent moral verdicts about particular cases. We have just seen how the principle of double effect serves to importantly qualify the theory's core and how some versions of natural law accept moral absolutism.

Let us now bring together the main components of natural law thinking—its core, the PDE, and moral absolutism—in order to present its theory of right conduct. We can do so by distinguishing direct from indirect violations of the basic values.

> D An action *directly violates* a basic value if and only if (1) the action will bring about the hindrance or destruction of a basic value, and (2) that action cannot be justified by the principle of double effect.

Actions that satisfy the first clause of D but can be justified by the principle of double effect count as *indirect violations*. Now we can present the theory of right conduct for the natural law theory.

Theory of Right Conduct

> An action A is *obligatory* if and only if failing to perform A would result in a direct violation of one or more of the basic goods.

> An action A is *wrong* if and only if performing A would result in a direct violation of one or more of the basic goods.

> An action A is *optional* if and only if neither performing A nor failing to perform A would result in a direct violation of one or more of the basic goods.

Thus, on the natural law theory, what *makes* an action right or wrong depends on whether it involves a direct violation of one or more of the basic human goods.

10. Some Sample Applications of the Theory

It will solidify our understanding of natural law thinking if we examine its implications in a range of cases.

Craniotomy

In some rare cases, a pregnant woman with a heart condition will die unless her unborn child is aborted. In such cases, the method of abortion involves performing a craniotomy—crushing the skull of the child—so that the fetus can be removed. What does the natural law theory imply about this case? Since the craniotomy has both a good effect (preserving the life of the woman) and a bad effect (the death of the unborn child), we can invoke the PDE to determine whether this sort of surgical procedure is morally permissible.[12]

First, as in the case of the hysterectomy, the operation is not itself morally wrong, and the loss of life involved here is not disproportionate to the good being aimed at. Thus, the first and third parts of the PDE are satisfied. But what about the second part requiring that the bad effect not be intended? In the hysterectomy case, it is reasonably clear that the death of the unborn is a mere unintended side effect, since it is the cancer that is life threatening and so its removal, and not the death of the child, is the means for saving the woman's life. But the craniotomy case is apparently different. It is the presence of the unborn that poses the threat to the woman's life, and so its removal (involving its inevitable death) is integral to saving her life. Hence, the death of the unborn child is a means to saving her life, and so this bad effect is intended. And since the bad effect is intended, the operation in question cannot be justified using the PDE. If the operation cannot be justified by the PDE, the craniotomy involves a direct violation of the value of human life and is thus prohibited by the natural law theory.

If we compare the hysterectomy and craniotomy cases, we see that they both involve choices whose outcomes are the same. In both cases, performing the operation will bring about the death of the unborn child and save the woman's life. In both cases, refraining from such procedures will result in the deaths of both individuals. Assuming that the PDE has been correctly applied in both cases, we see how, according to the natural law theory, an individual's intentions are crucial in determining the moral quality of the action. Actions whose outcomes are the same might still differ in their moral qualities owing to the agent's intentions (the diagram of the two cases shown in figure 4.2 may help).

For some, this result is hard to swallow. After all, as just pointed out, in both cases, either there is medical intervention that will save one life or there is not, in which case two lives are lost. So aren't they morally on a par? We will return to this matter in our critical discussion of the PDE in the final section.

End-of-Life Medical Decisions

In 1998, Dr. Jack Kevorkian gave Thomas Youk a lethal injection of drugs, an incident that was videotaped and broadcast on CBS's *60 Minutes*. Youk had been suffering from Lou Gehrig's disease and decided that he preferred death to the kind of painful life one experiences in the advanced stages of this disease. He enlisted the help of Kevorkian, who was later

Figure 4.2 Hysterectomy and Craniotomy Compared

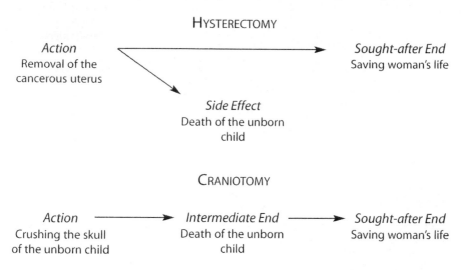

HYSTERECTOMY

Action
Removal of the
cancerous uterus

Sought-after End
Saving woman's life

Side Effect
Death of the unborn
child

CRANIOTOMY

Action
Crushing the skull
of the unborn child

Intermediate End
Death of the unborn
child

Sought-after End
Saving woman's life

found guilty of second-degree murder for his active role in causing Youk's death. Because the death was the result of an action (rather than an omission) and because the patient gave his consent to being killed, Kevorkian's bringing about Youk's death was a case of active voluntary euthanasia.

If we examine this case in light of the PDE, it is clear that what Kevorkian did was not morally justified. Although the ultimate, sought-after end was the cessation of the patient's pain, the means for bringing about this end was death. Here is the associated diagram:

ACTIVE EUTHANASIA

Action
Giving the lethal
injection

Intermediate End
Death of the patient

Sought-after End
Termination of the
patient's suffering

This case is to be distinguished from cases in which a patient with a terminal disease must take a particular drug (it is the only one available) in order to ease unbearable pain but where a foreseeable side effect of the drug is a shortening of the patient's life. If we assume that the easing of pain provides a proportionally serious reason for taking the drug, then the PDE implies that this sort of action is morally permissible. So, the appropriate diagram for this case is:

LIFE-SHORTENING DRUG

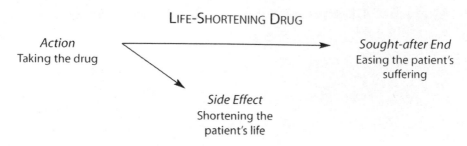

Action
Taking the drug

Sought-after End
Easing the patient's
suffering

Side Effect
Shortening the
patient's life

Self-Defense

As a final sample application, let us return to the self-defense case described earlier, because it was in connection with such cases that Aquinas
explicitly invoked the PDE. In answering the question of whether self-
defense is morally permissible, Aquinas wrote:

> The action of defending oneself may produce two effects—one, saving one's
> own life, and the other, killing the attacker. Now an action of this kind in-
> tended to save one's own life can not be characterized as illicit since it is nat-
> ural for anyone to maintain himself in existence if he can. An act that is
> prompted by a good intention can become illicit if it is not proportionate to
> the end intended. This is why it is not allowed to use more force than neces-
> sary to defend one's life. (*ST,* 70)

Here, Aquinas is saying that in cases of self-defense, if one's primary aim is
to save one's own life, and if one does not use more force against the attacker than is essential in protecting oneself, then one may use force to
bring about the good end being intended. With regard to the proportion-
ality requirement, the idea is that if one can escape the threat of the attacker
by running away or otherwise stopping that person by use of no or little
force, then one is not allowed, for example, to maim or kill the attacker.

But what about killing the aggressor? Although Aquinas thinks that it
can be morally correct for a proper public authority to carry out a sentence
of death against a justly accused and tried criminal, he denies that a private
individual may intentionally kill in self-defense.

> However, because killing is only allowed by action of public authority for the
> common good, it is not lawful for someone who is acting in self-defense to
> intend to kill another man. (*ST,* 71)

So, Aquinas's moral stance is that although one is allowed to use force
against an unjust aggressor in defense of one's own life, one may not intend
the aggressor's death, although one may foresee that death as an inevitable

side effect of using a certain amount of force. Here is the relevant diagram:

SELF-DEFENSE

Action
Using force against
an aggressor

Sought-after End
Saving oneself from
death or serious injury

Side Effect
Death of the aggressor

This use of the PDE may seem a bit strained since it requires that we distinguish between an action that involves a certain kind of harm to a victim and the effect of killing the victim. Suppose that all I have available to defend myself is a stick of dynamite. Are we to suppose that in lighting it and throwing it at my assailant I intend to blow him to bits, but that I only foresee his death as an unintended side effect? This raises a serious question, to which we will return in section 12, about how we are to distinguish between what one intends and what one merely foresees.

11. Brief Recap

We now have before us a version of the natural law theory derived mainly from the writings of Aquinas. Before we turn to its evaluation, it will perhaps help the reader's philosophical digestion if we pause for a moment to briefly review its three main components.

- The core of the theory involves a perfectionist account of the human good that is the primary basis for a theory of right conduct. Such value-based moral theories are versions of moral perfectionism. Aquinas defends his version of moral perfectionism—featuring life, procreation, knowledge, and sociability as the most basic human goods—by appealing to facts about human nature and, in particular, by appealing to facts about basic human inclinations.

- Because there is a plurality of basic values and the theory requires that we both promote these values and avoid the evil of their destruction, the natural law theory needs to address cases in which these values come into conflict. In particular, the theory must address the question of whether one is ever permitted to bring about or promote the good by doing or bringing about what is bad or evil. The principle of double effect (the second component) addresses this question by setting forth guidelines that permit some actions aimed at promoting good results even when some bad or evil effects will inevitably result. However, one is never permitted to intentionally do or bring about evil in order to promote what is good.

- In addition to these two components, the classical version of natural law ethics embraces moral absolutism—the idea that there are certain very general types of action that are morally wrong in all circumstances.

Putting this all together, the natural law theory makes human perfection the primary value to be respected and requires that we never act so as to directly violate any of the basic human values (life, procreation, knowledge, and sociability) whose realization perfects human nature. Thus, what *makes* an action right or wrong, on this view, are facts about whether an action directly violates one or more of the basic goods.

12. Evaluation of the Natural Law Theory

Because of the theory's complexity, its evaluation will likewise be somewhat complex. In what follows, I consider the three major components of the theory: (1) moral absolutism, (2) the principle of double effect, and (3) its core. Proceeding in this manner is necessary because, as I will explain, it is possible to accept any one of these elements while rejecting the other two. Before turning to the criticisms, let us pause for a moment to consider some of the advantages of natural law ethics.

Advantages of the Theory

The natural law theory has four apparent advantages. First, the theory develops the intuitively appealing idea that morality is grounded in facts about human nature. This makes sense, since one would expect that questions about what has worth for human beings and questions about what humans ought to do must reflect the essential nature of such beings. Indeed, as we have seen, Aquinas attempts to argue for his perfectionist account of value by appealing to nonmoral facts about human inclinations. These advantages of the theory involve the standards of intuitive appeal and external support, respectively (see section 6, chapter 1). (Later in this section, we shall consider in more detail the way in which the natural law theory attempts to ground morality in human nature.)

A second, related advantage of natural law ethics is that it represents a nonrelativist moral theory. The basic principles of value and right conduct featured in the natural law theory are supposed to be correct or valid for all individuals, in all historical and cultural contexts, and at all times. John

Finnis expresses this point nicely when, in commenting on such principles, he writes:

> Principles of this sort would hold good, as principles, however extensively they were overlooked, misapplied, or defied in practical thinking, and however little they were recognized by those who reflectively theorize about human thinking. That is to say, they would 'hold good' just as mathematical principles of accounting 'hold good' even when, as in the medieval banking community, they were unknown or misunderstood. (Finnis 1980, 24)

Having examined moral relativism in the previous chapter, we are in search of a theory that avoids its problems, and natural law ethics offers an initially promising nonrelativist account of value and right conduct.

Third, once properly qualified, the theory apparently satisfies the consistency standard. Moreover, given the specifications of the PDE, the theory also seems to yield fairly determinate moral verdicts in cases of conflict; so, again, the theory seems to satisfy the determinacy standard.

A fourth advantage of the theory, at least according to its defenders, is that its principles yield intuitively correct implications in a wide range of cases. This advantage represents an appeal to the standard of internal support for evaluating moral theories that was explained in chapter 1. In the previous section, we examined some of the theory's implications involving the application of the PDE. (Later in this section, we will see how the PDE, and absolutist moral rules, arguably fail to adequately satisfy this standard.)

Let us now proceed to evaluate natural law moral theory, beginning with moral absolutism.

Moral Absolutism

Moral absolutism is the thesis that there are some general types of action that, in all circumstances, it would be morally wrong to perform. Such moral prohibitions can be expressed by exceptionless moral rules. As we have seen, such rules are interpreted in light of the principle of double effect, which limits the scope of what the rules prohibit. The rule against killing and harming, for instance, absolutely prohibits *intentional* killing or harming individuals, thus allowing that under certain conditions nonintentionally causing death or harm may be permissible. The main challenge for the defender of moral absolutism is to provide a rationale or justification for such exceptionless rules. Why suppose there are any exceptionless moral rules? Don't all rules, including moral ones, have exceptions?

To examine these questions, let us simply focus on the moral rule against killing human beings. And to make the rule as plausible as possible, let us specify that it is the intentional taking of *innocent* human life that is absolutely prohibited.[13] After all, if there are any absolute moral prohibitions, the rule against killing surely expresses one of them. So, are there any clear cases in which it would be morally permissible to intentionally kill an innocent human being?

Arguably there are. Cases of active voluntary euthanasia and assisted suicide strike many reflective people as morally justified cases of intentionally killing the innocent.[14] For instance, many people, including the family of Thomas Youk, think that Kevorkian was morally justified in administering the lethal injection to his patient. Before the Youk incident, Kevorkian was arrested and tried four times for his role in cases of assisted suicide, but no jury would convict him. In the Tony Bland case (a case of *non*voluntary euthanasia) the British justices who decided that it was lawful to disconnect Bland from his feeding tubes judged that bringing about the death of an individual who can no longer benefit from treatment should be legally permitted.[15] These attitudes toward such cases indicate that upon reflection, many people see nothing wrong with intentionally killing the innocent in at least some cases. Thus many people see certain cases of euthanasia and suicide, which involve the intentional killing of innocent human beings, as morally justified exceptions to the rule against killing.

The defender of the absolute prohibition in question might argue at this point that the alleged counterexamples should not be given too much weight. After all, reasonable people disagree about such cases, and so the critic has not provided clear evidence of permissible cases of intentional killing of innocents.

But in addition to apparent counterexamples to the absolutist rule against killing, a commitment to this rule (and other absolutist rules) seems to be irrational. A way of bringing out the apparent irrationality involved in such rules is to consider cases in which, by engaging in a single violation of the rule, one can prevent a great number of violations of that same rule. Here is a well-known example from Bernard Williams that will help illustrate the point.

> Jim finds himself in the central square of a small South American town. Tied up against the wall are a row of twenty Indians, most terrified, a few defiant, in front of them several armed men in uniform. A heavy man in a sweat-stained khaki shirt turns out to be the captain in charge and, after a good deal of questioning of Jim which establishes that he got there by accident while on a botanical expedition, explains that the Indians are a random group of the inhabitants who, after recent acts of protest against the government, are just about to be killed to remind the other possible protestors of the advantages of not protesting. However, since Jim is an honored visitor from another land, the captain is happy to offer him a guest's privilege of killing one of the Indians himself. If Jim accepts, then as a special mark of the occasion, the other Indians will be let off. (Williams 1973, 98)

If, on the other hand, Jim refuses the offer, then the captain will proceed as originally planned and order that all twenty captives be shot. Jim must choose between killing one (presumably innocent) person and allowing all twenty captives to die. His killing one of them would be a violation of the rule against killing, but his refraining from this killing would result in many more violations of the same rule.

So we have a case in which a single violation of the rule will result in fewer violations of that same rule. If, by killing one innocent person, one can prevent the killings of nineteen other innocent persons, isn't it paradoxical, and thus irrational, to accept a rule against killing that, if followed in this case, would ensure many more violations of the rule? What rationale can be provided for such an absolute prohibition against killing?

Perhaps those sympathetic to absolutist moral rules will attempt to defend them by appealing to the claim that individuals are more responsible for what they *do* than for what they *allow* to happen, and so it is more important for Jim to avoid violating the rule against intentional killing than it is for him to prevent others from violating that principle. This rationale may sound reasonable, but upon closer inspection, it does not work. After all, the claim that individuals are more responsible for what they do than for what they allow to happen is a moral doctrine that is in just as much need of justification as the absolutist moral rules. Why, after all, are individuals more responsible for what they do than for what they allow, especially in cases where they can prevent a great number of violations of some rule?

There are certainly other ways in which one might try to justify absolutist moral rules, but it is doubtful that any of them will succeed.[16] So I think we must conclude that absolutist versions of natural law theory are implausible.

The Principle of Double Effect

Suppose that no plausible defense of moral absolutism can be given. Still, one might hold on to the rest of the natural law theory by accepting its core together with the principle of double effect. The result would be a nonabsolutist version of the theory. According to this version, there is no absolute prohibition against intentionally violating any of the basic goods. However, given the PDE, there is a morally relevant difference between acts that intentionally violate one or more of the basic goods and actions that foreseeably but nonintentionally result in the violation of one or more of these goods. Consider the morality of killing human beings. According to a nonabsolutist version of natural law theory, it is not always wrong to intentionally kill an innocent human being; however, in cases where such killing would be wrong, it is sometimes permissible (in otherwise similar circumstances) to bring about someone's death so long as the death is not intended. Since this nonabsolutist version of the theory depends on the PDE, let us proceed to evaluate the principle of double effect.

Let us begin by asking whether this principle makes intuitively correct moral discriminations in the cases to which it is typically applied. Consider the hysterectomy and craniotomy cases. In both cases the possible outcomes of operating compared to refraining from medical intervention are the same: operating in both cases will save the life of the woman and cause the death of the unborn child, while refraining will result in the death of both. To many this will seem just mistaken. In these cases, whether or not one performs the craniotomy, the unborn child will die. Since by performing the operation the woman's life can be saved, it seems clear that the operation is not morally forbidden and is perhaps even obligatory. The verdict reached about the craniotomy case using the PDE thus seems clearly mistaken. And if so, then there must be something wrong with the principle. Critics have raised similar worries about the euthanasia and life-shortening cases as well.[17]

Of course, the fact that many individuals upon reflection will judge that performing the craniotomy is not wrong does not *prove* conclusively that PDE is mistaken. After all, such cases are of interest partly because they are controversial. And so the defender of the PDE might well respond by insisting that it does give the correct moral verdict in this case and others as well. However, other defenders of the PDE argue that its correct application to the craniotomy case does not yield the conclusion that this medical procedure is wrong. These friends of the principle argue as follows. The death of the unborn is a merely foreseen, unintended side effect of the craniotomy because, strictly speaking, it is altering the shape of the unborn's skull that is the means for saving the woman's life. Of course the death of the unborn is an inevitable result of crushing its skull, but this result (say the defenders) is not part of the means but only a foreseen side effect of the craniotomy. Thus, contrary to how the PDE is standardly applied in this case, the principle does not yield the result that the craniotomy is morally wrong.

This response depends on being able to discriminate finely between what one strictly intends and what one merely foresees. But many critics find this way of handling the craniotomy case deeply problematic. Is it really plausible to claim that one can intend to crush someone's skull and yet not intend to kill him? Is it plausible to claim that one can intend to blow someone to bits with a bomb but that the resulting death is a merely foreseen side effect of being blown to bits? Is it plausible to suppose that one can intend to shoot someone through the heart and yet not intend to kill the individual?

None of these suggestions is plausible. Rather, the act of crushing someone's skull can also be described as killing him; blowing someone to bits can also be described as killing him; and shooting someone through the heart can be described as killing him. What we have here are alternative ways of describing the same action. This point helps reveal what seems deeply suspicious about the attempt to show how the PDE yields the correct result in the craniotomy case. If we describe the action of the physician one way—as the crushing of the unborn's skull, with the result that it dies—then it appears that the death of the unborn is not part of what the physician does but rather some separate effect of the act. But, of course, we can and often do correctly describe our actions in terms of what results from our basic bodily movements. If I move my finger so as to flip the light switch and thus cause the light in the room to go on, what I have done can be described in various ways: I moved my finger; I flipped the switch; I turned on the light.

Similarly, the physician who performs a craniotomy does what may be described as using a certain surgical instrument; crushing the skull; killing the fetus. It is quite proper, then, to describe the physician's intentional action as killing the fetus. So describing the action of the physician in one way yields the verdict that her action is an intentional killing, but when the action is described another way, the PDE yields the verdict that her action is not an intentional killing. This means that the verdict we get using the PDE depends on how we describe the physician's action. (See figure 4.3.) Clearly, something is wrong here. Either the physician's action is morally wrong or it is not morally wrong. It is nonsense to say that her action is wrong if described one way but not wrong if described another way, where both descriptions truly apply to her action. What the defender of the PDE owes us is a way of distinguishing intention from mere foresight in a way that marks a difference that is morally relevant for determining the rightness and wrongness of actions. This has proved difficult to do. Let us consider a few proposals.

One proposal is to claim that an effect is part of one's intention if it is

Figure 4.3 Alternate Descriptions of the Craniotomy Case

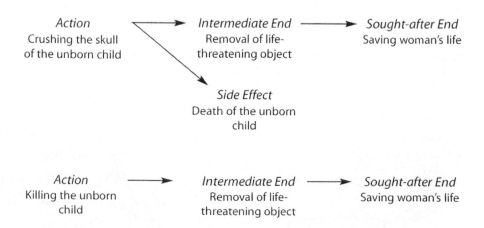

temporally close to the action that brings it about; that is, if the action and effect occur simultaneously, or if the temporal gap between the action and the effect is very small. Because the death of the unborn follows immediately after (or occurs at the same time as) the crushing of the skull, it is to be counted as part of what one intends.

But little thought is needed to see that this proposal does not help draw a morally relevant distinction between intention and mere foresight. For one thing, since the death of the unborn in the hysterectomy case is temporally close in time to the medical procedure of removing the uterus, its death would count as intended. But the hysterectomy case seems to be one of the clearest cases where the death of the individual is not intended. Furthermore, on this proposal, were I to give you a very slow-acting poison, my causing your death would be unintended; but clearly it isn't. The temporal immediacy of an effect following an action does not mark a morally relevant distinction.

Another proposal focuses on there being a close causal connection between action and effect. The idea is that if an effect is an *inevitable causal result* of the action, then one intends the effect. The death of the fetus is an inevitable causal result of the act of crushing the skull, so it is an intended effect.

Again, however, this proposal will not do. The PDE clearly allows that there can be inevitable and foreseen effects of our actions that are not intended. In the hysterectomy case, the death involved is an inevitable causal result of the action in question, but it is not supposed to be intended. In general, if one accepts this causal proposal, then one will not be able to draw a morally relevant distinction between the sorts of cases used to illustrate the moral significance of the principle.

The proposals just discussed appeal to temporal and causal relations respectively—objective relations in the external world between actions and effects. The next two proposals attempt to understand the distinction between intended and merely foreseen by appeal to an agent's psychology.

One such proposal is that an effect is intended if it is *desired* by the agent—if the agent who performs the action welcomes the effect. But again, there is an immediate problem with this proposal. If the distinction between what one intends and what one merely foresees is based on what one happens to desire, then if the physician performing a hysterectomy involving a previable child does not want or welcome the death of the child, then the death is not intended. On the other hand, if, for whatever reason, she does want the death of the child, then the child's death would be intended. But this makes things too subjective. Why should an agent's desires with respect to some effect make a difference in the rightness or wrongness of the action that produces that effect?

Another attempt to draw the desired distinction that might have occurred to readers involves appealing to a counterfactual claim about the physician's disposition toward the unborn. A *counterfactual* statement (also called a contrary-to-fact conditional) is a conditional "if ..., then ..." statement that has a false antecedent. Here is an example: Had Gore won the state of Florida in the 2000 presidential election, then he would have been elected president of the United States. Presumably, this counterfactual is true. So consider the following counterfactual claim: If the physician could perform the craniotomy without killing the unborn child, then she would do so. Now granted, given how things really are in the world, it is not possible to crush someone's skull and not kill them. Nevertheless, the proposal is that whenever a counterfactual of this sort is true, the effect is merely foreseen. The idea here is that if we would be willing to avoid a certain state of affairs if it were possible to do so, then that state of affairs is not intended.

This proposal may sound promising, but unfortunately it will not do, because it would imply that *any* means that produces an unwanted effect would not be intentional. Specifically, it would imply that if it were possible for the physician to save the woman's life without crushing the skull, then her action of crushing is not intended. But according to the PDE, one necessarily intends both the ends and one's chosen means of action. So this counterfactual test cannot be used by the defender of the principle to mark a morally relevant difference.

These proposals for distinguishing what is intended from what is merely foreseen do not exhaust the possibilities. But until the proponent of the PDE provides a criterion for making this distinction that marks a morally relevant difference, we may tentatively conclude that this principle is not sound.[18]

The Core

Even if we reject moral absolutism and the PDE, we need not reject natural law theory's core. We may, that is, embrace moral perfectionism by (1) giving a perfectionist account of the human good and then (2) using it as a basis for characterizing right and wrong action. In exploring the prospects for developing this sort of view, I want to consider three issues. First is the issue of how one might attempt to justify value perfectionism and, in particular, Aquinas's project of grounding a theory of value on facts about human nature. Second, any version of moral perfectionism that rejects moral absolutism and the PDE will have to deal with cases of moral conflict. Finally, there is the issue of whether a plausible moral theory can be based on considerations of human perfection. Let us take these up in order.

The Grounding Project. Aquinas is often read as attempting to justify his list of basic values by inferring them from facts about human inclinations. Perhaps this reading is encouraged when he writes:

[A]ll the things to which man has a natural inclination are naturally appre-
hended as good and therefore objects to be pursued, and their opposites to be
avoided. Therefore the order of the precepts of the natural law follows the
order of our natural inclinations. (*ST,* 49)

He then goes on, as explained earlier, to refer to natural human inclinations
toward self-preservation, preservation of the species, knowledge, and sociability in specifying the four basic human goods. Suppose for the time being
that Aquinas meant to infer basic values from claims about human inclinations. What are we to make of such attempted inferences?[19]

Let us first of all be clear about the aim or point of such inferences and
how they are supposed to work. Presumably, the idea here is to provide an
objective basis for morality—a basis grounded in nonmoral descriptive facts
about human nature. Aquinas (on the reading under consideration) is assuming that facts about human inclinations—inclinations characteristic of
the species—are a proper basis for inferring claims about basic human
goods. So, *without making assumptions about the good in relation to human beings,* we are to observe such beings, make note of species-wide inclinations,
and then on the basis of our observations, infer basic human goods. The key
idea here is that such inferences are supposed to feature only premises that
make nonmoral factual claims about human nature and conclusions that
make reference to what is intrinsically good.

There are two main problems with this project. One problem concerns
a logical gap between statements of nonmoral fact and statements of value,
and the other concerns a worry about circularity in reasoning from fact to
value. Let us take these in order.

To infer a claim about what is good or valuable *directly* from a premise
about some matter of fact is invalid: the conclusion does not follow logically from the premise. Thus, in the following argument:

1.   Human beings are inclined by nature to preserve their own lives;

therefore,

3.   Human life is intrinsically good

the conclusion does not follow logically. In order for the conclusion to follow, one would need to add this premise,

2.   If human beings are inclined by nature to preserve their own lives,
     then life is intrinsically good.

To avoid the logical gap between statements of nonmoral fact and statements of value, one must add a "bridge premise" to the sort of argument
displayed above that connects facts about human nature with value. But

then, one needs to provide a justification for this premise. And now the question becomes, why suppose that the claims expressed by such bridge premises are true? In general, why suppose that if human beings are naturally inclined toward some end or goal, then the end or goal in question is intrinsically good?[20] After all, there seem to be other widespread human inclinations—inclinations toward selfishness and aggression—that one would not be tempted to use as a basis for deriving human goods. So not just any old human inclination can be used as a basis for drawing a conclusion about what is intrinsically good. This point leads to the worry about circularity.

If there are such inclinations toward selfishness and aggression that are part of human nature, then in appealing to human inclinations as a basis for inferring what is good, one must be selective. But on what basis does one select some human inclinations (and not others) for purposes of inferring what is good? It begins to look as if the procedure is circular. The plan was to observe human inclinations *without making any assumptions about what is good or bad* and then use such information as a basis for inferring what is good (and bad). But, given the need to be selective in one's choice of human inclinations, it appears that one must first make assumptions about the human good in selecting those human inclinations that are to be a basis for inferring what is good. We thus go in a circle!

Perhaps there is a way of inferring claims about the human good from facts about human nature that does not involve arguing in a circle.[21] We will not pursue this further. But even if this kind of grounding project is doomed to failure, two points are worth keeping in mind.

Some critics make this sort of grounding project essential to any version of natural law ethics and therefore reject all versions of the theory because they think the grounding project is hopeless.[22] However, John Finnis, a contemporary advocate of natural law ethics, denies this characterization.[23] Moreover, Finnis claims that it is not even true of Aquinas's version of the theory that claims about morality are supposed to be derived from facts about human nature. On his reading of Aquinas, moral propositions identifying basic goods are not derived at all. So

> for Aquinas, the way to discover what is morally right (virtue) and wrong (vice) is to ask, not what is in accordance with human nature, but what is reasonable. And this quest will eventually bring one back to the underived first principles of practical reasonableness, principles which make no reference to human nature, but only to human goods. (Finnis 1980, 36)

According to Finnis's reading of Aquinas, claims about what are the basic human goods are *self-evident* in the sense that anyone of sufficient maturity, and thus able to understand the relevant concepts involved, can, by the use of reason, come to grasp the truth of such claims as "Life is intrinsically good," "Knowledge is intrinsically good," and so forth. I am calling attention here to the fact that there is some dispute about whether all versions of natural law ethics (including even Aquinas's) must involve the attempt to infer basic moral principles from facts about human nature.

My second observation is that even if it is not possible to infer values from nonmoral facts about human nature, this does not mean that we should reject moral perfectionism, which is at the core of natural law ethics. We should not confuse the perfectionist core of natural law ethics with a supposedly failed attempt to justify it by the sort of grounding project we have been examining. There may be other ways to justify moral perfectionism.

Revisiting the Problem of Moral Conflict. In presenting the version of natural law ethics we find in Aquinas, we proceeded in stages. We began with the perfectionistic account of the human good together with an initial account of right action but found that there are cases in which the view (unless qualified) leads to inconsistent verdicts about the morality of actions. As we also saw, the core of the theory, when augmented by moral absolutism together with the PDE, results in a theory that avoids inconsistency. If we now give up absolutism and the PDE but want to hold on to the core, we need a way of handling the problem of inconsistency generated by cases of moral conflict.

One proposal for developing the core so as to avoid inconsistency is to claim that the various intermediate moral rules—rules concerning killing, lying, and the rest—that are featured in the theory state presumptive moral reasons for engaging in or avoiding certain forms of behavior. Thus, the rule against lying is not absolute but can be expressed as follows:

> It is wrong to lie unless, in particular circumstances, there is some moral reason to lie that outweighs in importance the moral reason for not lying.

Suppose that the other moral rules featured in traditional natural law moral theory are similarly formulated. As before, we still have to deal with cases in which two rules apply to the same situation, one rule favoring doing some action while the other favors not doing the action. In other words, in cases of conflict, we have to decide which rule, in the particular circumstance under consideration, is overriding and thus should be followed.

Now one possibility is to find some sort of nonarbitrary rank ordering of the rules so that whenever there is a conflict, the rule higher on the list should always be followed. But suppose it is not possible to come up with a fixed ranking of this sort. In that case, another possibility is to claim that in cases of conflict we simply must appeal to the details of the case at hand and use good moral judgment to decide which rule, in that particular case, should be followed. For instance, if the situation is such that in order to save an innocent life, one must lie, then one must use good moral judgment to determine whether saving a life is a good moral reason for lying that outweighs the moral importance of not lying. The key idea here is that in cases of conflict, there is no supreme moral principle or superrule that determines what we are to do; rather, in such cases, moral judgment must take over.[24]

I maintain that the best way to develop the remaining core of the natural law theory—the way hinted at in the previous paragraph—will result in the theory being both pluralistic and limited in its power to generate verdicts about the morality of specific actions. The view will be pluralistic because it will feature a plurality of moral rules. It will be limited because the moral rules that make up the theory will not themselves determine (in cases where the rules conflict) which action is morally right. When, for example, in some circumstance, the rule against lying conflicts with the rule requiring that we help others in need, there is no higher rule or principle that can settle what we are to do in that circumstance. This is where theory is powerless to dictate some right answer to the question of what ought (or ought not) to be done in a particular circumstance and so lacks a measure of determinacy.

If we follow my suggestion for interpreting the core of the natural law theory, we end up with a kind of moral theory that I will call *limited moral pluralism*. Moreover, I shall argue that the most plausible versions of the theories to be considered in the remaining chapters will be versions of limited moral pluralism. (The idea of limited moral pluralism will become clearer as we go, especially when we come to the moral theory of W. D. Ross in chapter 8.)

Moral Perfectionism? But is the project of developing the perfectionistic core of the natural law theory worth pursuing? Moral perfectionism, recall, is the view that (1) considerations of value are conceptually prior to considerations of right conduct, and (2) the sort of value that is central to ethics is perfectionistic value. Thus, versions of moral perfectionism purport to explain the nature of right and wrong action in terms of how actions bear on perfectionistic value. But this view has been challenged by philosophers who would agree with the first claim made by the moral perfectionist but deny that perfectionistic value is central to morality. These critics would thus reject moral perfectionism's way of explaining what makes actions right or wrong and thus (appealing to the standard of explanatory power) reject it as a correct moral criterion.

Some moral philosophers hold the view that it is *welfare*—one's life going well for one—that is of primary concern in ethics and that one cannot understand the welfare of a human being (or other creature) solely in terms of its perfection. Their main reason for saying this is that the idea of the perfection of something is the idea of its being a good or excellent specimen of its kind. Arguably, this is an objective matter; it does not depend on the attitudes of the creature whose perfection is in question. By contrast, the notion of welfare or well-being is importantly subjective because it essentially involves the perspective of the agent in question. My life might satisfy the conditions for being a good or excellent specimen of humanity—I might be healthy and be quite knowledgeable about a range of issues—but it is still possible that *from my perspective* my life is not going well. But my well-being or welfare requires that from my perspective, my life is going well for me. Thus, achieving perfection does not guarantee my welfare. So, we can and should distinguish between perfectionist value and welfare (or what is often called prudential value). Here is how L. W. Sumner explains the contrast:

> [Y]ou can easily imagine yourself, at the end of your life, taking pride in your high level of self-development but none the less wishing you had got more out of your life, that it had been more rewarding or fulfilling, and thinking that it might have gone better for you had you devoted less energy to perfecting your talents and more to just hanging out and diversifying your interests. Whatever we are to count as excellences for creatures of our nature, they will raise the perfectionist value of our lives regardless of the extent to their payoff for us. There is therefore no logical guarantee that the best human specimens will also be the best off. (Sumner 1996, 24)

If one takes welfare (or prudential value) to be central to ethical concerns, then if Sumner is correct and welfare cannot be understood in terms of perfectionist value, we must reject moral perfectionism as giving us a correct moral criterion.

One type of moral theory that does take considerations of welfare to be central to ethical concerns is the utilitarian moral theory, which will occupy us in the next two chapters.

13. Conclusion

I have argued that there is reason to reject moral absolutism and the principle of double effect, which are associated with the natural law tradition in ethics. However, if we reject these components, we still are left with the core of the theory. The core consists of a perfectionist account of intrinsic value and an account of right conduct according to which we are to promote such value and not hinder or destroy it. Since there is a plurality of basic human goods, the remaining core instructs us to promote these goods and to avoid hindering or destroying them. For each of the basic goods, we can formulate moral rules that prohibit some forms of conduct and require others. I have suggested that in cases where these rules come into conflict, there is no supreme moral principle that will tell us which rule one should observe; rather we must rely on our moral judgment in deciding what ought to be done in such situations of conflict. Understood in this way, the natural law theory—its remaining core—is limited in its powers to tell us what ought to be done in many specific circumstances and so lacks a measure of determinacy. In the end, developing the theory in this way yields a version of limited moral pluralism.

Further Reading

Bole, Thomas J., ed. 1991. *Journal for Medicine and Philosophy* 16. A special issue, "Double Effect: Theoretical Function and Biomedical Implications," featuring various authors debating the PDE.

Boyle, Joseph. 1980. "Toward Understanding the Principle of Double Effect." *Ethics* 90: 527–38. A restatement and defense of the traditional principle.

Buckle, Steven. 1991. "Natural Law." In *A Companion to Ethics*, ed. Peter Singer. Oxford: Blackwell. A useful historical overview of natural law theorizing in ethics.

Davis, Nancy. 1984. "The Doctrine of Double Effect: Problems of Interpretation." *Pacific Philosophical Quarterly* 65: 107–23. Criticism of various attempts to draw the intended/merely foreseen distinction.

Haakonssen, Knud. 1992. "Natural Law." In *Encyclopedia of Ethics*, vol. 2, ed. Lawrence C. Becker and Charlotte B. Becker. 2d ed. New York: Routledge. Brief overview and critique of natural law ethics.

Finnis, John. 1980. *Natural Law and Natural Rights.* Oxford: Oxford University Press. One of the most important contemporary defenses of natural law theory.

———. 1998. *Aquinas.* New York: Oxford University Press. A penetrating study of the moral, legal, and political doctrines of Aquinas.

———. 1998. "Natural Law." In *Routledge Encyclopedia of Philosophy*, vol. 6, ed. Edward Craig, 685–90. London: Routledge. A helpful characterization of the rudiments of natural law theory.

Fried, Charles. 1978. *Right and Wrong.* Cambridge: Harvard University Press. A defense of moral absolutism.

George, Robert P. 1992. *Natural Law Theory.* Oxford: Oxford University Press. Essays by various authors on contemporary natural law theory in ethics and law.

Lisska, Anthony J. 1996. *Aquinas's Theory of Natural Law.* New York: Oxford University Press. A detailed interpretation of Aquinas's natural law theory of ethics. Includes discussion of contemporary versions of natural law ethics.

Marquis, Donald B. 1991. "Four Versions of Double Effect." *Journal of Medicine and Philosophy* 16: 515–44. Features criticisms of four versions of the PDE including those to be found in the writings of Boyle and Quinn.

Quinn, Warren. 1989. "Actions, Intentions, and Consequences: The Doctrine of Double Effect." *Philosophy and Public Affairs* 18: 334–51. An interpretation and defense of the PDE that attempts to justify it in terms of the idea of respecting persons.

Uniacke, Suzanne. 1998. "Double Effect." In *Routledge Encyclopedia of Philosophy*, ed.

Edward Craig, 3: 120–22. London: Routledge. A useful overview of the role, development, and problems for the PDE.

Notes

1. Aquinas, of course, was a theist, and his version of natural law theory is embedded in a theological framework. However, it is possible to interpret Aquinas's natural law ethic without relying on theological assumptions. See Lisska 1996, chap. 5 for a defense of this claim. In general, there are secular versions of the natural law theory, and so attempts to reject this type of theory on the basis of rejecting a religious outlook are a mistake.

2. To be precise, I am thinking of a certain category of knives that does not include such knives as butter knives and putty knives, neither of which are designed to cut.

3. It is important to distinguish these two types of perfectionism because it is possible to recognize value perfectionism as one kind of value but then go on to deny that this sort of value is central or even relevant to questions about right and wrong behavior. We will return to this matter at the end of the chapter.

4. Passages quoted from *Summa Theologiae* will be abbreviated *ST* followed by the page numbers from Paul Sigmund's translation of Saint Thomas Aquinas, *On Politics and Ethics* (New York: W. W. Norton, 1988).

5. In connection with suicide, Aquinas points out that it is wrong not only because it violates the value of life but also because it violates sociability, since "Man is part of the community and the fact that he exists affects the community. Therefore if he kills himself he does harm to the community" (*ST,* 70). In general, a type of action may be required or forbidden by more than one of the basic values.

6. If such rules can be known with certainty through deduction, then the premises from which they are deduced must be known with certainty, including claims about human nature featured in such deductions.

7. This claim about the moral status of the human fetus is widely accepted by members of the Catholic Church, including Catholic moral philosophers. While it is certainly controversial, let us grant it here and throughout the rest of this chapter.

8. The incommensurability of values does not mean that it is not possible to compare values for purposes of ranking them. One might rank them without supposing that there is some single scale of measure. As we shall see below in connection with the principle of double effect, the natural law theory does require that we compare values.

9. However, it might be, if, for example, someone has offered to buy me a new set of tires once mine are worn out and I want those new tires as soon as possible.

10. Defenders of moral absolutism may disagree over which types of action are absolutely prohibited.

11. As I will explain in section 12, moral absolutism is not an essential component of natural law ethics. But since it is an interesting and important doctrine in moral theory, it is worth considering, even if natural law ethics is not firmly committed to it.

12. Here, as in the hysterectomy case, we are assuming that if the operation is not performed, both the woman and her child will die. Sometimes the cases are described so that the choice is between saving the woman and saving her child. I prefer to work with the cases as I have described them because it helps bring out certain implications of this principle that we will consider in section 12.

13. In doing so, we sidestep any problems there might be in having to use the PDE (as does Aquinas) to justify killing in self-defense, since an unjust aggressor is not, by definition, innocent, and the rule only prohibits intentional taking of innocent human life.

14. See Buchanan 1996 for a discussion of the bearing of cases of voluntary euthanasia and assisted suicide on the prohibition against intentionally killing the innocent.

15. See Singer 1994 for an extensive critical treatment of the sanctity of life ethic, which upholds the absolute moral prohibition against intentionally killing the innocent. Singer discusses the Bland case in chap. 4.

16. For a critical discussion of a range of possible justifications, see Scheffler 1982, chap. 4.

17. Here, of course, we are appealing to the standard of internal support.

18. For a critical survey of attempts to draw the intended/merely foreseen distinction, see Davis 1984 and Marquis 1991.

19. Notice that the attempt to base a theory of value on facts about human nature is an attempt to satisfy the standard of external support.

20. Here is one place where Aquinas might appeal to God's design in creating human beings. In one place he writes, "God has implanted a natural appetite for such knowledge in the minds of men" (*Summa contra Gentiles*, in Aquinas 1988, 4). However, appealing to God's design will not, of course, help salvage the attempt to infer claims about intrinsic value *solely* from claims about human inclinations.

21. For a recent attempt to ground a version of moral perfectionism on non-moral facts about human nature, see Hurka 1993. Hurka's grounding project is trenchantly criticized by Kitcher (1999).

22. See O'Connor 1967, 68.

23. Finnis 1980, 33.

24. Moral judgment involves going beyond the application of rules in coming to correct moral verdicts. More will be said about moral judgment in the chapters to come, esp. chap. 8.

5

Classical Utilitarianism

In the previous chapter, we considered two cases featuring a woman and an unborn child, one involving a hysterectomy and the other a craniotomy. In the former case, a pregnant woman's life can be saved from cancer by removing her uterus, while in the latter case, a pregnant woman's life can be saved only by performing a craniotomy on the fetus. As the cases were described, the consequences of intervening to save the women's lives were essentially the same (the woman's life is saved, but the fetus dies), as were the consequences of not intervening (both woman and fetus die). Upon reflection, these cases strike many thoughtful individuals as being morally on a par; it seems reasonably clear (to many) that the right thing to do in both cases is to intervene and save the woman's life. In other words, there does not seem to be a morally relevant difference between the two cases, mainly because the choices involved are equivalent in the effects upon the lives of the individuals involved. Certainly, the effects or consequences of actions upon human beings and other sentient creatures are important considerations in determining the morality of actions. Approaching questions of right and wrong by considering the consequences of our actions is what utilitarianism is all about.

Because the utilitarian approach to morality has resulted in a variety of importantly distinct versions of utilitarian moral theory, it will be useful to break up our examination of this approach into two chapters. In this chapter, I shall begin by introducing some of the basic ingredients that go into a utilitarian moral theory and then focus on some of the views of two of its most historically influential proponents, Jeremy Bentham and John Stuart Mill. In the course of doing so, we will consider the objection that the utilitarian theory is useless in contexts of moral decision making and thus cannot satisfy the main practical aim of such theories. Utilitarian modes of response to this sort of objection can be found in the writings of Bentham and especially Mill.

In the following chapter, we continue our examination of utilitarianism by considering various theoretical objections to the view that challenge the idea that it represents a correct moral criterion. Examining such objections will lead us to consider some developments in contemporary utilitarian theorizing that have resulted in importantly different versions of the basic generic view.

1. Utilitarianism Characterized

We have already noted that competing moral theories differ importantly in their structure, that is, in how the notions of rightness and goodness are related to one another within the theory. Like natural law theory, utilitarian moral theories are *value-based:* considerations of value are prior to considerations of right and are the basis for a theory of right conduct. But unlike natural law theory, utilitarianism represents a version of *consequentialism* because it makes the rightness of an action depend entirely on facts about the values of consequences of actions.[1]

In addition, utilitarianism makes specific claims about (1) how actions are related to their consequences in determining their rightness, (2) which kinds of valuable consequences count morally, and (3) the scope of concern regarding such consequences. Let us take these up in order.

First, utilitarianism is characteristically understood to involve a *maximizing* conception of right action: right actions are those that, compared to the alternative actions open to one in a situation, would produce the *greatest amount* of value. The theory thus directs us to maximize the good; actions that do so are right, those that do not are wrong.

Second, the sorts of consequences that utilitarianism is interested in have to do with the *welfare* of individuals (including persons but also perhaps including other sentient creatures). The actions we perform can, and often do, have effects on the welfare or well-being of ourselves and others, and it is the goodness or badness of the consequences of our actions in relation to the welfare of individuals that determines the rightness or wrongness of an action. Thus, utilitarianism accepts *welfarism*—the view that the only kind of value that is of fundamental relevance for ethical evaluation is welfare.

Finally, the utilitarian theory is both *universalist* and *impartialist* with regard to the issue of whose welfare counts in determining the rightness of actions. It is universalist in the sense that the values of the consequences of our actions on *all* individuals who will be affected by them are counted as morally relevant. Of course, one might consider the welfare of all those who will be affected by one's action and yet give special weight to the welfare of one's family and friends. But the utilitarian theory rules out such special weighting; rather, it is impartialist: every individual whose welfare will be affected in some way by one's action is to count equally. No special preference can be given to oneself or one's family or friends in determining what the right course of action is. The universalist and impartialist elements of utilitarianism are encapsulated in Bentham's memorable slogan "Everyone to count for one, no one to count for more than one."

Thus, on the utilitarian theory, the deontic status of an action is determined entirely by how much value the action would produce (compared to other alternative actions one could perform instead), where value has to do with welfare, and where we are to give equal consideration to all individuals who will be affected by the action in question.

"Utility" is a technical term featured in utilitarianism that refers to the values of the consequences of actions. More specifically, I will be using the term to refer to the *net value* of the consequences of actions. The idea is this. An action can, and often will, have both good and bad effects upon the welfare of individuals. My making difficult paper assignments in my courses will predictably have good consequences: students will be challenged to extend themselves and many will in fact (I hope) improve their philosophical acumen. However, my making such assignments also results in an increased level of stress for many students, which, given the mental anguish involved, counts as a bad effect of my action. We might say, then, that my making tough paper assignments has some positive, or good, consequences and some negative, or bad, consequences. If we were to consider how much positive value (good) compared to how much negative value (bad) my action would produce, the overall net value of the consequences of my action is what we mean by referring to the utility of the action.

Notice that if some action were to produce a greater negative than positive value, then its utility would be negative. Indeed, in some cases, it might turn out that all of the alternative actions open to an agent have negative utilities. In this case, the utilitarian theory directs us to perform the action having the least amount of negative utility. This point helps make clear the guiding idea behind utilitarianism: we are obligated to bring about the best state of affairs bearing on welfare that we can in the particular situation in which we find ourselves. In some situations, the theory will direct us to make the best of a bad situation.

Here, then, is the theory of right conduct for utilitarianism:

Theory of Right Conduct

An action A is *obligatory* if and only if A has a higher utility than any other alternative action that the agent could perform instead.

An action A is *wrong* if and only if A has less utility than some other alternative action that the agent could perform instead.

An action A is *optional* if and only if (i) A has as high a utility as any other alternative action that the agent could perform instead, but (ii) there is at least one other alternative action that has as high a utility as A. (In other words, an action is optional if and only if in terms of utility production it is tied for first place with at least one other action.)

As we proceed in this chapter and the next, it will be convenient to be able to refer to a single principle that encapsulates the utilitarian theory just presented. So, making use of the category of right action (which includes both the obligatory and the optional), we can express the basic idea of the theory by what I will call the *generic principle of utility:*

GPU   An action A is *right* if and only if A has as high a utility as any alternative action that the agent could perform instead.

Utility, as we have said, refers to the value—the goodness and badness—of the consequences of actions as they bear on the welfare or well-being of individuals. But how are we to understand welfare?

2. Hedonistic Utilitarianism: The Classical View

The classic utilitarians, Bentham and Mill, accepted the following two claims:

1.   Welfare is identical with happiness.

2.   Happiness is identical with pleasure (and the absence of pain).

Individual welfare, then, was understood in terms of pleasure and pain. The resulting moral theory is called *hedonistic utilitarianism.* Let us consider it in a bit more detail.

In ethics, *value hedonism* is the view that experiences of pleasure *alone* are intrinsically good and experiences of pain *alone* are intrinsically bad.[2] All other things that have value are extrinsically good or bad. Money, health, power, knowledge, beauty, and other such desirable things are only good as means to the production of pleasure. To be more precise, we should say that *specific uses* of money, power, and knowledge are good as a means (and hence extrinsically good) whenever their use promotes pleasure, while their use on some occasion is bad as a means (extrinsically bad) when such use promotes pain. Otherwise they are intrinsically value-neutral.

As mentioned earlier, utilitarianism is committed to *welfarism,* according to which welfare is the only type of value that is of fundamental relevance in ethics. If we now combine welfarism with a hedonist account of welfare, we get *ethical hedonism:*[3]

EH Experiences of pleasure are intrinsically good and experiences of pain are intrinsically bad, and they are the only items of nonmoral intrinsic value with which ethics is concerned.

In connection with ethical hedonism it is important to stress that talk of pleasure and pain is to be understood broadly and includes not only bodily pleasures resulting from eating, drinking, getting a massage, and so forth, but also every sort of intellectual and aesthetic pleasure. Solving a difficult mathematical puzzle or viewing one of Edward Hopper's paintings can be a source of pleasure and is to be included in the utilitarian's calculations of utility.

Hedonistic utilitarianism, then, is the result of plugging ethical hedonism into the basic utilitarian conception expressed above in GPU. Bentham was an advocate of this brand of utilitarianism, and Mill, on some readings, was as well. We can begin our study of hedonistic versions of utilitarianism by defining a hedonistic conception of utility (net intrinsic value) as follows:

HU The utility of an action = the overall balance of pleasure versus pain that would be produced were the action to be performed.

If we now reformulate our generic principle of utility (GPU) to reflect a hedonist account of welfare, we have the basic principle of hedonistic utilitarianism:

PHU An action A is *right* if and only if A would produce at least as high an overall balance of pleasure versus pain as would any other alternative action.

How might we go about determining the utility of actions given this hedonistic theory of utility? This question is addressed in Bentham's "felicific calculus," to which we now turn.

3. Bentham's Felicific Calculus

Jeremy Bentham (1748–1832), who was among the most distinguished of the early proponents of utilitarianism, defended his version of the view in his 1789 work, *An Introduction to the Principles of Morals and Legislation*. As just mentioned, Bentham (like many utilitarians) accepts ethical hedonism. Of particular interest for our purposes is Bentham's so-called felicific calculus, which provides a checklist of seven features to be used in calculating the utilities of actions and thereby arriving at reasoned conclusions about their deontic status. Here is the list:

1. Intensity

2. Duration

3. Certainty and uncertainty

4. Propinquity and remoteness

5. Fecundity

6. Purity

7. Extent

Let us take a closer look.

The two items on Bentham's list that directly concern the calculation of the utilities of actions (where utility concerns episodes of pleasure and episodes of pain) are the *intensity* of such experiences and their *duration*. The key idea here is that pleasures and pains can be measured. That is, in principle at least, we can assign numerical values to episodes of pleasure and of pain based on their intensity and duration. Doing so allows us to add and subtract their values. Engaging in such hedonic arithmetic in turn allows us (again, in principle) to assign numerical values to the utilities of actions for purposes of arriving at judgments about their rightness and wrongness. Let us briefly elaborate this idea.

To carry out these calculations, we need to settle on some unit of measure for both episodes of pleasure and episodes of pain. Consider the pleasure that results from drinking lemonade for one minute on a hot day when one is thirsty. Let us stipulate that this will represent our unit for calculating pleasures. Thus, if drinking a beer yields pleasure that is twice as intense as drinking lemonade under the conditions specified, then drinking a beer for one minute equals two units of pleasure. Now we do a similar thing for experiences of pain: we stipulate some unit in terms of which all other pains can be assigned a numerical value. The idea, then, is that all experiences of pleasure (bodily, aesthetic, and intellectual) can be assigned a numeric value using our stipulated scale of measure, and the same can be done for experiences of pain. This means that such values are *commensurable*.[4]

The third entry on Bentham's list—*certainty and uncertainty*—has to do with the likelihood that an action will have some particular pleasurable or painful outcome. This dimension of utilitarian calculation will come up again in section 5, so we will skip over it for now.

Propinquity and *remoteness* have to do respectively with episodes of pleasure and pain that follow more or less immediately from an action and those that follow some time after the action. Since the utility of an action depends upon *all* of its consequences—including those that do not occur until some time has elapsed after the action—Bentham has us consider the propinquity and remoteness of episodes of pleasure and pain that an action would produce if performed.

In taking account of the long-range consequences of our actions, Bentham has us consider the *fecundity* and the *purity* of pleasures and pains in determining the utility of actions. Fecundity refers to the likelihood that episodes of pleasure will be followed by further episodes of pleasure, and similarly for pain. For instance, for many individuals the act of reading a fine novel will not only result in the immediate pleasures involved in the reading but also is likely to result in further pleasures experienced in reflecting on themes from the novel. For such individuals, the act of reading such a novel is fecund.

The purity of a pleasure or pain refers to the likelihood that such experiences will not be followed by experiences of the opposite sort. For instance, the immediate result of eating a chocolate bar may be one of pleasure. But suppose that as a result of eating the candy, one will experience a severe stomachache two hours later. In that case, eating the chocolate lacks, in Bentham's terminology, purity.

As I have explained these features, fecundity and purity have to do with calculating the remote effects of actions, and remoteness just has to do with considering all of the episodes of pleasure and pain that flow from some action. So, the intensity and duration of the episodes of pleasure and pain are fundamental in determining the utility of an action.

Finally, *extent* concerns the number of persons whose welfare will be affected by one's action. In describing a procedure for morally evaluating actions, Bentham recommends that we begin our calculations by considering any person who seems directly affected by the action in question. For this person, we consider all of the episodes of pleasure (both immediate and remote) that he will experience as a result of the action, and similarly for the episodes of pain.[5] We can then determine how much utility would accrue to this individual were the action to be performed. As Bentham explains, we next

> [t]ake an account of the *number* of persons whose interests appear to be concerned; and repeat the above process with respect to each. *Sum up* the numbers expressive of the degrees of *good* tendency, which the act has, with respect to each individual, in regard to whom the tendency of it is *good* upon the whole: do this again with respect to each individual, in regard to whom the tendency of it is *bad* upon the whole. Take the *balance;* which, if on the side of *pleasure,* will give the general *good tendency* of the act, if on the side of pain, the general *evil tendency,* with respect to the same community. (Bentham [1789] 1948, 31)

Calculating the utility of a single action is not sufficient for determining its deontic status for the utilitarian. Utilitarianism is a maximizing theory, and we are to perform the action with the highest utility. So we must calculate the utilities of the alternative actions open to us in some situation. We are morally required by the theory to perform the action with the highest utility (which might be negative); all other actions are forbidden. In cases where two or more actions are tied for first place in terms of their utilities, we are required to perform some one action from among this select alternative set, although each such action, taken individually, is optional.

This may all seem very tidy, but one may question whether such a calculus is possible even in principle. Is it theoretically possible to assign numerical values to episodes of pleasure and of pain that would allow the kind of hedonic arithmetic mentioned above? We explained this sort of measurement in terms of the duration of the experience and its intensity. The duration of pleasures and pains can, of course, be measured, but what about intensity? Consider the intensity of the pleasure involved in drinking a fine Bavarian pilsner beer, and compare it to the intensity of the pleasure involved in reading a good mystery novel. Can the intensities of these two very different experiences be put on some common scale of cardinal measurement? Of course, the problem is aggravated when we consider coming up with some unit of measure for making interpersonal comparisons of utility. Whether it is possible in principle to assign numerical values to episodes of pleasure and pain so that they can be added and subtracted will largely depend on the nature of such mental states. This is a difficult topic that we cannot pursue here.

But even if no such scheme of cardinal measurement is possible, this does not spell disaster for hedonistic utilitarianism. So long as there is some way to compare the levels of pleasure and pain experienced by different individuals, the utilitarian has all she needs for her theory. And we do seem to be able to make such comparisons. Consider first the comparisons we make in our own case. I judge that going to eat at Los Olivos would be a more pleasant experience than going to eat at the Pink Pony. I judge that staying home this evening and reading a Graham Greene novel would be more pleasant and yield more personal happiness than would going to Beale Street and being in a crowd. We make such *intra*personal comparisons of actual, remembered, and prospective pleasures and pains all the time.

Interpersonal comparisons also seem quite possible. That is, there seems to be no problem in comparing how much happiness I would derive from going to the restaurants in question with how much you would derive. And the same applies to reading a Graham Greene novel and going to Beale Street. I can sensibly judge, for example, that you would derive far more pleasure in going to Beale Street this evening than I would and that you would not enjoy reading a Graham Greene novel nearly as much as I. Such *inter*personal comparisons of pleasure and pain are commonplace and seem to be all one needs to make sense of interpersonal comparisons of utility.

Of course, in practice it may be difficult, if not impossible, to make interpersonal comparisons of utility for purposes of moral decision making, especially when one's action affects many people (a point that we consider in more detail in section 5). And even if the sort of felicific calculus envisioned by Bentham were possible, we could only hope to roughly approximate the rigor prescribed by his procedure. But our discussion of utility in terms of pleasure and pain has, thus far, taken for granted that the hedonic value of experiences of pleasure and pain is exhausted by considering their intensity and duration. This feature of Bentham's view prompted a certain criticism of the utilitarian doctrine that Mill was anxious to rebut. Mill's rebuttal involved rejecting Bentham's purely quantitative conception of utility, as we shall see in the next section.

4. Mill's Utilitarianism

The moral and political writings of John Stuart Mill (1806–73) continue to be extremely influential in the field of ethics in general and in the utilitarian tradition in particular. His 1863 *Utilitarianism* is as important for its forceful presentation and defense of utilitarianism as it is short. Two significant elements of Mill's theory are his conception of welfare and his attempted proof of the principle of utility. Let us briefly examine them.

Qualitative Hedonism

Like Bentham, Mill was committed to ethical hedonism as an account of welfare:[6]

> By happiness is intended pleasure, and the absence of pain; by unhappiness, pain, and the privation of pleasure. To give a clear view of the moral standard set up by the theory, much more requires to be said. . . . But these supplementary explanations do not affect the theory of life on which this theory of morality is grounded: namely, that pleasure, and freedom from pain, are the only things desirable as ends. (Mill [1863] 1979, 7)

However, Mill's version of hedonism makes an important departure from the version advocated by Bentham.

Bentham's hedonistic conception of the good for human beings (and other sentient creatures) is properly described as purely *quantitative*. As we have seen, the two aspects of experiences of pleasure in virtue of which such mental states have positive value are their intensity and their duration—properties of such states that can (so Bentham assumed) be measured in units. Bentham's quantitative hedonism (and hence the utilitarian theory generally) was attacked as being a moral philosophy unfit for humans, being more appropriate for lower animals like pigs. In response to this criticism,

Mill refined Bentham's purely quantitative version of hedonism by insisting that considerations of quality, along with quantity, represent an aspect of pleasurable mental states that help determine their value. Let us review the objection that prompted Mill's refinement and then consider his reply to it.

Here is how Mill characterizes what has come to be known as the *doctrine of swine objection*:

> Now such a theory of life [utilitarianism] excites in many minds, and among them in some of the most estimable in feeling and purpose, inveterate dislike. To suppose that life has (as they express it) no higher end than pleasure—no better and nobler object of desire and pursuit—they designate as utterly mean and groveling, as a doctrine worthy only of swine. (Mill [1863] 1979, 7)

The idea behind this objection is clear enough. Human beings are certainly capable of many fine and noble pursuits—we have capacities for intellectual and aesthetic endeavor, as well as a capacity for moral pursuits, that are quite beyond any capacities possessed by lower animals, which can experience only those pleasures associated with, for example, eating, drinking, sex, and (at least for pigs) wallowing in mud. Hedonistic utilitarianism, however, seems to ignore these facts about human beings, setting forth a life of pleasure and reduction of pain as the highest good for human beings and the end of moral conduct.

Now certainly, one sensible requirement of any plausible moral theory is that it reflect somehow the nature of human beings. A moral theory that sets forth severely demanding moral requirements might be fit for saints or some other superhuman creatures, but it would hardly be a theory fit for humans. Similarly, a moral theory that puts forth requirements that in effect represent human beings as creatures on a par with pigs errs in the other direction. Hedonistic utilitarianism does just that, according to the critics.

One obvious response to this criticism is that nothing in Bentham's version of hedonistic utilitarianism requires or advises human beings to pursue only those types of bodily pleasures that can also be experienced by lower animals. Certainly, given the enlarged capacities of humans compared to those of lower animals, nothing in Bentham's view conflicts or fails to comport with facts about distinctive human capacities. The fact that we are capable of intellectual and aesthetic endeavors means that we are capable also of experiencing the pleasures that typically result from pursuing such things. And furthermore, it is open to Bentham to claim that more often than not the pursuit of intellectual and aesthetic ends will yield longer-lasting pleasures and hence, on the whole, pleasures of greater quantity compared to pleasures resulting from such activities as drinking and eating.

Nevertheless, there is still a worry that can be raised against a purely quantitative hedonism that is brought out in a vivid and imaginative way by Roger Crisp in his story about Haydn and the oyster.

> You are a soul in heaven waiting to be allocated a life on Earth. It is late Fri-
> day afternoon, and you watch anxiously as the supply of available lives dwin-
> dles. When your turn comes, the angel in charge offers you a choice between
> two lives, that of the composer Haydn and that of an oyster. Besides compos-
> ing wonderful music and influencing the evolution of the symphony, Haydn
> will meet with success and honor in his own lifetime, be cheerful and popu-
> lar, travel and gain much enjoyment from field sports. The oyster's life is far
> less exciting. Though this is a rather sophisticated oyster, its life will consist
> only of mild sensual pleasure, rather like that experienced by humans when
> floating very drunk in a warm bath. (Crisp 1997, 24)

Haydn will die at the age of seventy-seven, but the angel in charge offers
you the life of an oyster for as long as you like—hundreds, even thousands,
of years. Clearly, the variety and intensity of the pleasures that fill Haydn's
life far exceed the pleasures that the oyster will experience in that same
seventy-seven year span of time. But on the sort of quantitative view held
by Bentham, if the oyster lives long enough, eventually the total quantity
of pleasure it will experience will exceed the total quantity experienced by
Haydn. If the only thing that counts in deciding matters of personal welfare is the product of the intensity and duration of one's pleasures (as Bentham's version of hedonism implies), then it follows that the extended life
of the oyster is to be preferred over a life like Haydn's. But this seems to
be an absurd result.

What the Haydn-oyster example reveals is that we normally think that
there is more to the value of pleasure than mere intensity and duration: facts
about *kinds* of pleasure also matter. And this is precisely what Mill's version
of hedonism—his *qualitative hedonism*—is intended to reflect.

> It is quite compatible with the principle of utility to recognize the fact, that
> some *kinds* of pleasure are more desirable and more valuable than others. It
> would be absurd that while, in estimating all other things, quality is consid-
> ered as well as quantity, the estimation of pleasures should be supposed to de-
> pend on quantity alone. (Mill [1863] 1979, 8)

It might help to understand Mill's position if we reflect a bit more on
hedonism as a theory of value. This sort of view makes two claims (sometimes not clearly distinguished).[7] First, hedonism makes a claim about what
sorts of items have intrinsic value: certain mental states and, in particular,
mental states of pleasure are intrinsically good, and mental states of pain are
intrinsically bad. Second, the view makes a claim about what *makes* such
states intrinsically good or bad: certain properties possessed by states of
pleasure make them intrinsically valuable, and similarly for states of pain.
According to Bentham's quantitative hedonism, the only good-making
properties of pleasures and pains are their intensity and duration. On Mill's
qualitative version, not only intensity and duration but also facts about the

very nature of the pleasure—its quality as a pleasurable experience—are good-making features of such states. (Again, similar remarks apply to states of pain.)

Of course, if we enrich hedonism in the way Mill suggests, we must have some way to determine the relative qualities of pleasures. Mill's proposal for dealing with this matter is that we are to consult the opinions of competent judges.

> If I am asked, what I mean by difference in quality of pleasures, or what makes one pleasure more valuable than another, merely as a pleasure, except its being greater in amount, there is but one possible answer. Of two pleasures, if there be one to which all or almost all who have experience of both give a decided preference, irrespective of any feeling of moral obligation to prefer it, that is the more desirable pleasure. If one of the two is, by those who are competently acquainted with both, placed so far above the other that they prefer it, even though knowing it to be attended with a greater amount of discontent, and would not resign it for any quantity of the other pleasure which their nature is capable of, we are justified in ascribing to the preferred enjoyment a superiority in quality, so far outweighing quantity as to render it, in comparison, of small amount. (Mill [1863] 1979, 8–9)

What do the experts have to say about matters of quality? According to Mill:

> Now it is an unquestionable fact that those who are equally acquainted with and equally capable of appreciating and enjoying both do give a most marked preference to the manner of existence which employs their higher faculties. (Mill [1863] 1979, 9)

Thus, according to Mill, the best evidence we have concerning the relative qualities of pleasures are the verdicts of those who have experienced a full range of types of pleasures, including bodily, intellectual, and aesthetic pleasures. Moreover, the experts apparently agree that, by and large, the pleasures flowing from the use of our intellect and from our aesthetic sense (the pleasures of the higher faculties) are more desirable and hence of a higher quality than those resulting from our lower, bodily faculties.

What is particularly important to recall from our previous discussion is that on a purely quantitative conception of utility, pleasures (and pains) of any sort could be put on a common numerical scale for comparison. So, for example, regardless of the fact that the pleasures that Haydn will experience are of far greater sophistication and intensity than the ones experienced by the oyster, it is possible, on a purely quantitative scale, to equate the total amount of pleasure that Haydn will experience in his lifetime with the total amount of pleasure that the oyster will experience during its lifetime. In short, on a purely quantitative version of hedonism, pleasures and pains are fully and completely commensurable.

The introduction of quality disrupts such commensurability: some types of pleasure cannot be equated with other types, whatever the quantity involved. In the very last sentence of the first of the above two passages, Mill claims that competent judges will rank some pleasures higher in value than others "and would not resign [them] for *any quantity* of the other pleasure." According to Mill, then, various types of pleasures are *incommensurable*—they can't be put on a cardinal scale of measurement.

How does the addition of quality help answer the doctrine of swine objection? Presumably, doing so blocks the claim that, for example, the extended life of an oyster is better (represents a greater source of welfare) than the life of Haydn. Haydn's life was filled with all sorts of nonbodily pleasures of a higher quality than the sorts of pleasures that would be experienced by the oyster. Take any one of Haydn's higher pleasures, such as the pleasure derived from composing a symphony. No amount of pleasure of the sort experienced by the oyster will outrank in quality this pleasure of Haydn's. Thus, by factoring in considerations of the quality of various pleasures, we can conclude that the life of a Haydn is certainly more desirable than the life of an immortal oyster.

I have been using the Haydn–oyster story for purposes of vivid illustration, but the point of Mill's qualitative hedonism can be brought to bear on the choices that human beings actually face. One can easily imagine having to choose between two paths in life. One path will result in a life of relative ease that will not put much strain on one's current intellectual abilities. The other path will be a life in the pursuit of scientific knowledge, which will no doubt involve many sacrifices and setbacks. Assuming the scientist enjoys some intellectual pleasures as a result of her scientific inquiries, her life is to be preferred to the life of the ne'er-do-well. By making quality one of the properties of experiences of pleasure and pain that determine the value of such experiences, Mill's moral theory fully respects the fact that humans have greater capacities than pigs and are thus "higher" than such beasts. Thus, Mill's qualitative hedonism helps the utilitarian theory avoid the charge that it is a moral philosophy fit for swine.

Objections to Qualitative Hedonism

Mill's qualitative hedonism has been roundly criticized. I shall mention two of the objections; the first challenges its intelligibility, the other raises worries about the appeal to experts.

A common objection to Mill's version of hedonism is that it faces a dilemma. Either quality has to do with the intrinsic nature of mental states of pleasure, or it does not. If it does, then it has to do with the pleasantness of experiences of pleasure, in which case the only basis for distinguishing various pleasures is their intensity and duration, and Mill ends up a pure quantitative hedonist after all. However, if quality does not have to do with the intrinsic nature of pleasure and has rather to do with something other than the pleasantness of the experience, Mill has forsaken hedonism. (Recall that the second claim made by the hedonist is that it is intrinsic properties of pleasures and pains that make them good and bad respectively.) Thus, there is no distinct position that can be described as qualitative hedonism.

The reply to this objection is that it begs the question against Mill's view. The first horn of the dilemma simply assumes without argument that the only aspects of pleasures that can affect their ranking are quantifiable. Mill would insist that the intrinsic nature of a pleasure—the quality of its pleasurableness—makes it more or less valuable than other types of pleasure. And appealing only to the pleasurableness of such states means that he can avoid the second horn of the dilemma as well. The idea might be put this way: for Mill it is a basic fact that the intrinsic nature of certain kinds of pleasures (apart from their intensities and durations) confers on them a value that is higher than the value conferred on other, "lower" pleasures of equal intensity and duration.

Critics have also raised doubts about Mill's use of competent judges as a basis for distinguishing higher from lower pleasures. As I have explained Mill's qualitative hedonism, the judgments of the experts do not *make* some pleasures higher than others; rather the role of the experts is *evidential:* their preferences represent the best evidence we have for judging the relative qualities of pleasures. Now, presumably, to be competent in judging matters of quality, one must have the developed capacities to enjoy the types of pleasures to be ranked. An uneducated individual, who is not able to appreciate works of literature and other works of art, is not competent to make comparative rankings between bodily pleasures and aesthetic pleasures. Only a select group will have the requisite competence. But how can Mill be so sure that those who are competent in the way he requires will reach universal or nearly universal agreement over matters of quality?

Consider Joe, a philosopher who is also a gourmand. One can imagine that Joe, under the appropriate conditions for making comparisons, may well rank the pleasure derived from consuming a meal prepared by one of the world's greatest chefs to be of a higher quality than the pleasure derived from reading (and contemplating) book Zeta of Aristotle's *Metaphysics.* If Joe is thereby disqualified from being among competent judges, the worry is that appeal to the experts is a cheat. That is, if it turns out that in order to qualify as a "competent" judge you must agree that the intellectual and aesthetic pleasures are of a higher quality than the bodily pleasures, then Mill's appeal to the experts is circular. We are supposed to appeal to the experts for unbiased testimony as to the comparative rankings of pleasures. But to count as an expert (so it seems) you must antecedently agree with a certain preferred ranking.

Despite such worries, there is something both plausible and attractive about Mill's attempt to sophisticate hedonism with the introduction of quality as a dimension of pleasure and pain. However, the main task seems to be one of blending such considerations of quality with considerations concerning the quantity of pleasures in arriving at judgments of overall relative value. It is simply not clear how considerations of both quantity and quality are to figure in determining the utilities of actions. Whether there is some way it can be done I will leave for the reader to ponder.

Mill's "Proof"

Bentham claimed that the principle of utility could not be proved, since "that which is used to prove every thing else, cannot itself be proved: a chain of proofs must have their commencement somewhere" (Bentham [1789] 1948, 4). The idea is that since the principle of utility is fundamental in the sense that all other moral claims are justified ultimately by appeal to it, there can be no further principle to which we can appeal in attempting to prove it. If there were, the principle of utility would not be fundamental. The assumption here seems to be that any genuine proof of a moral principle must appeal to some further, more basic *moral* principle.

Opposed to Bentham, many philosophers have thought that it is possible to prove, or at least provide justifying evidence for, a fundamental moral principle by appealing to nonmoral theories and assumptions.[8] However, Mill agrees with Bentham that "questions of ultimate ends do not admit of proof, in any ordinary acceptation of the term" (Mill [1863] 1979, 34). Nevertheless, Mill thinks that:

> We are not, however, to infer that its [the principle of utility's] acceptance or rejection must depend on blind impulse or arbitrary choice. There is a larger meaning of the word, 'proof' in which this question is as amenable to it as any other of the disputed questions of philosophy. . . . Considerations may be presented capable of determining the intellect either to give or withhold its assent to the doctrine; and this is equivalent to proof. (Mill [1863] 1979, 4–5)

Mill's "proof" (in the larger meaning of the term) is not so much an argument for the principle of utility as it is an argument for the claim that the general happiness is alone of intrinsic value. Mill assumes that if this can be shown, then since morality requires that we perform actions that produce as much positive value or goodness as possible, the principle of utility will have been (in the broad sense of the term) proved.

Mill's proof proceeds by attempting to establish three conclusions. First, he argues that each individual's happiness—that is, each individual's pleasurable experiences—is intrinsically good for that individual; second, that the general happiness (the happiness of all individuals) is an intrinsic good for the aggregate of individuals; and finally, that happiness is the only intrinsic good. Let us take a closer look at each stage.

Stage 1. Mill writes:

> The only proof capable of being given that an object is visible is that people actually see it. The only proof that a sound is audible is that people hear it; and so forth for the other sources of our experience. In this manner, I apprehend, the sole evidence it is possible to produce that anything is desirable is that people actually do desire it. (Mill [1863] 1979, 34)

We can elaborate Mill's line of thought as follows:

1. People desire their own happiness for its own sake.

2. If something is desired for its own sake, then it is desirable.

Thus,

3. Each person's own happiness is desirable for that person.

4. If something is desirable, then it is intrinsically good (by definition).

Thus,

5. One's own happiness is an intrinsic good for oneself.

Stage 2. Mill continues:

> No reason can be given why the general happiness is desirable, except that each person, so far as he believes it to be attainable, desires his own happiness. This, however, being a fact, we have not only all the proof which the case admits of, but all which it is possible to require, that happiness is a good, that each person's happiness is a good to that person, and the general happiness, therefore, a good to the aggregate of all persons. Happiness has made out its title as one of the ends of conduct and, consequently, one of the criteria of morality. (Mill [1863] 1979, 34)

So, the argument continues:

5. One's own happiness is an intrinsic good for oneself (conclusion of stage 1).

6. If each person's own happiness is an intrinsic good for that person, then the general happiness is intrinsically good for the aggregate of persons.

Thus,

7. The general happiness is an intrinsic good for the aggregate of persons.[9]

Before proceeding to stage 3, let us pause to consider the argument thus far. Both stages allegedly involve some basic logical fallacies. The argument of stage 1 seems to commit the fallacy of equivocation. This fallacy occurs when a line of reasoning trades on a word or expression being used with more than one of its meanings in the context of the argument. For instance, consider this bit of sophistry:

1. Philosophy is an art.

2. Art is studied by art historians.

Thus,

3. Philosophy is studied by art historians.

The problem here is obvious: the word "art" in English has more than one meaning. In the first premise, to say that philosophy is an art is to say that engaging in the activity of philosophy involves a kind of skill. But in the second premise, the word is referring to things like paintings, music, and film. Thus, the argument commits the fallacy of equivocation.

Now the word "desirable" has at least two meanings. It can mean "able to be desired" but it can also mean "worthy of being desired." Given the analogy Mill is drawing between what is visible and audible, on the one hand, and what is desirable, on the other, the occurrence of "desirable" in premise 2 is plausibly understood as meaning *able* to be desired. After all, to say that something is visible is to say that it is something people are able to see. But in order for step 4 in the argument to be true, the term must mean *worthy* of being desired. And certainly, from the fact that something is capable of being desired (a great many things are *capable* of being desired), it does not follow that it is worthy of being desired. Thus, stage 1 of Mill's argument commits the fallacy of equivocation. At least this is how it has often been read.

But notice that although the visible/desirable analogy is problematic, the conclusion of the argument is something that many are inclined to accept. And the fact that most everyone finds themselves desiring their own happiness as an end in itself might plausibly be said to be some evidence (though not iron-clad) that happiness is very likely something intrinsically good.[10]

But more problematic than the first stage is the second stage of the argument. There just seems to be a huge gap between the claim that my happiness is an intrinsic good to me, and your happiness is an intrinsic good to you (and so on for each and every person), to the conclusion that the total

sum of happiness of all individuals (the general happiness) is something intrinsically good to the aggregate of individuals. An egoist would admit the
premise, but why should he accept the conclusion?

The argument is typically understood to be an instance of the fallacy of
composition involving reasoning about parts and wholes. One commits this
fallacy when one illegitimately infers that some property possessed by each
part or member of a whole is thereby also possessed by the whole itself.[11]
From the fact that some machine is made up of parts and each part weighs
less than five pounds, it does not follow that the machine taken as a whole
weighs less than five pounds. To make such an inference is to commit the
fallacy in question. Similarly, Mill's argument here is diagnosed as going illegitimately from a claim about each member of the aggregate of human
beings to the same sort of claim about the aggregate. Whether this is a
proper diagnosis of Mill's argument, the problem of bridging the gap between the conclusion of stage 1 and the conclusion of stage 2 remains.

Stage 3. Mill recognizes that having argued that happiness is an intrinsic
good is not sufficient to secure his position; he also needs to provide reasons for claiming that it is the *only* thing of intrinsic value. Mill recognizes
that people do desire various things and states of affairs like virtue, knowledge, and power for their own sakes; and according to the mode of reasoning featured in the first stage of Mill's argument, this is evidence that these
items are intrinsically good. So the task that Mill sets for himself is to show
that although virtue and the rest are often desired as intrinsically valuable,
it is nevertheless the case that such items are really a part of an individual's
happiness. If he can show this, then happiness after all is the only thing of
intrinsic value. Continuing the argument, then:

8.   All other things besides happiness that are desired for themselves are
      really only desired as parts of the end of happiness.

Thus,

9.   Happiness is the sole intrinsic good.

Again, let us examine a passage from Mill.

> The ingredients of happiness are very various, and each of them is desirable
> in itself, and not merely when considered as swelling an aggregate. The prin-
> ciple of utility does not mean that any given pleasure, as music, for instance,
> or any given exemption from pain, as for example health, is to be looked upon
> as means to a collective something termed happiness, and to be desired on
> that account. They are desired and desirable in and for themselves; besides
> being means, they are a part of the end. Virtue, according to the utilitarian
> doctrine, is not naturally and originally part of the end, but it is capable of be-
> coming so. (Mill [1863] 1979, 35–36)

In addition to virtue, Mill makes similar remarks about money, power, and fame and concludes that such items are, or can be, "included in happiness. They are some of the elements of which the desire for happiness is made up. Happiness is not an abstract idea but a concrete whole; and these are some of its parts" (Mill [1863] 1979, 36–37).

To make sense of Mill's claim here, we should not understand him as claiming that virtue, power, money, and fame are themselves literally a part of happiness. Happiness is composed of pleasurable experiences, and these items are not identical to mere pleasurable experiences. Rather, the idea must be that our happiness is constituted of various types of pleasant experience, and so when people find virtue, power, or fame desirable in themselves, what they are really finding desirable are the pleasures that can be experienced from practicing virtue, from obtaining and making use of money and power, and from attaining and enjoying fame.

Again, we cannot pause here to enter into the scholarly debates that surround Mill's obviously complex conception of happiness. However, if we stand back from the details of Mill's proof and ask ourselves about the overall plausibility of his view, we can note two rather obvious things. First, the claim that happiness is the sole item of intrinsic value is not implausible. Many philosophers would agree (though philosophers differ in their conceptions of happiness). Second, the idea that taking the moral point of view requires that we take an impartial view of matters and, in particular, that we be concerned with the welfare of individuals regardless of whose welfare it is, is also initially plausible. Finally, the idea that it is rational to produce as much intrinsic value as possible (the basic idea behind the principle of utility) is also initially plausible. Combining these ideas naturally leads one to embrace some form of utilitarianism. So, whatever the verdict on Mill's proof, there are considerations that favor this sort of moral theory. (We examine the overall plausibility of utilitarianism in the next chapter.)

Having presented the basic elements that go into a utilitarian moral theory, as well as having examined some of the doctrines of Bentham and Mill, I will now turn from presentation to criticism.

5. Practical Objections to Utilitarianism

One objection to utilitarianism that may have occurred to many readers is that the principle of utility is not useful. In order to apply it in a concrete situation in an effort to determine the deontic status of an action, one would have to figure out the utilities of all of the available alternative actions one might perform in the situation. Given how many individuals might be affected by an action, and given that we don't have direct access to the experiences of other people, the calculation of utility seems beyond our powers. For instance, how many individuals do I affect in giving a lecture on Mill's utilitarianism to my students? Perhaps some of them, as a result of what I say, will tell others who are not in the class about some point I made. Perhaps my presentation will make a deep impression on one of my students and over time she will become a practicing utilitarian. Her conversion to this moral view may lead her to become an advocate for the underprivileged, eventually leading her to assume a prominent role in an organization devoted to famine relief. And so on and on. I can't possibly foresee such effects, so there is no chance that I can use the principle of utility to determine the morality of my actions.

This objection concerns what we identified in chapter 1 as the main practical aim of a moral theory—the aim of providing a decision procedure for arriving at correct moral verdicts about actions. We also explained in chapter 1 that the standards of consistency and determinacy are used to evaluate how well a moral theory satisfies this practical aim. However, the objection under consideration does not have to do with either of these standards; rather it has to do with what we might call the *standard of applicability* for evaluating a moral theory. According to this standard, a moral theory, in providing a decision procedure, ought to specify a procedure that human beings, with their various limitations, can actually use in moral deliberation. As just explained, the utilitarian theory fails to do this.

The Principle of Utility as a Moral Criterion, Not a Decision Procedure

The points featured in this objection are well taken, but utilitarians have ways of deflecting their force. In the first place, we need to recall the difference between the theoretical and practical roles associated with moral principles. In an investigation into the nature of the right and the good, many moral philosophers are primarily interested in the theoretical goal of providing principles that correctly express the most fundamental right-making and good-making features of actions, persons, institutions, and so on. That is, they are primarily interested in providing *moral criteria*—criteria that specify what makes an action right or wrong or something good or bad. But a moral principle functioning as a criterion of right action need not also serve as a *decision procedure* and so need not fill the practical role sometimes associated with such principles. In response to the above complaint, the utilitarian will point out that the principle of utility is intended as a moral criterion, and so the fact that it is not useful in practice (and thus does not satisfy the practical role of a moral principle) does not matter.

Actual versus Probable Consequences

Even though this response is plausible, it seems reasonable to expect a moral theory to address practical questions concerning proper moral thinking and decision making. One way the utilitarian can address this concern begins by distinguishing two versions of the generic principle of utility (GPU). Let me explain.

Notice that in explaining the utilitarian moral theory, I have been presenting what is called *actual consequence utilitarianism,* which makes the deontic status of actions depend on the actual consequences of the alternative actions. In this context, talk of actual consequences of actions refers, then, to those consequences that would (actually) occur were the action to be performed.

Now the complaint about the principle of utility being useless in practice is quite forceful against actual consequence versions of utilitarianism. But there is another version of the view, *probable consequence utilitarianism,* which may help the utilitarian deal with this issue. Let us consider this further.

Associated with any action we might perform are various possible consequences (or outcomes) that vary in their likelihood or probability of resulting from the action. For instance, suppose I shuffle a deck of regular playing cards. The probability of the queen of hearts being on top of the deck as a result of the shuffle is one out of fifty-two.

Suppose that for each possible consequence of an action, we could determine its chances or probability of resulting from that action. And suppose further that for each such possible consequence, we could determine its value or utility. These values together with the relevant probabilities are the basis for what is called the *expected utility* of an action. This idea is easiest to explain using an example.

Consider a simple game of chance involving a single die that costs you $1 to play. If you roll a three or a four, you get $12; otherwise you get nothing. With a fair die, there are six possible outcomes, each of which has a probability of one-sixth. If we simply let dollar amounts represent the values of the possible outcomes, we calculate the expected utility of playing the game by multiplying the probability of the various possible outcomes by their values, and then we sum the results. Since, in the game just described, the value of rolling anything other than a three or four is zero (and multiplying zero times one-sixth is still zero), we can simplify our calculation of expected utility as follows:

Outcome of rolling 3 + $2
(1/6 x $12)

Outcome of rolling 4 + $2
(1/6 x $12)

Cost of playing   – $1

Expected utility   = + $3

The actual utility of playing this game depends on the result of rolling the die. If it comes up a three or a four, the actual utility is + $11; otherwise it is − $1. Now if you are deciding whether to play this game of chance or another, similar game in which you get $6 if you roll an even number and nothing if you roll an odd, one way to rationally decide would be to calculate their expected utilities and select the game with the highest such utility. Since the expected utility of the second game is

    Outcome of rolling 2   + $1
    (1/6 x $6)

    Outcome of rolling 4   + $1
    (1/6 x $6)

    Outcome of rolling 6   + $1
    (1/6 x $6)

    Cost of playing   − $1

    Expected utility   = + $2

you would choose to play the first game with the higher expected utility.

Returning to the principle of utility, and with concerns about its application in mind, we can distinguish two versions of the generic view (GPU) presented earlier, actual consequence utilitarianism (ACU) and probable consequence utilitarianism (PCU):

ACU   An action A is *right* if and only if A has as high an actual utility as any alternative action that the agent could perform instead.

PCU   An action A is *right* if and only if A has as high an expected utility as any alternative action that the agent could perform instead.

Since expected utility is something we can apparently calculate (at least in many cases), PCU, unlike ACU, represents a useful version of the basic utilitarian principle that satisfies the applicability standard. In fact, in addition to the other six items on his list, Bentham's felicific calculus includes consideration of the certainty or uncertainty that some pleasure or pain will result from the action under consideration.

However, the proposal in question can be exploited in two very different ways. First, we might consider replacing ACU with PCU as a moral criterion—as specifying what makes an action right or wrong. But the problem with doing so is that we are led to apparently absurd results. Suppose that some action I might perform has, compared to other alternative actions open to me, the highest expected utility, but that as a matter of fact, were I to perform that action, it would have disastrous consequences—far worse than the actual consequences of any of the other actions. It is peculiar to conclude that this act is, objectively speaking, the right act to perform. Granted, one may not be in a position to foresee such disastrous consequences, but why should limits on human knowledge affect the objective rightness or wrongness of actions? Simply replacing actual consequence utilitarianism with its probabilist cousin seems implausible.

A quite different, and more plausible, way to exploit the distinction between actual and expected utility, and one intended to address the practical objection, is simply to take ACU as a moral criterion and propose PCU as a proper utilitarian decision procedure. Indeed, when you think about it, in most situations, we have no choice but to use PCU in engaging in utilitarian deliberation, since in most cases we cannot determine the actual consequences of actions and must rely on our estimates of the expected consequences of possible courses of action.

To understand more clearly the implications of all this, let us work with an example. Suppose that you are in charge of organizing some charity event this spring. You have to decide between having some outdoor event, involving a picnic, outdoor sporting events, rides for the kids, and so forth, and some sort of indoor event, perhaps a benefit dinner or whatever. Based on what has occurred in the past, you can reliably predict that there is far more utility to be gained, at least potentially, from holding the outdoor charity event. However, the problem is the weather. You happen to live in a part of the country where springtime is a rainy season, and there is an 80 percent chance that it will rain during the weekend in question. If it rains on your picnic, the charity event, in terms of utility production, will be negative (-10). Now let us suppose that the actual utility of having the event outdoors is +2000 (because as a matter of fact it will not rain) and the actual utility of having the event indoors is guaranteed to be +1000. Of course, you don't know that it won't rain, but you are aware of the fact that there is only a 20 percent (=.2) chance of good weather. What should you do? This chart summarizes your options.

	Actual Utility	Expected Utility	
Charity event held outdoors	+2,000	$+2,000 \times .2 = +400$ (shine) $-10 \times .8 = -80$ (rain)	
		$= +320$	
Charity event held indoors	+1,000	$+1,000 \times 1 = +1,000$ (rain or shine)	

Arguably, given your ignorance of what the weather will be like and the disastrous outcome if the outdoor event is rained out, you should play it safe, make use of PCU, and attempt to maximize expected utility. In doing so, it turns out that you in fact fail to maximize utility, but you neverthe-less chose the most reasonable course of action given your limited knowl-edge of the future.

If we distinguish between ACU and PCU and advocate the latter as a decision procedure, then we have the resources for distinguishing between the *objective rightness* (and wrongness) of actions and their *subjective rightness* (and wrongness). On the utilitarian theory, an action's actual consequences determine whether (in the situation) it is objectively right or wrong. If an action's actual consequences are higher than the actual consequences of all alternative actions in the situation, then it is objectively right (objectively obligatory); otherwise it is objectively wrong. If some action has the high-est expected utility, then it is subjectively right (subjectively obligatory); otherwise it is subjectively wrong. Clearly, some subjectively right actions will turn out to be objectively wrong (as in the case just considered), and vice versa. With this distinction in hand, we now are able to mitigate our moral evaluations of individuals by noting that someone who performs an objectively wrong action may not be a proper object of blame given that the action in question was subjectively right.

Although PCU is a principle that human beings can actually use in many contexts of moral deliberation, one might wonder, on utilitarian grounds, whether the principle *ought* to be used in such contexts. Moral deliberation (whether guided by utilitarian principles or not) is, after all, itself an activi-ty whose deontic status depends, for the utilitarian, on the values of its con-sequences. And clearly there are situations in which it would be morally wrong to engage in moral deliberation. If, for instance, I see that a child is about to be run over by a fast-moving car and I am close enough to pull the child to safety, I ought to spring into action and save the child. What I should not do is stop and begin to consider various alternative courses of action I might perform (grab the child, look the other way, yell at the child, run away and hide, etc.) and calculate the utilities of all the alternatives. Clearly, it is a mistake to suppose that the utilitarian theory requires that we use the theory as a decision procedure on every occasion in life.

The Two-Level Approach to Moral Thinking

This raises a question about the value of employing the principle of util-ity in other, nonemergency contexts. Should a utilitarian be in favor of a system of moral education in which individuals would be brought up so that they consciously, whenever possible, guide their behavior by reference to the principle of utility? The answer to this question depends, of course, on whether doing so would maximize utility, and no doubt it is difficult to say one way or the other with any degree of conviction. But it seems plau-sible to suppose that overall utility will not be maximized by training people to directly apply the principle of utility in figuring out what to do. Not only is there no time for such calculation, but the likelihood of miscalculation owing to self-interest seems very high indeed.

Therefore, many utilitarians, Mill included, have thought that when it comes to most situations in life, the moral thinking and choices of most individuals are properly guided by moral rules—rules having to do with lying, theft, killing, and so forth—that we learn in our early years. Such thought is *properly* so guided because as Mill explains, over time humans have "acquired positive beliefs as to the effects of some actions on their happiness; and the beliefs which have thus come down are the rules of morality for the multitude" (Mill [1863] 1979, 23). These rules of commonsense morality are thus by and large good utilitarian guides for individuals to learn and follow in a great many situations in life where employing a first principle of morality like the principle of utility would be wrong (because it does not maximize utility) or otherwise not feasible.

Still, there is a role for the principle of utility in moral thinking. Mill points out that, inevitably, we will confront situations in which the moral rules of common sense come into conflict. Indeed, Mill cautions that we "must remember that only in cases of conflict between [moral rules] is it requisite that first principles should be appealed to" (Mill [1863] 1979, 25). And, of course, his claim about such contexts is that "If utility is the ultimate source of moral obligations, utility may be invoked to decide between [moral rules] when their demands are incompatible" (Mill [1863] 1979, 25). When for example, a rule against lying conflicts with a rule against hurting others (because telling someone the truth about some matter will cause them great mental stress), one is to adjudicate the conflict by appealing to the principle of utility.

Utilitarians who advocate this approach to moral thinking distinguish two levels of moral thought.[12] First-level moral thinking, or what is called the *intuitive level,* proceeds (perhaps unreflectively in some cases) according to moral rules that we learn early on and that help us negotiate our social world. Such rules are taken to be more or less reliable guides to maximizing utility. Second-level moral thinking involves cases like the one just mentioned where ordinary moral rules come into conflict and we must deliberate about what to do. It is here at this second, *critical level* that utilitarians like Mill advocate employing the principle of utility for purposes of moral decision making.

What is crucial to notice about this two-level approach to moral thinking is the role that moral rules play. Here, they are taken to be useful guides to moral thinking in most situations where we are not confronted with moral conflict. However, even in those nonconflict situations, the rightness or wrongness of actions does not depend on whether or not they conform to these rules; (objective) rightness or wrongness depends on the values of the consequences of actions. (When we consider rule utilitarianism in the next chapter, it will be important to bear this point in mind.)

Let us sum up. The main practical challenge to utilitarianism has to do with how the theory is to be used in guiding moral thought and decision. We have made the following observations.

- The utilitarian is going to insist that the principle of utility is being proposed as a moral criterion and not as a decision procedure.

- Further, the utilitarian distinguishes actual consequence utilitarianism from probable consequence utilitarianism and notes that while the former represents a criterion of objective rightness, the latter represents a principle of subjective rightness that can be used by humans with limited foresight.

- Finally, the utilitarian may propose a two-level approach to moral thinking that allows the rules of commonsense morality to provide moral guidance in many situations and reserves use of the principle of utility for circumstances of moral conflict and uncertainty.

6. Conclusion

This chapter has been devoted to a presentation of the elements of the utilitarian approach to moral theorizing, including an exposition of some of the main ideas and arguments of the classical utilitarians, Bentham and Mill. We ended the chapter with an examination of a kind of practical objection to the utilitarian theory and saw how the utilitarian can plausibly defend against this sort of objection. In the next chapter, we consider some of the developments in the utilitarian approach to moral theory; this will involve a discussion of various theoretical objections to the theory.

Further Reading

Brink, David O. 1989. *Moral Realism and the Foundations of Ethics*. Cambridge: Cambridge University Press. See chapter 8 for a defense of utilitarianism that makes use of the distinction between a moral principle functioning as a criterion and as a decision procedure.

Crisp, Roger. 1997. *Mill on Utilitarianism*. London: Routledge. A lucid introduction to Mill's moral philosophy.

Donner, Wendy. 1998. "Mill's Utilitarianism." In *Cambridge Companion to Mill*, ed. John Skorupski. Cambridge: Cambridge University Press. A concise overview of Mill's moral theory, including an illuminating discussion of Mill's qualitative hedonism.

Hare, R. M. 1981. *Moral Thinking*. Oxford: Oxford University Press. Chap. 1 defends the two-level approach to moral thinking mentioned in section 5.

Quinton, Anthony. 1973. *Utilitarian Ethics.* Chicago: Open Court Press. A mainly
historical treatment of the utilitarian tradition with chapters devoted to Bentham and Mill.

Schneewind, J. B., ed. 1968. *Mill: A Collection of Critical Essays.* Garden City, N.Y.:
Anchor Books. Includes some classic essays on Mill's moral philosophy.

Scarre, Geoffrey. 1996. *Utilitarianism.* London: Routledge. Includes a historical
overview of the development of utilitarian doctrine.

Notes

1. In the next chapter, we will introduce a version of utilitarianism, *rule utilitarianism,* that makes the deontic status of actions depend on facts about the consequences associated with rules. For the time being, we will only be considering
versions of utilitarianism that focus on the consequences of actions.

2. Value hedonism, which makes claims about what is intrinsically valuable,
should be distinguished from *psychological hedonism,* which claims that all human
actions are ultimately motivated by concern for pleasure and avoidance of pain.
One can embrace the former yet deny the latter.

3. Strictly speaking, ethical hedonism does not imply value hedonism, because
one might embrace the former (and think that pleasure and pain are the only
things having intrinsic value that *are relevant for ethical evaluation*) and yet deny that
they are the only things having intrinsic value, thus denying the latter.

4. Recall the discussion of commensurability of value from chap. 4, sec. 6.

5. Of course, some actions may only result in episodes of pleasure for some affected individual, while some may only result in episodes of pain.

6. This claim has been disputed by some recent interpreters. For a brief critical overview of such interpretations, see Donner 1998.

7. See Crisp 1997, 26; and Donner 1998.

8. Recall from chap. 1 that the standard of external support for evaluating
moral theories assumes that nonmoral theories and assumptions can be used to
support (and to criticize) moral principles. We have seen this assumption at work
in the divine command theory, moral relativism, and natural law theory.

9. Here, in stating the conclusion in this way, I am following what Mill says.
One might think that what Mill needs as a conclusion is the claim that the general happiness is of intrinsic goodness *for each individual.* One of Mill's critics, Henry
Jones, thought so, but Mill (in a letter quoted by Crisp) denies that his argument
should be reinterpreted that way. See Crisp 1997, 77–78.

10. See Crisp 1997, chap. 4.

11. Not all arguments involving wholes and parts are fallacious. From the fact
that each piece of a jigsaw puzzle is uniformly the same shade of red, it does follow that the puzzle as a whole is uniformly red.

12. See Hare 1981 for a developed version of this two-level approach.

6

Contemporary Utilitarianism

In this chapter, we consider some developments in utilitarian moral thinking that have been largely prompted by certain objections to classical versions of the theory that we examined in the previous chapter. The objections in question—theoretical objections—challenge the idea that utilitarianism represents a correct moral criterion of right action. The next two sections explain these objections, and the remaining sections consider utilitarian responses to them, including, as we shall see, versions of utilitarianism that differ importantly from the views of Bentham and Mill.

1. Theoretical Objections to Utilitarianism

Theoretical objections to utilitarianism (often referred to as moral objections) have to do with the main theoretical aim of a moral theory—the aim of providing a theoretical account of the nature of right and wrong and thereby providing a moral criterion of right action. This section will be concerned with certain stock-in-trade objections to the theory that challenge its theoretical correctness.

A very common method of criticizing utilitarianism involves thinking up cases in which the theory is dramatically at odds with ordinary moral thinking about the issue at hand. Appealing, then, to the standard of internal support for evaluating moral theories, the claim is that since the utilitarian theory conflicts with our considered moral beliefs in a wide range of cases, it fails to be a correct moral criterion.

Here are four cases of the sort often featured in this kind of objection.

Punishment

Suppose a series of horrible unsolved crimes has been committed and the townspeople are up in arms, demanding that the culprit be found and brought to justice; otherwise they will riot. The foreseeable result of a riot would be a great loss in overall utility, given the predictable loss of life, injury, and damage to property. Unfortunately, the police have no suspects. The chief of police is pondering the situation and, as a good utilitarian, is considering alternative courses of action he might take.

One option would be to do what one can to quell the rising fear and anger, and intensify the investigation. But another, more devious option is to frame someone who is innocent of the crimes in question—someone with no family or friends, preferably a social outcast with a long police record. The chief happens to know of just such a person against whom a plausible case could easily be concocted. He is also quite certain that this individual is innocent of the crimes in question. Of course, taking this second alternative would result in severe hardship for the outcast, but when one considers the overall utility of such a course of action compared to the other main alternative, it seems pretty clear to the chief that as a good utilitarian he ought to proceed with the case against the innocent outcast. Let's suppose that the police chief is correct in his assessments of the utilities of his options. Utilitarianism thus implies that the chief has a moral obligation to proceed with framing and punishing the innocent person. But, so the objection goes, it would clearly be morally wrong for him to bring punishment upon someone known to be innocent of the crimes in question. Thus, the utilitarian theory yields an incorrect moral verdict in this case.

Medical Sacrifice

A physician with a strong utilitarian conscience finds herself in the following situation. A perfectly healthy patient has been admitted to the hospital for alcohol abuse. The physician knows about the personal history of this patient. She knows, for example, that the patient has no family, is homeless, and so forth. Except perhaps for the patient's liver, his bodily organs are in excellent shape. Now suppose that under the physician's treatment are three individuals who need an organ donor, each needing a different organ. Moreover, time is quickly running out for these patients. You see how the story goes from here. Our physician does some utilitarian calculation and concludes that since it would be easy and (let us suppose) not at all risky for her to cause the death of the alcohol abuser, she ought to do so, since she would then have at her disposal the needed organs for her three patients. (We are assuming that there is a match in blood types so that the transplants are medically feasible.) Suppose the chances of successful transplant are very high and that proceeding would in fact yield success. From the utilitarian perspective (whether we consider the probable or the actual consequences) our physician ought to kill the one patient to save the other three. But doing so would be murder! Again, the theory leads to obviously incorrect moral conclusions.

Distributive Justice

Distributive justice has to do with how the benefits and burdens of society are spread among its citizens. Now consider two schemes of distribution for a society as they bear on two groups that together compose the society.

Scheme 1		**Scheme 2**	
Group 1	Utility = +500	Group 1	Utility = +1,300
Group 2	Utility = +500	Group 2	Utility = -200
	Total = +1,000		Total = +1,100

Suppose that the numbers for each group represent the total amount of utility that would be produced within the group given the relevant scheme. Assume also that within each group utility is fairly evenly distributed and that at a level of +500, the members of such a group can live comfortably. According to scheme 1, the members of both groups can live comfortably. However, members of groups having a total utility below 0 are below poverty level and must struggle against disease, poor education, poor job opportunities, and other social ills. So, were scheme 2 implemented, the members of group 1 would be well enough off, but not the members of group 2.

Since the utilitarian theory is only concerned with total aggregate utility, it clearly favors the second scheme, ignoring considerations of equal distribution of benefits and burdens across the members of society. In doing so, the theory runs afoul of our sense of fairness. Certainly, considerations of equality are morally important, and scheme 1 is to be morally preferred over scheme 2, contrary to utilitarianism. (Some critics like to employ this same mode of reasoning to show how, at least in principle, utilitarianism could, under the right conditions, morally require that a certain segment of the population be enslaved in order to produce the greatest total aggregate utility in society.)

Promising

It is often pointed out that utilitarianism does not square with our considered moral beliefs about promising. Suppose that Jones, who is terminally ill, has secretly entrusted to me as his financial adviser a large sum of money, which I have promised to give to his young daughter when she turns twenty-one. I am to keep tabs on her until then. In the meantime, the daughter comes into a huge fortune and by the time she is twenty-one has no need of the money her father has entrusted to me. However, my own situation is financially desperate. My wife is suffering from a debilitating disease that has eaten away at our savings and has forced us to sell our house. I am on the brink of financial ruin and realize that the money entrusted to me by Jones would essentially bail me out. So it appears as if the correct thing to do from the utilitarian perspective is to keep the money and thereby break my promise. But can this be right? Wouldn't it be morally wrong to break my promise to Jones?

All of these examples involve actions that, at least as the cases are described, are intuitively morally wrong but morally obligatory according to utilitarianism. However, other counterexamples involving actions that we judge to be morally optional reveal that utilitarianism is too demanding. Let us consider some of them.

2. Further Objections

Utilitarianism is often criticized as being excessively demanding. There are various ways in which this kind of objection can be pressed. One way has to do with the value we naturally attach to our personal projects and plans. Another way has to do with the moral category of the supererogatory. In this section, I want to focus on such complaints, but before doing so, we should begin with a clarification.

Morality is demanding. Moral constraints are often at odds with what we want to do. Any moral theory that adequately captures and makes sense of what we take to be moral obligations will sometimes impose demands on agents that they do not welcome. So the objection to utilitarianism under consideration is not that it is demanding but that it is *over*demanding. Let us take a closer look.

The Overdemandingness Objection

In describing some of the general characteristics of utilitarianism (chapter 5, section 1), we noted that it is both *universalist*, holding that everyone whose welfare will be affected by one's action counts morally, and *impartialist*—everyone's welfare counts equally in determining the deontic status of an action. Here is a passage from Mill in which he comments on this kind of strict impartialism:

> I must repeat, what the assailants of utilitarianism seldom have the justice to acknowledge, that the happiness which forms the utilitarian standard of what is right in conduct, is not the agent's own happiness, but that of all concerned. As between his own happiness and that of others, utilitarianism requires him to be as strictly impartial as a disinterested and benevolent spectator. (Mill [1863] 1979, 16)

This kind of universal impartialism places extreme demands on us. Let us take a simple example. Suppose that I could spend my Sunday afternoon at Wrigley Field watching the Cubs play the Giants—something that, as a baseball fan (and specifically a Cubs fan), I would enjoy doing. I thus have a reason, based on my own "partialist" concerns, to go to the game. But suppose also that I could spend my time on Sunday afternoon doing some volunteer work for the city, which, from an impartial perspective, would be the best course of action to engage in at the time in question. I thus have a reason, based on the sort of impartialist perspective represented in utilitarianism, to do the volunteer work.

So far, we have simply noted the possibility of a clash between two sorts of reasons for action. But add to this two further claims. First, moral requirements are typically taken to be *supremely authoritative* in the sense that they provide individuals with overriding reasons for action. Anytime we have a moral reason to perform some action and a nonmoral reason for not performing that same action, the former trumps the latter. Second, seemingly there are many occasions in life where there is a clash between our partialist concerns (and the reasons for action they generate) and impartialist reasons flowing from the perspective represented by utilitarianism.

Putting all of this together, the implication is that utilitarianism is extremely demanding—so much so that according to its standard of right conduct, we are often doing something morally wrong in pursuing our own personal projects and interests. Thus, many actions that strike us intuitively as morally optional are forbidden according to utilitarianism.

A related objection concerns acts of supererogation.

The Supererogation Objection

We have not had occasion to refer to supererogatory actions until now, but this moral category of action is familiar. We sometimes hear about someone who performed an action that was "above and beyond the call of duty." As this description suggests, such actions, because they are *beyond* the call of duty, are not, strictly speaking, one's duty and so they are not obligatory. Because they are *above* the call of duty, agents who perform such actions deserve moral praise. Since the actions in question are neither obligatory nor forbidden, they are optional actions—but, of course, optional actions of a very special sort. Such actions are called supererogatory (from the Latin *erogare*, meaning "to demand").

One particularly memorable example of supererogation was the young man who, after witnessing a jet crash into the icy waters of the Potomac River, risked his life to pull survivors from the wreckage. This story made newspaper headlines and was featured on television news shows because the man went beyond what morality requires of anyone in that situation.

It cannot be said of every supererogatory action that, from among the agent's options, it has the highest utility. After all, some acts of supererogation are not successful. Suppose the young man had actually drowned while trying to rescue survivors and his efforts proved entirely fruitless—he tried but saved no one and consequently lost his own life. However, it is a good bet that in many cases in which the right opportunities present themselves, the supererogatory action will maximize utility. But if so, then such actions are, according to the utilitarian, morally obligatory and not, according to the definition, supererogatory after all. But any theory that turns many (if not all) of what we ordinarily suppose to be supererogatory actions into obligatory actions, is overly demanding. Call this the *supererogation objection.*

These two objections concerning the demanding nature of utilitarianism prompted J. L. Mackie to complain that this theory represents an "ethics of fantasy": a theory that sets standards of right action that are simply too high for normal human beings, given our deeply ingrained concern for ourselves, friends, and family.[1]

The overdemandingness and the supererogation objections, like the other theoretical objections, have been presented as variations on a central critical theme, namely, the utilitarian theory has implications regarding the deontic status of various actions that are at odds with our considered moral beliefs about those actions. The punishment, medical sacrifice, distributive justice, and promising scenarios all concern actions that are forbidden but are classified as obligatory or optional (depending on how the utilities work out) by utilitarianism. The other two objections focus on the category of the optional, making the same general point about the deontic implications of the theory.

So the objection to utilitarianism as a moral criterion based on such examples is just this. One way of testing the correctness of a moral criterion is to see whether it implies, or is at least consistent with, our considered moral beliefs about a range of cases. This way of testing the correctness of a theory appeals to the standard of internal support for evaluating moral theories, which was explained in section 6 of chapter 1. Now we need not insist that our considered beliefs about such cases are always correct; if a moral theory is otherwise very attractive but conflicts with our considered moral beliefs in a few cases, then we might have good reason to revise our beliefs about the specific cases in question. But in connection with utilitarianism, the theory seems to conflict with a whole range of very deeply held and widely shared moral beliefs. Thus (so this objection goes) the theory fails the standard of internal support and gives us reason to reject it as providing a correct moral criterion.

3. Two Utilitarian Responses

One way of responding to such objections is to challenge some of the claims made in the examples. Either one can deny the moral verdict being offered about the case under consideration, or one can challenge the claims made about the utilities of the various options. Let us consider these responses in order.

Bold Denial

In responding to the objections in question, the utilitarian might just boldly deny the moral verdicts made by the critic. Go back for a moment to the example about promising in which I can either keep my promise and inform the intended beneficiary of her inheritance or break the promise and keep the money for myself. In that example, the critic first of all claims that the action of breaking the promise would have the highest utility in the imagined circumstances but that, contrary to what the utilitarian theory implies, this action would be morally wrong.

But is it so clear that it would be wrong for me to break my promise (under the circumstances) and keep the money? Remember, I need the money desperately, but the intended heir has all the money she will ever need. I suspect that this case will prompt a good deal of disagreement among thoughtful individuals, and so the critic's objection is somewhat blunted because the antiutilitarian moral verdict in the case at hand is questionable. Indeed, a very bold utilitarian might also go on to deny the moral verdicts being passed on the actions featured in the punishment, medical sacrifice, and distributive justice examples. In doing so, she might challenge the validity of appealing, as the critic does, to our moral intuitions about such extraordinary cases and argue that we should not put much weight on such intuitions. However, there is another, not so bold, option for the utilitarian.

Appeal to Remote Effects

Utilitarianism makes the rightness or wrongness of an action depend on the values of all of its consequences, including both immediate and long-term consequences. (Recall from the last chapter that Bentham's felicific calculus includes propinquity and remoteness as one dimension of utilitarian calculation.) A second strategy for answering at least some of the theoretical objections is to challenge the critic's claims about the utilities of the options featured in the examples. The critic more or less stipulates, for example, that in the case of the threatening mob, utility will be maximized by framing and then punishing an innocent person. But how plausible is this stipulation, give the possible long-term consequences of engaging in such behavior? How easy will it be for the police chief to keep his deed a secret? Realistically, won't he need some cooperation from a prosecuting attorney? Won't he have to engage in a whole web of lies and deception, which again, realistically speaking, will be uncovered eventually?

Once we begin to think through this case (and the others) by factoring

in plausible empirical assumptions about possible consequences of punishing innocent persons (and the disutility associated with such consequences), it is no longer clear that the police chief's best option (on utilitarian grounds) is to engage in such obviously immoral behavior. Similar
remarks can be applied to the other cases as well. By questioning assumptions about utilities in this way, the defender of utilitarianism hopes to de-
flect theoretical objections to her theory.

How successful are these two strategies in combating the alleged counterexamples to utilitarianism? Here is a quick (mixed) assessment. On the
one hand, the utilitarian is correct in demanding that potential counterexamples to her theory involve plausible real-world assumptions and that
the moral judgments being rendered in such cases be as uncontroversial as
possible, as well as contrary to the utilitarian theory.

On the other hand, it does seem *in principle possible* that cases of the sort
the critic aims to describe can (and probably do) turn up in the real world.
Granted, in complex social settings like hospitals and law enforcement
agencies, the kinds of immoral actions featured in the examples are unlikely to maximize utility. But transfer such cases to a rural setting, for example, where deception by an individual acting alone is not nearly as likely to
be found out. In such settings, the kinds of long-term effects that are featured in the second of the two strategies are perhaps much less likely to
occur. If the critic can plausibly describe cases like the kind I am suggesting, then the two strategies in question may not be enough to turn back
the sorts of theoretical objections under consideration. I will leave this as
something for readers to think about.

We turn next to a more radical kind of response to these objections, one
involving the development of a different strain of utilitarianism that features
references to rules in its criterion of right action.

4. Rule Utilitarianism

So far in this and the previous chapter, we have been focusing on *act utilitarianism*, according to which the utilities of individual concrete actions
that might be performed in some situation determine the deontic status of
those actions.

In the 1950s and 1960s, an apparently distinct form of utilitarianism, *rule
utilitarianism*, was put forward and defended as superior to its act utilitarian cousin. The alleged superiority of this version of the view has to do with
its ability avoid the kind of theoretical objection we have just examined.
What is rule utilitarianism? How does it avoid the objection?

The basic idea behind the view can be summarized by two claims.

1.   The rightness or wrongness of some individual action depends upon

whether it is mentioned in a correct moral rule that applies to the situation in question.

2. A moral rule applying to a situation is correct if and only if the utility associated with the rule is at least as great as the utility associated with any other alternative rule.

Thus, as a basic formulation of the view, we have:

RU   An action A is *right* if and only if A is mentioned in a moral rule whose associated utility is at least as great as the utility associated with any alternative moral rule applying to the situation.

Mention of utilities *associated* with a rule is deliberately vague because there are varieties of the generic theory that differ primarily over how they define the utility associated with a rule. For our purposes, it will be enough if we consider one prominent version of RU.

First, we need to define the sort of utility associated with rules. What we may call the *acceptance utility* of a rule is defined as the utility that would result were individuals generally to accept the rule in question. To say that individuals generally accept a rule is to say that by and large most people conform their behavior to the rule in question as a result of internalizing it.

To explain further, let us work with a very simple example. Suppose that I have promised to help you clean out your garage on Saturday. Saturday comes and among my options are these:

A1   Keep my promise

A2   Break my promise

Now for each alternative action, we can formulate a rule that mentions the action in question (and thus a rule that applies to the situation). Thus,

R1   Whenever one has made a promise, one is to keep the promise.

R2   Whenever one has made a made a promise, one may break the promise.

We now consider the acceptance utilities for each of these rules. That is, we consider the utility that would result were individuals in society to accept R1 and compare it to the utility that would result were individuals to accept R2. Pretty clearly, R1 has associated with it a higher utility than is associated with R2, thus (restricting our alternatives to just these two rules) R1 is the correct moral rule in this situation. Finally, the rule utilitarian theory tells us that the action of keeping my promise is obligatory in this particular situation, since it is mentioned in the rule with the highest acceptance utility.

Now suppose that in the situation just sketched, if I break my promise and shoot pool with some friends at the local pub, I would thereby bring about a greater amount of utility than if I were I to keep my promise. Act utilitarianism implies that the objectively right act is to shoot pool and thereby break the promise. But intuitively, this seems incorrect. Rule utilitarianism, by contrast, has us calculate, not the utilities of individual actions, but rather the utilities of whole patterns of action, and so in this case yields a correct moral verdict.

Return now the examples in the previous section. The rule utilitarian theory gives us morally correct results when applied to those cases. Individual actions of punishing an innocent person, committing murder to benefit others, unequally distributing benefits and burdens in society, and breaking promises, though they may, in rare instances, maximize utility, nevertheless are morally wrong according to RU.

Moreover, RU helps make sense, from a utilitarian perspective, of the very common idea that breaking promises is wrong because of the kind of act it is—an act of promising that violates a moral rule against such actions. And the same goes for other actions like murder and lying. Of course, the rule utilitarian offers an account of why such actions are wrong in terms of utility, but the view allows moral weight to attach to moral rules in terms of which we often justify our actions.

A couple of clarifying remarks are in order before we proceed further. In the first place, although R1 would have a higher acceptance utility than R2, we can expect that a more complex rule than either of these two will, in contexts like the one in question, yield the highest utility. After all, in situations where I can save an innocent life by breaking a promise, the rule

R3 Whenever one has made a promise, one will keep the promise unless by breaking it one can save innocent lives

would no doubt have a higher utility than R1. After all, in cases where there are no innocent lives to be saved, R3 would agree with R1 in implying that one ought to keep one's promise. But in those rare cases in which one can save lives by breaking a promise, acceptance of R3 would no doubt produce a greater amount of utility than would acceptance of R1. Thus, overall, R3 would have a higher acceptance utility than R1.

It is clear that there are other circumstances in which breaking one's promise and performing some competing action would (in general) produce more utility than acceptance of a rule like R3 with only one exception built into it. Thus, some rule more complex than R3 would have the highest acceptance utility for situations of the relevant sort.

But now one might suspect that the following rule will produce the highest acceptance utility for situations involving promises:

> R4 Whenever one has made a promise, one will keep it unless there
> is some alternative action open to the agent that, in the situation,
> would produce a greater amount of utility.

But R4 in effect prescribes that in such situations we perform the action
that would maximize utility. And, of course, for every situation, there will
be, from among the set of alternative rules, a rule like R4. But then one is
led to the conclusion that rule utilitarianism is extensionally equivalent to
act utilitarianism; that is, it will necessarily agree with act utilitarianism
about the deontic status of actions. And this result means that rule utilitarianism cannot, after all, avoid the kinds of theoretical objections described
in the previous section!

Now some versions of rule utilitarianism are indeed extensionally
equivalent to act utilitarianism, but the version under consideration is not
one of those.[2] You may recall from section 5 of the previous chapter that
it is very unlikely, given how human beings are, that a rule requiring individuals to maximize utility would, if consciously followed, actually yield
as much utility as would simpler rules that are easier to follow and less
likely to encourage self-interested biases from inappropriately affecting
one's moral decisions. In other words, rules like R4 have arguably less acceptance utility than other, more easily applied rules, and so the version
of rule utilitarianism under consideration does not reduce to act utilitarianism.

So assuming that RU represents a moral theory that is truly distinct from
act utilitarianism, how plausible is it?

One sort of objection often raised against this particular version of RU
is that it faces theoretical objections of its own because it leads to counterintuitive results with regard to nonmaximizing practices of one's own
society. Suppose, for instance, that there is some other marriage institution
with a set of rules differing from the institution (and associated rules) that
governs our current marriage practices, and that the rules governing this
alternative marriage institution have a higher acceptance utility than the
moral rules governing our current marriage practices. (Perhaps polyga-
mous marriage practices would yield more utility than do monogamous
ones.) It seems incorrect to conclude that individuals who abide by the
rules of the current institution of marriage are engaging in morally wrong
behavior. In general, the fact that there may be some set of utility-
maximizing rules governing a practice that a society might adopt in place
of the current rules does not mean that those conforming to the current,
nonmaximizing rules are doing anything morally wrong. Perhaps there is a
way around this problem for the rule utilitarian, but I shall not pursue this
matter further.

In any case, although rule utilitarianism made a splash in the 1950s and 1960s, many moral philosophers have since concluded that it is, as Brad Hooker puts it, "tried and *un*true."[3]

5. Nonhedonistic Versions of Utilitarianism

According to utilitarianism, right acts maximize the good, and the good to be maximized is the welfare of individuals. As we saw in the last chapter, classical utilitarianism understands welfare in terms of happiness and understands happiness hedonistically. A happy life is one filled with experiences of pleasure and lacking (so far as possible) experiences of pain. But even granting that pleasure and pain are among the items that have intrinsic value and disvalue respectively, and granting also that they are at least part of what makes a person's life go well, are they the only items that have this status? Many moral philosophers reject hedonism as an account of welfare. One reason for the rejection is nicely illustrated by a thought experiment devised by Robert Nozick:

> Suppose there were an experience machine that would give you any experience you desired. Superduper neuroscientists could stimulate your brain so that you would think and feel you were writing a great novel, or making a friend, or reading an interesting book. All the time you would be floating in a tank, with electrodes attached to your brain. Should you plug into this machine for life, preprogramming your life's experiences? (Nozick 1974, 42)

If the only items of positive intrinsic value are mental states of pleasure, why not plug in?

But, of course, most people (and maybe all people whose lives are not utterly miserable) will not plug in. Presumably this reveals that there are items other than experiences of pleasure that we take to have intrinsic value and that are an important part of what makes an individual's life go well for her. Nozick points out that there are things we want to *do*, and not just think we are doing. We also want to *be* persons of a certain sort, and not just think we are. A fantasy life in which I merely think I have written a great novel or have many friends is clearly inferior in value to a life in which such things really occur. But if all that matters is how everything seems from the inside, then there is no difference in value between my thinking I have done something and my truly having done it. In short, hedonism does not do justice to our considered moral beliefs about what it is in life that makes up a person's welfare. Pleasure may be one item that has intrinsic value and contributes positively to one's welfare, but it does not seem to be the only kind of thing that does.

As explained in the last chapter, the generic principle of utilitarianism

GPU An action is *right* if and only if A has as high a utility as any alternative action that the agent could perform instead

does not itself specify a theory of utility or value and so it does not commit one to hedonism. Because value hedonism seems implausible, contemporary versions of utilitarianism typically embrace some nonhedonistic theory of welfare.

One prominent nonhedonist account of welfare to be developed and defended in the last half of the twentieth century is the *desire fulfillment theory of welfare.* Its basic idea is that what makes a person's life go better is the fulfillment of her desires, and what makes it go worse is the nonfulfillment of her desires. If we plug this theory of welfare into the generic utilitarian scheme, we have *desire fulfillment utilitarianism.* Utilitarianism, of course, is concerned with the general welfare, and hence desire fulfillment, of all those affected by one's action. So we can formulate this version of the theory as follows:

DFU An action A is *right* if and only if A would result in at least as much general desire fulfillment as any alternative action that the agent could perform instead.

One attractive feature of this theory is that it avoids the main objection to hedonism. Many of our desires are for things and activities other than pleasurable experiences. I desire to travel to Italy, and this desire will only be satisfied if I really travel there, not just think I'm doing so. Thus, my actually traveling has intrinsic value for me and contributes directly to my welfare because (according to the desire fulfillment view) such activity is the object of one of my desires. So on this theory of welfare, how things really are—what I am really doing and how I really am—is important for one's welfare; I am not doing well if I am merely hooked up to Nozick's experience machine.

However, the desire fulfillment theory of welfare has its share of problems. I will mention but two of them. First, some restrictions must be placed on those desires whose fulfillment plausibly contributes to one's welfare. After all, I might desire that the music of the Beatles still be popular in the twenty-second century, long after I am gone. It is hard to see how the fulfillment (or nonfulfillment) of this desire could contribute in any way to my well-being. Presumably, the theory needs to make welfare depend only on those desires whose fulfillment (or nonfulfillment) will affect one's own life. We need not pursue this matter further.[4]

A second, more serious problem for the theory is that desire fulfillment *as such* does not seem to contribute to one's welfare. Suppose that someone's guiding desire in life is to count blades of grass.[5] The pleasure this person derives from counting contributes to his welfare, but it is hard to see how the mere fact that his desire is being fulfilled contributes to his welfare. It would seem that it is only when the "right" desires are fulfilled that our welfare is enhanced. But what are the right desires? Aren't they for things and activities that have value for us independently of our desiring them? If so, then the desire theory cannot be a correct account of the nature of welfare.

These reflections on the desire fulfillment theory suggest an account of welfare—a pluralist account—that promises to be an adequate account of welfare as well as help the utilitarian answer the theoretical objections to her theory. Let us consider this version.

6. Pluralistic Utilitarianism

If the strategies of bold denial and appeal to remote effects for answering the various theoretical objections to utilitarianism are not wholly convincing, there is a strategy that may work. It involves appealing to a pluralist theory of intrinsic value of a special sort—what I will call *morally constrained value pluralism*—in attempting to show how the utilitarian theory can be made to fit with our considered moral beliefs about punishment, sacrifice, promising, distributive justice, and the importance of our own personal projects. The strategy, then, is to develop and defend this sort of pluralistic theory of intrinsic value (as an account of welfare) and then show how a utilitarian theory that makes use of this particular theory of value fits with our considered moral beliefs about the sorts of cases discussed above.

In what follows, I will briefly explain the pluralist theory of value in question and how it works to the advantage of the utilitarian. Then I want to suggest (if not fully argue) that embracing this strain of utilitarianism will be at the cost of determinacy in the resulting theory and will, in effect, make the theory a form of what I have called limited moral pluralism.

The version of utilitarianism under consideration is developed and defended by David Brink (1989). According to Brink's pluralist account of welfare, there are three main components of human welfare that are intrinsically good: (1) reflective pursuit of one's reasonable projects, (2) realization of those projects, and (3) certain personal and social relationships, including family relations, friendships, and other social connections.[6] But it is crucial to Brink's theory of welfare that for the pursuit (and realization) of a personal project to be truly valuable, and for personal and social relationships to be truly valuable, they must *respect persons*. Since the notion of respect for persons is a moral one, it is *morally constrained* pursuit (and realization) of personal projects and personal and social relationships that have intrinsic value in the first place. Here is how Brink puts the point (he calls his theory "objective utilitarianism," "OU" for short):

> [T]here are moral constraints on valuable projects; in order for the pursuit and realization of a project to be of value, that project must, among other things, respect other people at least in the minimal sense of not causing significant and avoidable harm. Moreover, personal and social relationships involving mutual concern and respect form an important part of human good, according to OU's theory of value. (Brink 1989, 264)

If value attached to the pursuit of any personal project, no matter what, then a racist's project of genocide would have to count as having positive value. And if there are enough such racists and few enough members of the group targeted by the racists, it might turn out that maximizing utility would justify racist activity. Obviously, this result is blocked on Brink's version of utilitarianism. Since racist projects fail to respect persons, those projects do not have value in the first place.

As an example of how this version of utilitarianism can avoid the various sorts of moral objections we have examined, let us consider Brink's response to the distributive justice objection. According to that objection, utilitarianism can in principle require patently unjust, and hence immoral, allocation of benefits and imposition of burdens whenever the greatest aggregate utility would thereby be produced. For instance, the theory would justify gross inequalities in such basic goods as health, nutrition, and shelter in the interests of maximizing overall welfare. In short, utilitarianism is insensitive to matters of distribution.

In response to this objection, Brink argues that according to his version of utilitarianism,

> inequalities in basic goods cannot be justified as maximizing the total amount of welfare. It will always be better (i.e., more valuable) to give basic goods to one more person than to increase someone else's supply of nonbasic goods. Moreover, OU's insistence on respect for persons constrains accepting inequalities in nonbasic goods. In order for pursuit or realization of one's personal projects to be valuable, they must respect the interests of others, and the development and maintenance of personal and social relationships involving mutual concern and commitment are intrinsically valuable. For distributions of goods and services to respect persons, they must express fair terms of social cooperation. . . . OU's theory of value is thus itself distribution-sensitive. (Brink 1989, 272)

In general, then, by embracing a morally constrained account of intrinsic value, Brink is able to argue plausibly that his version of utilitarianism fits nicely with our considered moral beliefs about punishment, promising, distributive justice, and the importance of personal projects and thereby nicely satisfies the standard of internal support for evaluating a moral theory.

Now the observation I wish to make about this pluralist version of utilitarianism is that it seems to lack the kind of determinacy possessed by more classical versions of the theory. Let me explain.

The classical version of utilitarianism, involving value hedonism, makes the deontic status of an action depend on how much overall utility would be produced by the action (compared to how much would be produced by alternative actions). Utility is a matter of the net balance of episodes of pleasure over episodes of pain. Thus, the classical principle of utility enjoys a high degree of determinacy since (in a wide range of cases) there is going to be a determinate fact of the matter about the utilities of actions, and the principle of utility specifies how such utilities determine the deontic status of actions.

Although I cannot fully argue the case here, I believe that Brink's version of utilitarianism will lack the kind of determinacy characteristic of the classical version. The reason for this is that in order for the pursuit of personal projects, their realization, and the realization of personal and social relationships to have positive value at all, they must respect persons. Sometimes, for instance, when the choice is between pursuing one's own projects and maintaining or promoting certain social relationships, the pursuit of personal projects would fail to respect persons. Suppose a young woman, interested in pursuing her artistic ambitions, strongly desires to move from the United States to Paris to study art. However, suppose she has a sick family member whose care falls to her, thus requiring that she stay in the United States indefinitely. Arguably, in this context, consideration of respect for persons favors the promotion of the good of a family relationship. In other cases, it may be the other way around. But I doubt there are any principles or methods that fix or determine what counts as respecting persons in all contexts. And if not, then moral principles that make substantial use of this notion will lack a measure of determinacy both as decision procedures and as criteria for right action. In making this claim I am anticipating what I will be arguing in the next chapter in relation to Kant's moral theory—a moral theory that makes the idea of respect for persons central in its account of right conduct.

There is a further point to be made here. If my speculation about Brink's theory is correct, then the main injunction of the utilitarian theory to maximize utility really amounts to the injunction to produce as much good as one can that is compatible with respect for persons (including oneself). But if so, then the differences between the utilitarian theory and the theories of Immanuel Kant and W. D. Ross, which are supposed to be striking, seem to evaporate.

In chapter 4, I argued that the natural law theory, once it is purged of implausible elements, lacks determinacy as a moral theory and is plausibly interpreted as a version of what I called limited moral pluralism. I am making the same point about plausible versions of utilitarianism, a point that I will go on to make about Kant's moral theory. W. D. Ross's version of moral pluralism and virtue ethics, which we take up in chapters 8 and 9 respectively, are clear versions of limited moral pluralism—limited in their determinacy. Thus, one of the main themes to emerge from this book is that plausible versions of many of the theories we examine are indeterminate in what the principles of the theory imply about the deontic status of a wide range of actions. This fact about those theories is not so much a defect to be somehow overcome as an acknowledgment of the limit on the degree of determinacy we can expect from any plausible moral theory, given the complexity of moral phenomena.

7. Evaluation of Utilitarianism

An overall evaluation of utilitarianism is difficult because there are many versions of the theory that vary in their plausibility, and because utilitarians under fire have met the various challenges with responses that have some degree of plausibility (so I think). However, a few general observations can be made in coming to a tentative evaluation of the theory.

Utilitarianism captures three intuitively plausible ideas about morality. First, its commitment to welfarism accommodates our sense that morality has to do with human well-being. Second, it is based on a very plausible view of practical rationality. When it comes to rationality in the realm of choice and action, the idea that we ought to bring about as much good as possible seems irresistible. And finally, utilitarianism captures the idea that impartiality is at the heart of morality. Thus, according to the standard of intuitive appeal, utilitarianism has a lot going for it.

In the last chapter, we saw how the utilitarian can deal with the main practical objection to the theory by denying that it represents a decision procedure. We also saw how utilitarians can, like Mill, adopt a two-level approach to moral thinking and decision making.

However, the theoretical objections that challenge the claim that utilitarianism represents a correct moral criterion are not so easily dealt with. In this chapter, we have explored four strategies that utilitarians have offered in response: (1) the strategy of bold denial, (2) the strategy of appealing to remote effects, (3) the move to rule utilitarianism, and (4) the strategy of appealing to a morally constrained pluralist theory of welfare. I have suggested that the fourth strategy seems to work best in helping the utilitarian square her theory with our considered moral beliefs and thus overcome the various theoretical objections. However, this strategy comes at a cost. While classical versions of the theory offer a simple and highly determinate theory of morality, pluralist versions (in order to deal with the theoretical objections) lack simplicity and determinacy. Moreover, a pluralist version like Brink's seems hardly identifiable as an alternative to other competing theories (as we shall see in the coming chapters).

8. Conclusion

In closing I want to consider briefly a claim often made against utilitarianism that is supposed to reveal what is really wrong with it. Utilitarianism, so the complaint goes, fails to respect the separateness of persons. Presumably, this fact about the theory underlies its problems with punishment, distributive justice, overdemandingness, and other such cases. Let me explain.

We normally take ourselves to be, in some deep sense, distinct from one another. We have separate identities and think of ourselves as separate centers of care and concern. Moreover, we think that this fact about ourselves ought to be respected by a sensible moral theory. Now the way in which utilitarianism supposedly fails to respect the separateness of persons is often explained by noting that the theory can be viewed as taking a perfectly plausible method of prudential choice and decision making and extending it to moral choice and decision making. Prudential rationality seems to require that we maximize our own welfare over time by discounting, as it were, temporal considerations. In maximizing one's own welfare, that is, it is rational to make intrapersonal trade-offs in which one forgoes indulging in an immediate pleasure in order to enjoy something more worthwhile at a later time. In short, in cases of intrapersonal rational choice, if we look at our temporally extended lives as a series of stages of a single individual, it makes perfect sense that my welfare at one stage be sacrificed for my greater welfare at some other stage.

Now the idea is that utilitarianism takes this conception of rational intrapersonal choice and extends it to social choice by treating different individuals as though they were parts of one great big person. Just as prudence is indifferent with respect to different times at which one experiences welfare, so the utilitarian theory, in its approach to social choice, is indifferent toward individuals, allowing the welfare of some individuals to be sacrificed for the good of the whole. Thus, so the complaint goes, utilitarianism does not respect the separateness of persons.[7]

Moreover, its failure to do so explains why it has counterintuitive implications about the sorts of cases considered previously. For instance, the utilitarian theory is susceptible to the objection based on distributive justice because it allows (and even sometimes requires) that for the greater overall good we impose unequal burdens on some individuals that intuitively seem grossly immoral. It allows for such treatment because it does not respect the separateness of persons. And because it does not properly respect persons, it ultimately fails to *explain why* right actions are right and wrong ones wrong: it thus fails to satisfy the standard of explanatory power.

One way around this objection is to follow Brink and build into the utilitarian theory considerations of respect for persons. Whether doing so results in a moral theory that is a version of utilitarianism and represents a fully adequate moral criterion, I will not try to determine here.

There is little doubt, however, that the idea that morality, and moral requirements in particular, must reflect respect for persons is a very intuitively appealing belief about morality that most of us share. It is at the very center of the moral theory that we consider in the next chapter, the theory of Immanuel Kant.

Further Reading

Bayles, Michael D., ed. 1968. *Contemporary Utilitarianism*. Garden City, N.Y.: Anchor Books. A collection of important essays by various authors debating utilitarianism.

Brandt, Richard B. 1979. *A Theory of the Good and the Right*. Oxford: Oxford University Press. Includes a systematic defense of a version of rule utilitarianism.

Brink, David O. 1989. *Moral Realism and the Foundations of Ethics*. Cambridge: Cambridge University Press. See chapter 8 for a defense of a version of utilitarianism that employs a pluralist theory of value.

Brock, Dan. 1973. "Recent Work on Utilitarianism." *American Philosophical Quarterly* 10: 241–76. A somewhat dated but still useful overview of developments in contemporary utilitarian theory.

Hooker, Brad. 2000. *Ideal Code, Real World*. Oxford: Oxford University Press. A defense of a version of rule consequentialism.

Hooker, Brad, Elinor Mason, and Dale E. Miller, eds. 2000. *Morality, Rules, and Consequences: A Critical Reader*. Lanham, Md.: Rowman & Littlefield. A collection of articles by scholars debating rule utilitarianism and related issues in moral theory.

Lyons, David. 1965. *Forms and Limits of Utilitarianism*. Oxford: Oxford University Press. Critical discussion of utilitarian generalization (see Singer 1961 below) and versions of rule utilitarianism.

Miller, Harlan B., and William H. Williams, eds. 1982. *The Limits of Utilitarianism*. Minneapolis: University of Minnesota Press. Wide-ranging anthology of articles on utilitarianism.

Scheffler, Samuel. 1982. *The Rejection of Consequentialism*. Oxford: Oxford University Press. Chapter 1 includes a penetrating discussion of the overdemandingness and distributive justice objections to utilitarianism.

———, ed. 1988. *Consequentialism and Its Critics*. Oxford: Oxford University Press. A collection of essays by various authors critical of consequentialism generally and utilitarianism in particular.

Sidgwick, Henry. [1907] 1966. *The Methods of Ethics*. 7th ed. New York: Dover. Book 4 of this masterpiece defends a version of utilitarianism.

Singer, Marcus G. 1961. *Generalization in Ethics*. New York: Alfred Knopf. A defense of a kind of utilitarian moral theory akin to rule utilitarianism called "utilitarian generalization."

Smart, J. J. C., and Bernard Williams. 1973. *Utilitarianism: For and Against.* Oxford: Oxford University Press. An important, relatively short book with Smart defending a version of act utilitarianism and Williams objecting.

Sumner, L. W. 1996. *Welfare, Happiness, and Ethics.* Oxford: Oxford University Press. An illuminating discussion of competing theories of welfare plus a defense of welfarism.

Notes

1. See Mackie 1977, 129–34. Notice that Mackie's complaint based on the overly demanding nature of utilitarianism contrasts sharply with the doctrine of swine complaint that we considered in chap. 5.

2. If we define utility in terms of the results of everyone actually conforming their behavior to a rule—call this *conformance utility*—then RU turns out to be extensionally equivalent to act utilitarianism. After all, for any situation, if we consider the values of the consequences were everyone actually to conform to some rule (regardless of whether or not such rules are understood or accepted), the result will be that rules like R4 will always have the highest (conformance) utility. Hence we get extensional equivalence between rule and act utilitarianism.

3. However, see Hooker 2000 for a recent defense of rule consequentialism, a near cousin of rule utilitarianism.

4. See Sumner 1996, chap. 5 for further discussion.

5. This example is from Rawls 1971, 432.

6. In addition to these basic items of intrinsic value, Brink also recognizes goods that are necessary conditions for the basic intrinsic goods and goods that are of extrinsic value. See Brink 1989, 231–36.

7. Rawls (1971, 22–27) develops this line of criticism.

7

Kant's Moral Theory

Immanuel Kant (1724–1804) made important contributions to all of the major fields of philosophy and ranks as one of history's most influential philosophers. He wrote three important books in moral philosophy: *Groundwork of the Metaphysics of Morals* (1785), *Critique of Practical Reason* (1788), and *The Metaphysics of Morals* (1797). His work in philosophy generally and in ethics in particular is marked by its originality, subtlety, and difficulty. This chapter will provide an overview of some of the main ideas in Kant's theories of right conduct and value.

A leading idea of Kant's moral theory is that moral requirements are requirements of reason. To act immorally is thus to act in a way that is not rational. In Kant's terminology, moral requirements can be expressed as "categorical imperatives"—imperatives grounded in reason and which can be derived from a supreme moral principle—the Categorical Imperative.[1] The place to begin in coming to understand Kant's moral theory is with his conception of duty.

1. Kant on the Idea of Duty

Kant's moral theory attempts to make sense of what Kant takes to be the ordinary, commonsense idea of duty. He expresses this idea in the following passage from the preface of the *Groundwork:*

> Everyone must grant that a law, if it is to hold morally, that is, as a ground of an obligation, must carry with it absolute necessity; that, for example, the command "thou shalt not lie" does not hold only for human beings, as if other rational beings did not have to heed it, and so with all other moral laws properly so called; that, therefore, the ground of obligation here must not be sought in the nature of the human being . . . [but] simply in the concepts of pure reason. (G, 3/389)[2]

A main point that Kant is making here concerns the *scope* of moral obligation: such obligations, like the duty not to lie, hold not just for human beings but for all rational agents. Although at this time in our history, we are
only acquainted with human rational agents, there may be nonhuman
species of intelligent life whose members are rational agents, and Kant is
claiming that those rational nonhumans (assuming there are some) are subject to moral requirements just as we are. Why does Kant say this?

The answer is that he thinks that moral requirements are requirements
of reason, specifically *practical reason*. Practical reason has to do with one's
capacity to deliberate and make free choices. Principles of practical reason
set forth requirements for deliberating and choosing rationally, and Kant
holds that some of these principles are moral principles specifying moral requirements. If Kant is right about this, then moral requirements, as requirements of reason, would have to be valid for every rational agent, regardless of whether such agents are *Homo sapiens.*

A comparison may help make the point. What is called *theoretical reason*
concerns that use of reason involved in coming to rational beliefs about
how things really are.[3] The use of theoretical reason is involved in, for example, scientific and mathematical reasoning where there are principles expressing requirements that govern rational thinking in these areas. Consider the following principle governing rational inferences about some object
of study (called a population) based on a sample:

> If x percent of a sample taken from some population has a certain
> characteristic, then one may infer (assuming the sample is representa-
> tive of the population) that approximately x percent of the entire
> population has the characteristic in question.

Now this principle may need some refinement, but the point is that it does
not hold just for human beings; rather, it represents a universally valid standard for rationally drawing conclusions about a population on the basis of
a sample and thus holds for all rational beings. Kant's idea about moral principles is the same: they purport to express rational requirements on choice
and action that apply to all rational agents.

Notice that Kant's idea that moral obligations represent requirements of
reason concerning choice and action contrasts with how other moral theories we have examined understand such requirements. Mill's utilitarian
moral theory attempts to base the principle of utility (and hence moral
obligation) on facts about what human beings desire. The natural law theory attempts to base moral obligation on facts about natural human ten-
dencies—the promotion of individual life, the continuation of the species,
knowledge, and social relations. In the passage quoted above, Kant claims
that the basis, or ground, of obligation cannot be discovered by appealing
to facts that pertain specifically to human beings since in attempting to do

so, one misses the idea that moral requirements hold for all rational agents, human and nonhuman.

Let us explore in more detail Kant's views about the demands of practical reason.

2. Kant and the Demands of Practical Reason

According to Kant, moral requirements represent demands on rational agents that are, in a sense to be explained below, "unconditional." The unconditional demands are properly expressed by what Kant calls *categorical imperatives.* Furthermore, he claims that underlying all particular moral requirements is a supreme principle of morality that he calls *the Categorical Imperative.*

In order to appreciate and explain these points, it will help to begin with a discussion of some of the kinds of rational requirements on choice and action that are *nonmoral* in character, requirements that Kant expresses by what he calls *hypothetical imperatives.*

Let us begin by noting that we sometimes evaluate the choices and actions of individuals as being either rational or irrational (even though we may not use these terms in expressing our evaluation). For example, suppose that I very much want to earn a degree in mathematics at a particular university, so I make earning it one of my ends. Now suppose further that taking a particular calculus course, say Calculus 500, is a requirement for earning a mathematics degree at the university in question and that I am aware of this requirement. Then it seems clear that I ought to take the calculus course in question. If I refused to do so yet persisted in my goal of earning the degree in math, I would be acting irrationally. Here we have a case of what philosophers call means–end rationality: given some end or goal that one intends to achieve, one ought to perform those actions that are necessary (perform the necessary means) for achieving that end, or else give up the end. In the particular case under discussion we can express the main idea in terms of this principle:

H If you intend to earn a mathematics degree and taking Calculus 500 is necessary for earning the degree, then you ought to take Calculus 500 (or give up the goal of earning a mathematics degree).

It should be clear that for any goal or end someone might attempt to achieve, relative to which there are actions that must be performed to realize the goal, there will be principles like H that tell the agent to either perform the necessary actions or give up the goal. Since failing to conform to such a principle would be manifestly irrational, it should be clear that H and principles like it are principles of rationality pertaining to choice and action—that is, they represent principles of practical rationality.

It is particularly important to grasp here that principles like H specify what it is rational to do *given certain goals that one has.* People vary widely in the goals they have. Thus, whether or not a specific principle like H applies to an individual depends on whether she has the particular goal featured in the principle. If you don't intend to earn a mathematics degree, then it is not true of you that you ought to take Calculus 500 or give up your end (unless, of course, the achievement of another of your goals requires taking this course).

We can express the idea that principles like H only apply to, and have binding force for, persons relative to their goals by saying that such principles are *conditionally valid* for agents: a principle of the sort in question imposes rational constraints on one's behavior only on the condition that one has the goal or end specified in the principle. As we shall see, Kant thinks that principles of practical rationality expressing moral requirements are *unconditionally valid.*

Kant calls practical principles like H *hypothetical imperatives.* Calling them hypothetical is another way of indicating that for Kant they are conditionally valid—they apply to, and have binding force on, an agent only on the condition (hypothesis) that the agent has the end in question. He calls them imperatives because although H and other such principles are expressed in terms of what an agent *ought* to do, given certain ends she has, we can also express such requirements in a way that more clearly brings out their action-guiding force by replacing talk of what an agent ought to do with an imperative directing her to do it. Thus, according to Kant, H can alternatively be expressed this way:

H★ If you intend to earn a mathematics degree and taking Calculus 500 is necessary for earning the degree, then take Calculus 500 (or give up the goal of earning a mathematics degree).

Given the pattern exemplified by H and H★, it should be clear that underlying all specific hypothetical imperatives is the following formal principle:

HI If one intends E and recognizes that doing A is necessary for bringing about E, then do A (or give up E).

Clearly H and other principles of the same form are instances of HI, and so if HI is a correct principle of practical rationality, so are all of its specific instances.[4]

One might ask how it is that we come to recognize principles like H to be principles of practical rationality. One way to approach this question is to think about the very concept of rational choice and action and imagine an ideally rational agent—an agent who necessarily reasons and acts in a perfectly rational manner—and then ask what principles would in fact govern the behavior of such an ideal agent. Upon reflection, it seems intuitively clear that a fully rational agent who sets for herself a certain end E and who recognizes that doing action A is necessary for her bringing about E would (insofar as she is fully rational in her deliberation and choice) do A.[5]

Of course, we are not fully rational agents. For one thing, even in cases where we know what reason requires of us when it comes to choice and action, we can fail to take the rational course of action. Sometimes, for instance, we act irrationally under the influence of some desire. So, for human beings who are not by nature always and unfailingly rational, principles that *describe* how in fact a completely rational agent would behave are presented to humans as principles that *prescribe* how we ought to behave (if we are to be rational in our choices and actions).

3. Morality Is Not a System of Hypothetical Imperatives

Because requirements flowing from hypothetical imperatives are only *conditionally binding* on an agent, they cannot express genuine moral requirements since, according to Kant, the very idea of a *moral* requirement or duty involves there being some action (or omission) that one must do (or omit) regardless of what one might happen to desire.

In making this claim about the concept of duty, Kant takes himself to be saying something true about our ordinary, commonsense idea of duty. Is Kant right about this? Consider a couple of cases. Suppose first that you come into my office for advice about what courses to take next semester and I say to you that you really ought to take Logic 101. When you ask me why, I point out that this course is a requirement for getting a degree in philosophy, to which you respond that you have no intention of earning a philosophy degree. Upon hearing this, I would naturally retract my claim about your having to take logic; it does not truly apply to you.

But now think for a moment about your reaction to someone who, in response to a claim that she has a duty of gratitude to care for her sick relative, responds by saying, "You know, caring for my sick relative just does not serve any of the personal goals I happen to have." I think a common (and proper) reaction would be to say that this kind of response is irrelevant: whether or not someone morally ought to do something does not depend on how the required action fits with the goals and ends the person happens to desire. So in striking contrast to the previous case, we would not retract the claim about what one morally ought to do just because of what that person happens to desire. The kind of requirement expressed by a moral duty is, in Kant's terminology, unconditionally valid, and part of what this means is that its validity is not dependent on one's desires.

To summarize this discussion: Our desires for various ends are the basis for conditionally valid requirements on choice and action that can be expressed as hypothetical imperatives. But for Kant, such imperatives, because they are only conditionally valid, cannot express genuine moral requirements. Morality is not a system of hypothetical imperatives governing the rational pursuit of our chosen ends.

A related point concerns the pursuit of our own happiness. Kant claims that as human beings we necessarily have our own happiness as an end. (See G, 26/415.) But happiness, on Kant's view, results from the fulfillment of certain ends or goals, which, again, we form on the basis of our desires.[6] As we have just explained, the ends or goals we adopt on the basis of desire cannot be the ground of moral requirements. Furthermore, it is obvious that moral requirements often conflict with what would contribute to our personal happiness. So, even though all human beings necessarily have their own happiness as an end, this fact about us cannot be the basis for moral requirements: morality is not a doctrine of personal happiness.

These conclusions about the basis of moral requirements are negative. We need a positive account of their basis, to which we now turn.

4. The Supreme Principle of Morality: The Categorical Imperative

If moral requirements are unconditionally valid for all rational agents, then there must be requirements that are, in Kant's terminology, categorical. But how can there be such categorical imperatives? What could be the basis for such requirements? Answering this question takes us to the heart of Kant's theory of right conduct.

A leading idea in Kant's thought about the basis of moral requirements is that there must be something of unconditional worth or value, some end of action, that can be a source of the unconditionally valid requirements of morality. Now those ends that we adopt on the basis of our desires only acquire worth or value for us as a result of being objects of our choice. Their worth or value is conditional. We are looking for some end whose worth is not acquired in this way but is valid for all rational agents independently of their various desires. Such an end would be an *end in itself*—something possessing unconditional, intrinsic worth. And, according to Kant, there is such an end: "Rational nature exists as an end in itself" (G, 37/429). Rational nature as an end in itself possesses a kind of unconditional, intrinsic value—what Kant sometimes calls "dignity"—that can be the basis of a supreme principle of morality and thus a basis of moral requirements derivable from such a principle.

But what is it about rational nature in virtue of which it has this kind of dignity? In response, Kant claims that "*Autonomy* is . . . the ground of the dignity of human nature and of every rational nature" (*G*, 43/436). Autonomy, for Kant, refers to a capacity, inherent in all rational agents, to act freely on the basis of reason and independently of our desires. Autonomy, or freedom of choice, is thus the basis of moral requirements that can be expressed as categorical imperatives. As Kant remarks:

> The ground of the possibility of categorical imperatives is this: that they refer to no other property of choice (by which some purpose can be ascribed to it) than simply to its *freedom*. (*MM*, 15/222)

Unfortunately, Kant's conception of autonomy and its relation to categorical imperatives are difficult topics and the subject of much controversy among ethics scholars. Here is not the place to examine these topics. Rather, let us make do with a summary of some of the main connections Kant is making among the concepts just introduced.

These connections can be summarized by the following chain of reasoning: Since (1) our rational natures make us ends in ourselves, and (2) we have this status because we possess autonomy, it follows that (3) our nature as autonomous agents makes us ends in ourselves. (4) Anything with the status of an end in itself has unconditional value, and so (5) our autonomous rational natures have unconditional value. (6) If something has unconditional value, then there is an unconditional requirement to respect it. (7) Thus, there is a basic unconditional requirement to respect the autonomy of agents. This basic requirement is expressed in Kant's supreme moral principle, the Categorical Imperative.

Kant uses the term "humanity" to refer to the sort of autonomy that is part of our natures as rational creatures. Here, then, is one formulation of his supreme moral principle that we may call the *Humanity as an End in Itself* formulation (HEI, for short).

HEI So act that you use humanity, whether in your own person or in the person of any other, always at the same time as an end, never merely as a means. (G, 38/429)

As we shall see, Kant offers more than one formulation of his supreme principle of morality. But the main idea expressed by the HEI formulation is that a person's autonomy (humanity) serves as a supremely authoritative constraint on the pursuit of her desire-based goals. I treat someone as a means to my own ends when, for example, I gain their cooperation in helping me achieve what I want. There is nothing necessarily morally wrong in doing so. However, treating people *merely* as means to one's own ends involves treating them in ways that fail to respect their humanity. So, for instance, getting someone's assistance through coercion or deception obviously involves treating that individual as a mere means.

But there are many other ways in which, according to Kant, we can fail to treat ourselves and others as ends in themselves. To get a clearer understanding of the implications of Kant's supreme moral principle, let us briefly consider his system of duties, in which he spells out in some detail the meaning of his principle.

5. Kant's System of Duties

According to Kant, then, moral requirements are properly expressed as categorical imperatives. Kant claims that from his fundamental moral principle, the Categorical Imperative, we can derive all other duties and that they can be organized into a system. First, using the Categorical Imperative, we can derive two very general duties, and then from these derived duties, we can derive further, more specific duties.

The two most general duties are (1) the duty of self-perfection and (2) the duty to promote the happiness of others. Two things need explanation here: first, how Kant arrives at the claim that perfection and happiness are duties; and second, why we do not have a duty to promote our own happiness and why we do not have a duty to bring about the perfection of others. Let us take these one at a time.

The guiding idea contained in the Categorical Imperative is the requirement to treat oneself and others in ways that protect and promote one's own humanity and the humanity of others. Kant claims that "The capacity to set oneself an end—any end whatsoever—is what characterizes humanity" (*MM,* 154/392); this capacity, as we have noted, refers to our autonomy. In order, then, to fully protect and promote our capacity to set ends, we obviously need to develop certain powers that would enable us to effectively set and pursue ends of our choosing. Developing such powers is a matter of perfecting oneself. Hence, from the Categorical Imperative we can derive a general duty to perfect ourselves.

Furthermore, our nature as autonomous agents essentially involves using our end-setting capacities to pursue various projects in life that are aimed at achieving our own happiness. Just as we recognize our own happiness as a legitimate end, consistency demands that we recognize the happiness of all other individuals as having a similar legitimacy. Hence, from the Categorical Imperative we can derive the general duty of promoting the happiness of others. This does not mean that we must help others in their goals no matter what those goals happen to be. Rather, according to Kant, we have a general duty to promote the *morally legitimate* goals of others.

Now the reason we do not have an obligation to promote our own happiness is that, as already noted, by nature we necessarily have our own happiness as an end and so we are strongly naturally inclined to act in ways that promote our happiness. But the idea of a moral duty involves the idea of being morally *constrained* to act in ways that we are not naturally inclined to act. Hence, we do not have a moral duty to promote our own happiness.

Furthermore, since our own perfection is something that must be achieved by our own efforts (I can't do it for you), I don't have a duty to develop your various natural and moral powers (though my actions can help or hinder you in your efforts at self-perfection).

Thus, for Kant, once we bring into view what would, in general terms, be involved in respecting our own humanity and in respecting the humanity of others, we can arrive at two general duties: duties to adopt as guiding aims our own perfection and the happiness of others. Kant calls them *ends that are at the same time duties*. Let us refer to them simply as *obligatory ends*.

These obligatory ends provide, respectively, the basis for deriving more specific duties to oneself and to others. Consider, first, duties to oneself regarding self-perfection. This obligatory end of action is the basis for duties of omission (negative duties) and also for duties of commission (positive duties). After all, there are actions we should avoid in order to maintain and not destroy or otherwise degrade our autonomy, but there are also actions the performance of which would positively promote our autonomy, thus increasing its powers. Furthermore, it is part of Kant's view of human beings that for purposes of moral theory, we can distinguish between humans considered as natural creatures (and thus part of the animal world) and humans considered as rational agents capable of autonomous choice. He thus divides duties to oneself into duties one has considered as a natural being and duties one has considered as a moral being. Figure 7.1 summarizes Kant's duties to oneself as presented in *The Metaphysics of Morals*.

In defending each of these duties, Kant appeals to considerations of respecting one's own humanity. For instance, he argues that suicide is wrong

Figure 7.1 Duties to Oneself Regarding Self-Perfection

	DUTIES OF OMISSION Perfect (narrow) duties	DUTIES OF COMMISSION Imperfect (wide) duties
	To avoid:	*To develop:*
As a Natural Being	Suicide (and self-mutilation) Carnal self-defilement Intemperance in the use of food and drink	Natural powers of Spirit Soul Body
As a Moral Being	Lying Avarice Servility	Moral powers

because it involves "disposing of oneself as a mere means to some discretionary end [which] is debasing humanity in one's own person" (*MM*, 177/423). With regard to lying, the central claim is that "By a lie a human being throws himself away and, as it were, annihilates his dignity as a human being" (*MM*, 182/429). Suicide, lying, and other duties of omission involve actions whose performance would destroy or at least degrade humanity in the person.

As figure 7.1 indicates, Kant (following tradition) distinguishes "perfect" from "imperfect" duties. Perfect, or narrow, duties are so called because the kinds of actions forbidden are fairly precisely specified and presumably we are to refrain from such types of action in all or most circumstances.

By contrast, duties of commission, listed on the right in the chart, are imperfect or "wide" duties because, although they require that agents adopt certain ends as general guiding objectives in life, agents have a great deal of leeway in deciding how and when to act on those ends. Compared to the narrow, perfect duties, imperfect duties are more wide open in terms of what agents can do to fulfill them. For instance, powers of the spirit involve those capacities having to do with the exercise of our reason, powers of soul have to do with those capacities involving memory and imagination, while powers of the body are those physical capacities that must be developed for all sorts of purposes. Now it is up to the individual to decide which specific powers of spirit, soul, and body to develop and how much time she will devote to their development. Presumably such decisions will be partly based on what one plans to do in life. Obviously, someone who aspires to be a mathematician is going to concentrate mainly (but not exclusively) on developing certain powers of spirit. An athlete will no doubt concentrate instead on developing certain powers of body.

Finally, perfecting our moral natures has to do with striving to make the thought of duty the sole motive in dutiful action—in other words, it has to do with progressing toward a state of moral virtue. (The topic of moral virtue is taken up in section 10 below.) This duty seems much more specific than duties connected with our natural powers, but Kant claims that nevertheless working on becoming morally virtuous (something we need not be doing at all times) involves a kind of latitude or leeway and so counts as an imperfect duty.

Regarding the other main obligatory end—the happiness of others—Kant distinguishes duties of love, which are not strictly speaking owed to another person, from duties of respect, which are. And, as before, he distinguishes negative duties of omission from positive duties of commission. Figure 7.2 summarizes duties regarding the happiness of others. Kant argues that duties of omission involve actions the performance of which fails to respect humanity as an end in itself, while promoting humanity as an end in itself requires that we develop attitudes of beneficence, gratitude, sympathy, and respect for others.

Figure 7.2 Duties to Others Regarding Their Happiness

	Duties of Omission Perfect (narrow) duties	Duties of Commission Imperfect (wide) duties
	To avoid:	*To develop:*
Of Love	Envy Ingratitude Malice	Beneficence Gratitude Sympathy
Of Respect	Arrogance Defamation Ridicule	Respect for others as ends in themselves

To bring before us clearly the different levels of duty in Kant's system, the visual aid in figure 7.3 may help.

Level 1 represents the most general moral principle of the system, level 4 represents duties in concrete situations. In between are levels of varying generality, which we have been summarizing (level 3 is summarized in figs. 7.1 and 7.2). There are two important things to keep in mind about the relations between these levels.

First, going from level 1 to 2 and from 2 to 3 requires that we appeal to facts about the specific nature of human beings. Kant makes this clear when he writes:

> [A] metaphysics of morals cannot dispense with principles of application, and we shall often have to take as our object the particular nature of human beings, which is cognized only by experience, in order to show in it what can be inferred from universal moral principles. (*MM*, 10/216–17)

As explained earlier, because the Categorical Imperative is a principle of practical rationality, it is valid for all rational creatures, human and nonhuman. Kant's point is that its implications for human morality require that we take into account various facts about the nature of human beings. For instance, it is because as human beings we have powers of body, mind, and spirit that need development that we have a duty to perfect ourselves.

A second, related point is that going from level 3 to level 4, in which rules are applied to particular circumstances, is not a mechanical procedure. Kant fully recognizes that the application of rules requires the use of good judgment, including being sensitive to the details of individual cases. This point is made especially clear in Kant's casuistical remarks that he appends to his presentation of the various duties in his system.

Figure 7.3 Levels of Duty in Kant's Moral System

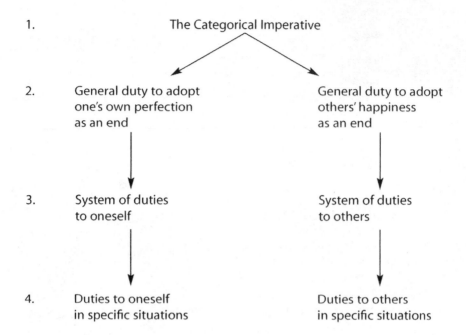

1.   The Categorical Imperative

2.   General duty to adopt   General duty to adopt
      one's own perfection   others' happiness
      as an end   as an end

3.   System of duties   System of duties
      to oneself   to others

4.   Duties to oneself   Duties to others
      in specific situations   in specific situations

Casuistry is the art of applying principles to specific cases to reach justified moral conclusions about those cases. In doing so, the details of one's situation are important. For instance, in connection with the duty not to commit suicide, Kant asks whether it would be morally wrong "to hurl oneself to certain death (like Curtuis) in order to save one's country" (*MM*, 177/423), or whether it would be right for someone suffering from a form of madness (that makes him a danger to others) to commit suicide (*MM*, 178/423–24). Obviously, here and elsewhere in his remarks on casuistry, Kant is considering how particular facts pertaining to situations might affect the rightness or wrongness of various actions. So we should avoid supposing that because the basis of Kantian duties is an abstract moral principle that supposedly holds for all rational agents, it therefore must ignore the important particularities of human beings and the particular circumstances in which they find themselves.

Considering the various duties featured in his ethical system, it should be clear that Kant thought that the Categorical Imperative is rich in its implications. Moreover, its application in our world requires knowledge both about human nature and about the morally relevant details of particular cases. Unfortunately, Kant's theory has sometimes been misunderstood on these points.

6. Kant's Theory of Right Conduct

Now that we have examined some of the detail of Kant's system of duties, let us summarize his theory of right action, using the HEI formulation of the Categorical Imperative. The main idea is that morality requires that we treat all human beings, including ourselves, as ends in themselves and never merely as means to an end. We can shorten this by saying that morality requires that we respect humanity. As we have been doing with the other theories, we can set out Kant's theory as a set of principles:

Theory of Right Conduct: Humanity Formulation

An action A is *obligatory* if and only if failing to perform A would fail to respect humanity.

An action A is *wrong* if and only if performing A would fail to respect someone's humanity.

An action A is *optional* if and only if neither performing A nor failing to perform A would involve failing to respect humanity.

We can fill out Kant's theory by adding principles of perfect and imperfect duty.

Actions whose performance would interfere with someone's humanity violate perfect duty.

Actions whose performance would fail to promote or respect humanity violate (or at least fail to fulfill) imperfect duty.[7]

It is important to note that as I am interpreting Kant's moral theory, it is the HEI formulation of the Categorical Imperative that functions as a moral criterion, telling us what *makes* an action right or wrong. Thus, facts about the action as it bears on treating persons as ends in themselves or, equivalently, respecting their humanity represent the most fundamental right- and wrong-making properties of all choice and action.

7. The Universal Law Formulation of the Categorical Imperative

As mentioned above, Kant expresses his supreme principle of morality in various ways. According to the Universal Law (UL) formulation of that principle:

UL   Act only in accordance with that maxim through which you can at
the same time will that it become a universal law. (G, 31/421)

Those familiar with Kant's ethics might be surprised that I have said nothing so far in this chapter about the UL formulation. Typically, ethics texts
focus mainly on this formulation in expounding Kant's moral theory, since
in the *Groundwork* it seems to be featured over the others and since Kant
seems to recommend it over the others when he says that "one does better always to proceed in moral appraisal by the strict method and put at its
basis the universal [law] formula of the categorical imperative" (*G*,
44/436–37).

I have said that I take the HEI formulation to represent Kant's fundamental criterion of right action, and thus I have featured it in my presentation of his moral theory. The UL formulation, as I understand it, provides
a *decision procedure* to guide moral deliberation rather than a moral criterion.[8] (Notice that in the passage just quoted, Kant recommends the UL formulation for use in contexts of *moral appraisal*, when we are deliberating
about what to do.) With this in mind, let us proceed to consider the UL
formulation.

Since the UL formulation mentions an agent's maxims and employs the
idea of consistent willing, we first need to say something about these notions.

Maxims

Kant defines a maxim as "a subjective principle of volition" (*G*, 14/402)
on which an agent acts whenever she acts intentionally. When one acts, one
represents to oneself the action one is proposing to do (or has done) and
the circumstances in which the action is to take place. Furthermore, one
acts for some purpose or end. To take a simple case, suppose I am having
trouble with the spelling of a word and I finally decide to look it up in a
dictionary to get the spelling straight. My act of looking up the word
flowed from my intention to perform this action in certain circumstances
in order to achieve a certain purpose. My intention is what Kant means in
talking about one's maxim associated with the actions one performs. A
maxim is thus a psychological state expressing one's intention to perform
(or omit) some action and thereby represents the agent's view of what she
is doing. Maxims can be expressed in thought and language by sentences
having this form:

I will _____, if/when _____ in order to _____.

where the first blank is filled by a description of the action, the second blank
with a description of the circumstances in which the agent is contemplating

doing (or has done) the action, and the last blank with a description of the agent's purpose or end to be achieved by the action. We will consider some sample maxims below.

Notice three points about maxims. First, Kant is not committed to the idea that we all go around mentally rehearsing maxims and then acting on them. One need not be consciously attending to the maxim on which one acts, though one could presumably, upon reflection, become aware of the maxim. While driving my car I am acting on a maxim, but normally when I drive, I'm thinking about where I'm going, the road conditions, the traffic, and so forth; I am not thinking about or rehearsing the maxim or intention from which my driving actions flow. Second, since maxims represent the agent's view of the circumstances and action, they may involve mistaken beliefs. I might falsely believe that I have a bad heart and act accordingly and thus be acting on a maxim that does not correctly represent my circumstances. Finally, a maxim, as a principle of volition, expresses what one *wills* to do; adopting a maxim involves setting oneself to do (or omit) some action or pursue some end.

Consistent Willing

We can distinguish between direct and indirect willing. Direct willing involves setting oneself to do some action (or to refrain from doing one) that is within one's direct voluntary control—like willing your arm to move. But one can also will in the sense of setting for oneself some end or goal that is not immediately under one's control—like earning a college degree. This latter is an example of indirect willing.

There are at least two ways in which one might be inconsistent in what one wills. First, if one wills to perform some action or bring about some end where the very idea of the action or the end is self-contradictory, one is guilty of inconsistent willing. Thus, to set out to draw a four-sided triangle involves an inconsistency in willing since one is aiming at bringing about something that in its very conception is self-contradictory. We can refer to this as the *first pattern* of inconsistent willing. As we shall see below, the lying promise example that Kant uses to illustrate the application of the UL formulation of the Categorical Imperative involves this sort of inconsistency.

One might also be guilty of inconsistent willing when there is a conflict between different actions or ends that one wills. Suppose, for example, one intends to donate money to all charitable organizations that help the poor. Suppose also that one refuses to help any organization that contributes to global warming. Now if we suppose that there is some organization, O, that both helps the poor and contributes to global warming, we have an inconsistency in the will. One both wills to contribute money to O (since it is a charitable organization) and does not will to contribute money to O (since it contributes to global warming). Call this the *second pattern* of inconsistent willing. Again, as we shall see, Kant's example involving refusing to help others in need involves this kind of inconsistency in willing.

Let us now turn to Kant's UL formulation of the Categorical Imperative (and the two tests associated with it), where we will encounter both types of inconsistent willing.

Kant's Tests

Kant claims that the UL formulation of the categorical imperative can be used to test the morality of one's actions by determining whether one can consistently will that the maxim of one's action could become a universal law of nature. Kant's test employs the idea that for a proposed course of action to be morally permissible, it must be such that, as a rational agent, one could consistently will that everyone act in the way one is proposing to act. And this amounts to determining whether one could consistently will that everyone adopt and act on the maxim associated with the action in question. This will be made clearer when we turn in a moment to some of Kant's examples.

Let us introduce a bit of terminology. To say that a maxim is *universalizable* is to say that it can be consistently willed as a law of nature. Let us distinguish between maxims of commission and maxims of omission associated with some action. If, for example, the action is one of keeping a promise, then the action of commission would be described by:

I will keep my promise whenever _____.

The corresponding maxim of omission, then, would be:

I will omit to keep my promise whenever _____.

Making use of this distinction, we can formulate principles for determining the conditions under which an action is obligatory, optional, or forbidden.

Principles of Right Conduct: Universal Law Formulation

An action A is *obligatory* if and only if one cannot universalize the maxim of omission associated with A.

An action A is *wrong* if and only if one cannot universalize the maxim of commission associated with A.

An action A is *optional* if and only if one can universalize the maxims of commission and omission associated with A.

Let us now examine some of the details of Kant's test.

In the *Groundwork,* Kant illustrates how his test works by considering four examples: committing suicide, making false promises, letting one's talents rust, and refraining from helping others. He also claims that the UL formulation really embodies two tests that can be used to distinguish perfect from imperfect duties. Rather than work through all four illustrations, it will be enough for our purposes if we just consider the false-promising case (which is supposed to violate a perfect duty) and the case of refusing help to others (which is supposed to violate an imperfect duty).

The False-Promising Example

Regarding the case of false promising, Kant has us imagine someone who

> finds himself urged by need to borrow money. He well knows that he will not be able to repay it but sees also that nothing will be lent him unless he promises to repay it within a determinate time. He would like to make such a promise, but he still has enough conscience to ask himself: is it not forbidden and contrary to duty to help oneself out of need in such a way? (G, 32/422)

The maxim associated with this contemplated action is:

M1 I will get money on a false promise whenever I am in need of money and I have no other way of getting it.[9]

Now Kant's test has agents consider whether they could consistently will that everyone perform the type of action mentioned in the maxim under the circumstances. The idea is to ask yourself whether you could, without contradicting yourself, will that it be a law of nature that everyone do what you are proposing to do. In asking yourself this question, you are, in effect, asking yourself whether you could consistently will as a universal law of nature the following generalized version of your maxim, in this case, M1:

GM1 Everyone will get money on a false promise whenever they are in need of money and have no other way of getting it.

Kant then argues:

> I then see at once that it could never hold as a universal law of nature and be consistent with itself, but must necessarily contradict itself. For, the universality of a law that everyone, when he believes himself to be in need, could

promise whatever he pleases with the intention of not keeping it would make the promise and the end one might have in it itself impossible, since no one would believe what was promised him but would laugh at all such expressions as vain pretenses. (G, 32/422)

Kant's claim is that we cannot conceive of the maxim as a universal law (we cannot conceive of GM1 as a law of nature without falling into contradiction) and so we cannot consistently will the maxim as universal law. And so, concludes Kant, the action mentioned in the maxim is forbidden—a violation of duty.

Unfortunately, Kant's reasoning in this passage is compressed, and it isn't clear exactly how the false-promising maxim, were it to be a universal of nature, "must necessarily contradict itself." Scholars of Kant's ethics disagree over how (if at all) there is a contradiction here. But assuming there is some sort of contradiction, the main idea seems to be this.

Kant's test has us consider whether we can imagine, without contradicting ourselves, a world in which the maxim in question functions as a universal law of nature. To imagine the lying-promise maxim as a universal law of nature apparently requires that we imagine a world like ours except that it is a law of nature that everyone who believes he or she is in need of money will get the money by making a false promise. In attempting to conceive of such a world, we end up in contradiction. After all, if everyone who thinks that he or she needs money makes a lying promise to get the money, eventually this will be found out, with the result that those who believe themselves to need money will not be able to get the money on promise, "since no one would believe what was promised him." Thus, in attempting to conceive of a world in which the false-promising maxim is a universal law governing the behavior of those who think they need money, we are attempting to do the following:

1. Imagine a world in which there is a law according to which everyone who thinks he is in need gets the money on a promise, but also

2. Imagine a world in which (because of the results of widespread false promising) it is not the case that everyone who thinks he is in need gets money on a promise.

Putting (1) and (2) together, we are attempting to:

3. Imagine a world in which everyone believing himself to be in need of money both (by law) gets the money on a promise, but where it is not the case that everyone in those circumstances gets the money on a promise.

By this line of reasoning we have thus uncovered a contradiction in attempting to conceive of the maxim as a universal law of nature. Hence, the maxim in question is not universalizable, and the action mentioned in the maxim is wrong.

The false-promising maxim presumably cannot even be conceived without contradiction as a universal law of nature, and maxims that fail this test—the *contradiction in conception test* (CC test)—feature actions that are violations of perfect duty.

This case, where the state of affairs one is attempting to will cannot even be consistently conceived, fits the first pattern of inconsistent willing that was presented above. However, some maxims corresponding to actions that violate one's duties can be conceived as universal law without contradiction but are such that they still cannot be consistently willed as a universal law of nature, thus fitting the second pattern of inconsistent willing. Such actions are violations of imperfect duty.

The Example of Refraining from Helping Others

The example of refraining from helping others illustrates Kant's second test, the *contradiction in the will test* (CW test). Kant considers a person whose life is going well and who realizes that he is in a position to help others but refuses to do so, thus adopting and acting on the maxim:

M2   I will refrain from helping those in need whenever I am in a position to help and despite the fact that I am well off.

The associated generalized version of M2 is:

GM2 Everyone will refrain from helping those in need whenever they are in a position to help and despite the fact that they are well off.

Here is what Kant says about such a person and the associated maxim:

[A]lthough it is possible that a universal law of nature could very well subsist in accordance with such a maxim, it is still impossible to will that such a principle hold everywhere as a law of nature. For, a will that decided this would conflict with itself, since many cases could occur in which one would need the love and sympathy of others and in which, by such a law of nature arisen from his will, he would rob himself of all hope of the assistance he wishes for himself. (*G*, 33/423)

According to Kant, the nonhelping maxim passes the CC test—one can consistently conceive of a world in which (by law) those who are well off refuse to help those in need. However, one is still involved in an inconsistency in attempting to will the maxim in question as a universal law of nature. Kant's idea here seems to be this. First, if one wills GM2, then by implication one is committed to willing the following:

I   Everyone will refrain from helping *me* whenever they are in a position to help and despite the fact that they are well off.

But, according to Kant, as a rational agent, one necessarily wills that one be helped whenever one is in need. That is, it is a constraint on being a rational agent that one adopt the following maxim:

RM   I will that I be helped whenever I am in need and others are in a position to help me.

But RM is inconsistent with I: RM involves willing that you *be helped* in certain circumstances, while I (which one necessarily wills in willing GM2) involves willing that you *not be helped* in those same circumstances—a contradiction. Thus the maxim in question is not universalizable; attempting to will the original nonhelping maxim as a universal law exemplifies the second pattern of inconsistent willing. Since the nonhelping maxim passes the CC test but fails the CW test, the action mentioned in the maxim violates an imperfect duty to help others.

Are these arguments about false promising and helping others convincing? Perhaps the false-promising case is persuasive, but I suspect that many readers will be suspicious of Kant's insertion of what I have labeled a maxim of rationality (RM) into the helping-others example. After all, consider the diehard individualist who would rather die than accept any form of charity from others. This individual may be acting imprudently, but in failing to adopt RM is he guilty of being irrational? It is perhaps difficult to say without saying much more about what is involved in being rational. I will let the reader mull this over.

Before we consider the plausibility of Kant's tests, I wish to make two remarks about them. First, Kant's tests should be distinguished from rule utilitarianism, which was briefly discussed in chapter 6. Although some versions of rule utilitarianism, like Kant's tests, involve considering what would happen if everyone were to act in a certain way, they are very different. The rule utilitarian is interested in the *values* of the consequences of everyone acting in some way or accepting a certain rule, while Kant's tests focus on whether, in willing one's maxim as universal law, one is caught in some sort of inconsistency. As I have been interpreting Kant's tests, the projected consequences (results) of willing one's maxim as a universal law play a role in determining whether the maxim passes the tests, but it is not the goodness or badness of the consequences that is of concern. Kant does not argue that because the consequences of everyone (in need of money) making a lying promise would be bad or undesirable, acting on the false-promising maxim is wrong.

The second remark I wish to make concerns the difficult issue of how the UL formulation of the Categorical Imperative is related to the HEI formulation. Kant claims that they are equivalent in that they represent different ways of expressing the same supreme law of morality, but it is by no means obvious that they are equivalent. I am proposing that the HEI formulation expresses a moral criterion and thus that it expresses what it is that most fundamentally makes an action right or wrong. But I am also proposing that we think of the UL formulation, not as a moral criterion telling us what makes actions right or wrong, but rather as a decision procedure for use in arriving at justified conclusions about the rightness or wrongness of actions. The HEI formulation then, addresses the main theoretical aim of a moral theory, while the UL formulation addresses the main practical aim of a moral theory.

If this interpretation of the two formulations is plausible, then the UL formulation must be somehow deeply related to the HEI formulation if it can be used as a decision procedure. The idea would have to be that the universalizability of one's maxim is a reliable indicator of whether or not the action featured in the maxim treats humanity as an end in itself. But this idea needs to be defended and would take us beyond the aims of this chapter.

8. Objections to Kant's Tests

Kant thought that his universalization tests would yield results that are consistent with commonsense views about the rightness and wrongness of various actions. But critics have argued that Kant's tests yield the wrong moral conclusions over a range of cases where commonsense notions about right and wrong seem fairly clear and accurate. In some cases a maxim will fail one of Kant's tests (yielding a negative verdict about the corresponding action) but the action is not morally wrong (false negatives), and in other cases a maxim that features a wrong action will pass Kant's tests, yielding a mistaken positive verdict about the act (false positives).

As an example of the first kind of case, consider the investor who intends to withdraw all of her money from the bank once the stock market index climbs another two hundred points.[10] One cannot consistently conceive of this maxim being a universal law of nature, for reasons similar to those presented in connection with the case of false promising. If one attempts to imagine a world in which this maxim functions as a law, one ends up attempting to imagine a world in which everyone withdraws their money under the conditions specified. But since banks do not have the necessary funds on hand to support massive withdrawals, one is also attempting to imagine a world in which it is not the case that everyone in the circumstances in question withdraws their money from a bank. Thus, because the maxim cannot be universalized, the action in the maxim is morally wrong. But surely adopting and acting on this maxim is not morally wrong, so Kant's CC test yields a false negative.

Here is an example of a false positive. Suppose that I plan to make a false promise in order to get money from someone named Igor Cycz on March 8 so that I can make a down payment on a metal detector. I thus formulate my maxim as:

> M3 I will get money on a false promise whenever it is March 8 and I can get it from someone named Igor Cycz in order to buy a metal detector.[11]

Now if I consider whether this maxim can be universalized, I ask whether I could consistently conceive of a world in which everyone in the circumstances in question obtains money on a false promise. Since the circumstances mentioned in my maxim are extremely rare, this maxim will pass the CC test, and so we must conclude that the action mentioned in the maxim is morally permissible (at least in the circumstances so specified), but surely it isn't.[11]

The problem of false negatives and false positives is related to a more general problem for Kant's universalization tests, namely, the *problem of relevant maxims*.[12] A maxim represents an agent's conception of what she is doing or proposes to do, and for every action there are innumerable possible maxims on the basis of which the action in question might be performed. To make this point more clearly, suppose that I am hiding an innocent person who is being hunted by some killers. The killers come to my door and ask me whether I know where the hunted person might be hiding. Suppose I lie and deny that I know anything of the whereabouts of their intended victim. Here are a couple of the possible maxims on which I might act:

> M4 I will tell a lie whenever I am asked a question and don't want to give the correct answer.

> M5 I will tell a lie whenever I am asked a question whose truthful answer will likely lead to the death of an innocent person.

Both maxims fit my circumstances in the sense that they both contain correct (or what I believe to be correct) information about my circumstances.

Now presumably, if I test the first maxim by Kant's tests, it will fail to be universalizable, thus implying that an act of lying in this case would be wrong. (I leave the details as an exercise for the reader.) However, if I test M5 by Kant's tests, it will (arguably) pass with the implication that the action in question is not morally wrong. Intuitively, we judge that the second maxim is (of these two) the one that should be used in testing the morality of lying in this case. What we need from Kant is a principled reason for selecting one possible maxim for purposes of testing the morality of an action over the many others that also apply to the same action. This is the problem of relevant maxims.

Critics often allege that Kant's UL version of the Categorical Imperative is useless without a solution to the problem of relevant maxims. It is useless and hence fails to satisfy the main practical aim of a moral theory—the aim of providing a useful decision procedure—because, given the multiplicity of maxims associated with any action, one can use Kant's tests to derive inconsistent moral verdicts about the same action. We just noted this in connection with maxims M4 and M5. Without a solution to the problem of relevant maxims, that part of Kant's moral theory having to do with providing a correct decision procedure fails the consistency standard for evaluating a moral theory.

Here is how the problem of relevant maxims is related to the problem of false negatives/false positives. For instance, the maxim of making a false promise to someone named Igor Cycz on March 8 includes morally irrelevant information of a detailed sort that has the effect of ensuring that the maxim will pass Kant's tests. After all, there will be very few occasions on which anyone could act on this particular maxim. If everyone who planned to borrow money on March 8 from someone named Igor Cycz in order to buy a metal detector made a false promise, this would not (as in Kant's original example) result in the collapse of the practice of promising. No contradiction in conception would result. Formulating maxims with a lot of true but irrelevant detail will allow almost any maxim to pass Kant's tests. Intuitively, such maxims are not relevant for purposes of morally evaluating the actions they mention.

A maxim like M4 suffers from the opposite problem: it fails to include morally relevant information. If we could supply a theory of relevant maxims on Kant's behalf, we would have a principled basis for determining just what information about one's circumstances and action is morally relevant and should be included in one's maxim and what information should not be included. We would then presumably have a way of eliminating the false negatives/false positives problem.

I hope what I am about to say about the problem of relevant maxims is obvious. A moral theory is in the business of specifying what features of an action and circumstances are the most fundamental morally relevant features—features that make an action right or wrong. If we examine Kant's moral philosophy asking ourselves what features of actions and one's circumstances are the most basic morally relevant features, the answer seems to be provided by the HEI formulation: facts about how one's action (in the circumstances) would bear on humanity in the person—on our capacities as autonomous agents—are the most fundamental morally relevant features in determining the moral status of actions.

So, for instance, the reason the second of the two maxims featured in the example about lying to the would-be killers (M5) is to be favored for use in Kant's tests over the first one (M4) is that it contains some morally relevant information that is not present in M4. The fact that one's telling the truth or even being otherwise evasive might well lead to the death of an innocent person, thus annihilating that person's autonomy, is a morally relevant feature of the circumstances in question.

In general terms, I am suggesting that we look to the HEI formulation of the Categorical Imperative and, in particular, to the derived duties that make up Kant's system of ethical duties (to oneself and to others) as a basis for deciding which features of actions and circumstances are morally relevant and thus should be included in a specification of one's maxim. In other words, the duties featured in Kant's system specify the main ways in which actions and omissions bear on respecting the humanity of persons. Whether an action would be an instance of suicide, or an instance of a lie, or an instance of defamation, or an instance of nonbeneficence, and so forth for the other duties, has to do with respecting humanity in oneself and others. In circumstances where one can save an innocent life only by telling a lie, the fact that by lying one would be saving someone has to do with protecting humanity and so is obviously morally relevant. But facts about the proposed time of some action and the names of individuals involved in the circumstances are not relevant; such facts are not reflected in any of the types of actions featured in Kant's ethical system.[13]

If, following my earlier suggestion, we view the HEI formulation of the Categorical Imperative as a moral criterion specifying what makes an action right or wrong, and if we think of the various duties that Kant attempts to derive from this formulation as specifying the main ways in which actions can affect respect for humanity, then we might ask of what use the UL formulation is. After all, it appears as if we can simply appeal to the HEI formulation to figure out what we ought to do, and thus the rather complicated testing procedure associated with the UL formulation is unnecessary.

Those interpreters of Kant's ethics who think that there are serious problems with the UL formulation would be glad to ignore it and simply concentrate on the HEI formulation. However, following my suggestion, one might also view the UL formulation as primarily a decision procedure that looks to the HEI formulation as a basis for properly formulating maxims to be tested. The idea would be that the UL formulation involves thinking about a course of action from the point of view of morality. In particular, it provides a method for agents to follow when they are considering whether certain facts about their circumstances can justify performing an action that, in other contexts, would be wrong. Ordinarily, acts of lying are wrong, but what about lying to save a would-be murder victim? Does this fact about the action justify lying? Determining whether one could universalize the relevant maxim is perhaps a way of deciding the issue from the moral point of view.

9. Kant's Theory of Value

To complete our presentation of Kant's moral theory, let us turn briefly to Kant's theory of value, including his accounts of nonmoral and moral value and his doctrine of the "highest good."

Nonmoral Value

In presenting his theory of right conduct, we have already touched on the idea that for Kant, autonomy, or the capacity for free choice, has intrinsic (nonmoral) unconditional worth and is thus the basis for categorical requirements on choice and action.[14]

Moral Value

Recall from chapter 1 that *moral* value concerns the kind of value attaching to responsible agents who are appropriately praised or blamed for what they do. A morally good (or bad) person is one who has certain character traits. Those traits that confer goodness on a person are called "virtues," those that confer badness on a person are called "vices."[15]

According to Kant, there is only one moral virtue, which he describes as "the moral strength of a human being's will in fulfilling his duty" (*MM*, 164/405). The idea is that being a morally good person involves being disposed to act from the sole motive of duty whenever duty calls. Being so disposed requires an inner strength that enables one to resist the temptation to transgress the requirements of duty. Such persons have what Kant calls a *good will*.

Although moral goodness attaches primarily to a person's character in the manner just described, Kant also characterizes actions that are done solely from the motive of duty as having moral worth. Thus Kant distinguishes actions that fulfill one's obligations (actions in accordance with duty) from actions that are not only in accordance with duty but also are done from the motive of duty. The shopkeeper who gives correct change to young and inexperienced customers because he is interested in guarding his good business reputation fulfills a moral obligation and so does his duty, but since his motive is one of self-interest, his dutiful action does not possess moral worth. Only when the act of giving correct change is motivated solely by the thought that the action is a duty does the shopkeeper's action possess moral worth.

Moral goodness plays a key role in Kant's conception of the highest good for human beings.

The Highest Good

Kant's view about the *highest (complete) good* for human beings is not only interesting in itself but also leads Kant to certain "practical postulates" concerning human immortality and God. While virtuous character or a good will is the *supreme good* for Kant, it is not the highest good.

> [F]or this [the highest good], *happiness* is also required. . . . For to need happiness, to be also worthy of it, and yet not to participate in it cannot be consistent with the perfect volition of a rational being that would at the same time have all power, even if we think of such a being only for the sake of experiment. (*CPR*, 92/110)

Kant's point seems to be that human beings are (in part) essentially creatures with needs and desires whose satisfaction constitutes each such being's happiness. If we reflect on a situation in which an individual who possesses virtue is also happy and compare it with a situation in which that same virtuous person lacks happiness, we see that the former situation is better than the latter. Thus, according to Kant, the highest good for human beings involves two components: the possession of virtuous character (which, as the supreme good, represents a limiting condition on other components of the highest good) together with happiness (understood as a reward for one's virtuous character).[16]

However, for Kant, as we have seen, the demands of duty and the pursuit of one's own happiness are often in conflict. Certainly, coming to have a good will is no guarantee that in this life one will be happy. But since Kant insists (for reasons we shall not go into here) that the highest good must be attainable, he is led to two postulates, the *postulates of practical reason*. Since coming to have a truly virtuous character is something that one cannot fully and completely accomplish during this lifetime—it is always in progress—we must recognize that

> [t]his endless progress is, however, possible only on the presupposition of the *existence* and personality of the same rational being continuing *endlessly* (which is called immortality of the soul). Hence the highest good is practically possible only on the presupposition of the immortality of the soul, so that this, as inseparably connected with the moral law, is a *postulate* of pure practical reason. (*CPR*, 102/122)

This postulate takes care of the possibility of the first element of the highest good. But as already noted, there is no necessary connection (at least in this life) between being virtuous and being happy. And this point leads to

> the supposition of the existence of a cause adequate to this effect [happiness as a reward for virtue], that is, it must postulate the *existence of God* as belonging necessarily to the possibility of the highest good. (*CPR*, 104/124)

Thus, the possibility of the highest good—virtue rewarded with happiness—is only possible on the assumption that we are immortal and that there is a God. Those who are familiar with the epistemological doctrines of Kant's *Critique of Pure Reason* (1781) will recall that in that work, Kant argues that human knowledge about the world is limited to what can be based on experience using our five senses plus introspection. In particular, Kant claims that although we can consistently conceive of such metaphysical things as freedom, immortality of the soul, and God, nevertheless, human beings cannot have knowledge of such things. In his moral writings, Kant still insists that humans cannot have knowledge of freedom, immortality, and God. However, freedom (autonomy) is a presupposition of the possibility of morality, and immortality and God must be postulated in order allow for the possibility of the highest good.

10. Brief Recap

This completes my presentation of Kant's moral theory, including his theory of right conduct and of value. As I mentioned at the outset of this chapter, Kant's views in ethics are complex, and I have only attempted to go over some of the basic elements of his theory. Since we have covered a good deal of territory, it might be useful, before turning to evaluation, to recall the major ideas in Kant's overall moral theory.

- *Kant's conception of moral requirements.* For Kant, moral requirements are categorical and apply to us in virtue of our reason and independently of our desires. They are expressed as categorical imperatives.

- *The supreme principle of morality.* Kant's Categorical Imperative, understood as a moral criterion specifying what makes an action right or wrong, is expressed by the Humanity as an End in Itself (HEI) formulation of Kant's supreme principle. Basically, it requires that we always treat humanity as an end in itself and never as a mere means to our ends. The system of duties implied by this principle involves both duties to ourselves and to others.

- *The universality tests.* Kant's theory includes a decision procedure for coming to justified conclusions about the rightness and wrongness of actions. This procedure is expressed by Kant's Universal Law (UL) formulation of the Categorical Imperative.

• *The theory of value.* Kant's account of intrinsic nonmoral value is based on the idea that our capacity for free choice (autonomy) has the sort of unconditional value that can ground unconditional, categorical moral requirements. According to Kant's account of moral goodness, virtue is a matter of possessing a certain kind of strength—the strength required to do one's duty from the sole motive of duty (on occasions where duty calls). Finally, Kant's notion of the highest most complete good is that of an individual being happy in proportion to her being virtuous. The possibility of the existence of this highest good requires that we postulate our own immortality and the existence of God.

11. Evaluation of Kant's Moral Theory

Some advantages of Kant's theory are mentioned in the next, concluding section. In this section, I mainly focus on objections to this theory, partly because doing so helps deepen our understanding of Kant's complex views in ethics. The objections I wish to consider concern (1) Kant's conception of duty, (2) his account of moral virtue, and (3) his theory of right conduct. Let us take these up in order.

Moral Requirements (Duties) as Requirements of Reason

Kant, as we have seen, believes that moral requirements are requirements of reason on choice and action. In particular, he thinks that there are certain ends of action that reason, apart from any of our desires, prescribes for us as rational agents. The ends of self-perfection and the happiness of others are the two most basic obligatory ends in Kant's ethical system. But are there really any ends that it would be *intrinsically irrational* to fail to adopt? Whether there are such rationally required ends is a difficult and complex issue over which contemporary philosophers disagree.

Many philosophers interested in questions about practical rationality are in basic agreement with the Scottish philosopher David Hume (1711–76), who argued that when it comes to what it is rational and irrational to do, reason can only function to help us discover ways to best satisfy our desires. As Hume dramatically put it: "Reason is, and ought only to be the slave of the passions, and can never pretend to any other office than to serve and obey them" (Hume [1739] 1978, 415). On Hume's instrumentalist view of practical reason, there cannot be any truly valid categorical imperatives since they purport to set forth requirements on choice and action not based on desire. But if all reasons for action are based on desire, then the only sorts of requirements possible are those expressed by mere hypothetical imperatives.

Suppose that Hume and his followers are right and there are no intrinsically rational requirements of reason on choice and action, that all reasons for action are based on our desires. What then?

In that case, we have two options in relation to Kant's moral theory. The first is that we can agree with Kant that our ordinary notion of duty is based on the assumption that there are categorical requirements of reason; then, if Hume is right, we have to conclude that the ordinary conception of duty rests on a false assumption. And if our ordinary conception rests on a false assumption, we would have to conclude that there really are no moral duties (given what we mean by a moral duty). Consider a parallel. Ordinary religious claims of Christians presuppose that there is a God of a certain sort. Suppose there is no such God, what then? Clearly, we would have to conclude that religious claims about God are false—there is no such being about which such claims are true.

The other option in response to Hume on this matter is to question whether the ordinary conception of duty really does presuppose that there are categorical requirements of reason on choice and action. Some philosophers have claimed that we should understand ordinary moral claims about duty as involving a system of hypothetical imperatives.[17] One way to make sense of this suggestion is to suppose that insofar as we value and desire human flourishing, certain kinds of actions should be avoided and other sorts of actions should be encouraged. Moral requirements, on this conception, get their binding force from the desire for personal flourishing and the recognition that one's chances of flourishing are greater if individuals accept a code of behavior that protects the interests of individuals in certain ways and positively promotes everyone's interests.

I have not rehearsed any of the specific criticisms that Hume and his followers might press against the Kantian view of practical reason; I have simply noted that this issue deeply affects the overall plausibility of Kant's moral theory and is an issue of ongoing philosophical concern.[18]

Kant on Virtue

According to Kant's account of moral virtue, the virtuous person—the person with a good will—(1) is someone who possesses moral strength of will in being able to overcome temptation and (2) is someone who acts from the sole motive of duty (when duty calls).

According to critics, Kant's account of moral virtue is problematic on both counts. First, Kant seems to portray the truly virtuous person as someone who is in a state of conflict in having to overcome temptation in the face of duty. But this conflict model of the virtuous agent is contrasted by the critics with the picture of someone whose desires and feelings are in complete harmony with her moral obligations, someone who does not suffer from the kind of conflict that is characteristic of the Kantian virtuous person. Critics making this point often look to the work of Aristotle, who distinguishes the person of mere continence from the truly virtuous person. Someone is continent if he is able to muster the moral strength of will to overcome temptation, while the truly virtuous person for Aristotle does not (in general) suffer from such conflict. If we reflect on which of these two sorts of persons seems morally preferable, it is clear that we think the latter more desirable than the former. The person who has to resist the temptation to steal is in a less morally desirable state than someone who does not consider stealing as a serious option. If this is correct, then Kant's account of the virtuous person seems defective as a moral ideal.

The second objection to Kant's account of virtue has to do with his claim that only the motive of duty has moral value and hence that motives like love and benevolence lack such value. Suppose that you are convalescing in a hospital and one of your friends, Megan, comes to visit. Compare two cases.[19] In the first, Megan comes to see you because of her genuine care and concern for you—you are someone she very much likes. In the second, Megan comes to see you only because she thinks it is her duty to do so. Now even if we think that acting from the sole motive of duty is of moral value, it seems clear (from the case I've described) that we place value on motives other than the motive of duty. Reflection upon such cases has led many philosophers to claim that altruistic motives and emotions like care, compassion, and direct concern for others possess moral value.

I will not attempt to evaluate these criticisms. However, it is worth noting that in recent years scholars of Kant's ethics have increasingly turned their attention to Kant's later moral writings, especially *The Metaphysics of Morals,* where his developed views on moral virtue are arguably closer to the Aristotelian harmony conception of the morally virtuous person.[20] Also, the austere Kantian doctrine that only the motive of duty confers moral worth on actions has been defended against those who would claim that other motives and emotions have moral worth.[21] At this time, it seems to me that our understanding of Kant's account of virtue is in transition, so it would be premature to either endorse or dismiss this aspect of Kant's overall moral theory.

Theory of Right Conduct

Let us now turn to Kant's theory of right conduct and, in particular, his supreme moral principle, the Categorical Imperative. I wish to raise questions about its justification and about its role in moral theory.

On Justifying the Categorical Imperative. In the *Groundwork,* Kant tells his readers that the twofold aim of the book is to set forth and *establish* the supreme principle of morality. Kant attempts to establish his supreme principle by arguing that (1) human beings must presuppose that they possess autonomy (freedom of the will) and that (2) the principle governing autonomy is the Categorical Imperative. In presenting the HEI formulation of the Categorical Imperative, we noted the deep connection between morality and autonomy in Kant's thinking. However, we did not explore Kant's difficult and controversial argument connecting autonomy and the Categorical Imperative, and this is not the place to take it up.

Instead, let me suggest that even if Kant's attempt to establish the Categorical Imperative fails, one might attempt to justify it by showing that it fits well with, and helps explain, our considered moral judgments. In other words, one might appeal to the standards of internal support and explanatory power in attempting to justify this principle. An exploration of these matters would take us well beyond our survey of Kant's moral theory and so cannot be pursued here.

On the Role of the Categorical Imperative in Moral Theory. Kant's Categorical Imperative is supposed to function as the supreme principle of morality, serving both as a moral criterion and as a decision procedure. Can it plausibly do so?

Some critics complain that the Categorical Imperative, because it is so abstract, is necessarily insensitive to morally relevant details of concrete particular situations calling for moral decision. The idea is that the Categorical Imperative seems to yield a kind of moral absolutism according to which certain general types of action are always morally wrong.[22] But such absolutism, because it is insensitive to morally relevant details of particular situations, overlooks exceptional cases, cases in which suicide, lying, and other such actions are not wrong.

I do not think this sort of objection, based on an appeal to the standard of internal support, has much force against Kant's theory. In presenting his system of duties, I made a point of explaining how particular facts about concrete situations calling for a moral decision play a role in Kant's considered view. This point emerges clearly from Kant's various casuistical questions which we noted at the end of section 6. Since we have already dealt with this issue, we need not revisit it here.

A second objection has to do with indeterminacy. According to my interpretation, the HEI formulation of the Categorical Imperative represents Kant's fundamental moral criterion of right action. But critics have expressed skepticism about the possibility of basing a system of duties on a moral principle that features the concept of respecting humanity. The problem is that this concept is quite vague and there will be many actions where it is doubtful that there is a determinate fact of the matter about whether it respects humanity. Kant's theory thus fails to satisfy the determinacy standard for evaluating moral theories.

To take just one example, consider the action of killing a human being. A pacifist might claim that any instance of intentionally killing a human being (even in war and self-defense) is wrong because all such killing involves a violation of respect for humanity. Kant and many others would no doubt disagree. But is the concept of respecting humanity clear enough in what it involves to decide *on the basis of the concept of respecting humanity* whether or not the pacifist is right about killing humans? This is but one example, but it illustrates the worry about determinacy stemming from the fact that the notion of respecting humanity is so vague.

This worry is nicely expressed by James Griffin:

> Every moral theory has the notion of equal respect at its heart: regarding each person as, in some sense, on an equal footing with every other one. Different moral theories parlay this vague notion into different conceptions. . . . [M]oral theories are not simply derivations from these vague notions, because the notions are too vague to allow anything as tight as a derivation. (Griffin 1986, 208)

Griffin's talk of "equal respect for persons" is equivalent to talk about respecting humanity. We can illustrate Griffin's point by noting that in developing and defending a version of utilitarianism, Bentham claimed that on his theory, every person counts equally in determining the morality of an action. In short, many, if not all, of the moral theories we have already considered can fairly claim to capture the idea that persons are to be treated with equal respect.

The upshot is that although the idea of respecting humanity, or, equivalently, treating persons as ends in themselves, is an intuitively attractive moral ideal, it is too vague to be the basis for a supreme moral principle that one can use to *derive* a system of moral duties. What this implies for Kant's ethical system is that when it comes to understanding what it is that makes actions right or wrong, the real work is done at the level of the various duties to oneself and duties to others that were summarized in figures 7.1 and 7.2. That is, instead of thinking of Kant's moral theory in terms of a very general moral principle that can be used to derive more specific duties, think of his system as involving a plurality of moral rules—rules that forbid suicide, lying, defamation, and other duties of omission, as well as rules that require self-development, beneficence, and other duties of commission. We end up with a theory of right conduct that is properly described as a version of moral pluralism—there is a plurality of basic morally relevant features of actions and circumstances whose presence bears on the deontic status of actions.

But moral pluralism of this sort leads to questions about conflict of duty situations. Conflict of duty situations are ones in which one must choose between satisfying two or more duties, because they can't all be satisfied. In the example of the would-be killers who are inquiring into the whereabouts of someone you are hiding, you must choose between observing the duty not to lie and observing the duty of beneficence to help those in need (in this case the innocent would-be victim). Conflict of duty situations are particularly important since moral quandaries about such issues as abortion, euthanasia, capital punishment, treatment of animals, and others involve conflicting values and obligations. How can Kant's theory deal with such cases?

One suggestion (mentioned earlier) would be to use the UL formulation of the Categorical Imperative where the maxim to be tested mentions all of the morally relevant information pertaining to the situation. Perhaps testing such maxims will determine how one is to act, and thus determine which of the competing duties should be observed. This possibility needs to be explored, but we cannot pause here to do so.

Another suggestion is that we make use of Kant's distinction between perfect and imperfect duties. Kant indicates that perfect, narrow duties are *strict* while imperfect, wide duties are not. Applied to conflict of duty cases, the idea would be that when we must choose between fulfilling a perfect duty and fulfilling an imperfect duty, the former, stricter duty is to be observed. After all, imperfect, wide duties allow latitude as to the time and manner of fulfillment. So when any such duty conflicts with a perfect duty, doesn't it make sense to comply with the strict duty?

This proposal has two rather obvious difficulties. First, we have already described a case in which, arguably, the duty to render aid to someone (a duty of beneficence) outweighs one's duty not to lie. Again, if I have made a promise to meet someone at a specific time to help with some project of theirs, wouldn't I be doing the right thing if, on my way to keep my appointment, I break my promise in order to help an accident victim? Here, an imperfect duty seems to outweigh a perfect duty.

A second obvious problem arises in cases where a perfect duty conflicts with a perfect duty or an imperfect duty conflicts with another imperfect duty. The proposal under consideration says nothing about such cases. I have an imperfect duty to develop my moral powers and, in particular, a duty to strive to have a good will. But what if I am a budding young artist and recognize that the only way to ascend to the top of my field is to become the protégé of a great artist of dubious character? I judge that being under the direction of this great artist will no doubt lead me to adopt a way of life that will conflict with developing my moral powers. In short, my imperfect duty to develop my natural talents conflicts with my imperfect duty to develop my moral character. Now it seems pretty clear what Kant would say about this matter, but in claiming that the duty to develop one's moral self outweighs the other duty, we have gone beyond the proposal under consideration.

What, then, should we say about conflict of duty situations in relation to Kant's moral theory? Here, again, I think the most plausible route is to admit that any moral theory, including Kant's, is limited in its power to resolve such conflicts. I thus propose that we interpret Kant's theory as being a version of what I have been calling limited moral pluralism.

It is a version of pluralism because (as explained earlier) when it comes to specifying those features of actions that make them right or wrong, the real work is done (so I claim) by the moral rules featured in Kant's system of duties. On my proposal what we have is a set of moral rules—rules featuring the various duties to oneself and to others—and when they conflict, there is no superprinciple or rule that can adjudicate the conflict. In short, I propose that if we are skeptical of the idea that Kant's Categorical Imperative can function, as he seems to have thought, as a very general moral criterion with determinate implications for the deontic status of actions, what we are left with is a version of limited moral pluralism.

12. Conclusion

Let us conclude with a brief overall assessment of Kant's moral theory, beginning with his account of moral virtue.

In criticizing Kant's theory of moral virtue, we have raised some standard objections that question the austerity of Kant's picture of the virtuous agent. However, we have also noted that in recent years Kant's ethics scholars have been paying more attention to his later, somewhat neglected moral writings, which seem to indicate a less austere and thus more plausible conception of virtue.

Regarding Kant's theory of right conduct, I think we can agree that his guiding idea that morality has to do with treating humanity as an end in itself has a great deal of intuitive appeal. It also has some comparative advantages over some of its main rivals. Unlike the natural law theory, it is not embroiled in sticky questions about intending versus merely foreseeing; and unlike utilitarianism, it is not guilty of being overdemanding in its requirements. Moreover, because Kant's theory features both duties of self-perfection and duties concerning the happiness of others, it combines the best of natural law and utilitarian traditions.

Against Kant's theory of right conduct, we noted that unless there is a solution to the problem of relevant maxims, the UL formulation of the Categorical Imperative will lead to inconsistent verdicts about the morality of specific actions. My suggestion for dealing with this problem is to recognize that the HEI formulation of the Categorical Imperative is supposed to specify fundamental morally relevant features of actions—features that should be reflected in maxims appropriate for moral testing.

We also raised questions about how Kant's theory of right conduct is to be justified. We did not explore Kant's notoriously difficult attempt to justify the Categorical Imperative. We did note, however, that if this principle can be shown to fit with our considered moral beliefs and can plausibly explain what makes actions right or wrong, then in satisfying the standards of internal support and explanatory power, it will be strongly justified. Rather than pursue such matters, I suggested that the central idea of respecting humanity that is featured in the HEI formulation of the Categorical Imperative is too vague to yield determinate moral verdicts about a wide range of cases. I furthermore suggested that Kant's theory of right conduct might best be viewed as a system of moral rules—some rules specifying duties to oneself, others specifying duties to others—without there being a super-principle from which these various rules might be rigorously derived. This means that in cases in which the moral rules conflict, Kant's theory (that is, my proposed reworking of the theory) is limited in its power to resolve such conflicts and generate determinate moral verdicts.

I have not argued at length for this way of viewing Kant's ethics and will not be able to do so here. But since my proposal in relation to Kant's moral theory is greatly influenced by the pluralist moral theory of W. D. Ross, let us now turn to Ross's theory.

Further Reading

Aune, Bruce. 1979. *Kant's Theory of Morals.* Princeton, N.J.: Princeton University Press. An accessible presentation of the main doctrines of Kant's *Groundwork* and *The Metaphysics of Morals.*

Baron, Marcia W. 1995. *Kantian Ethics Almost without Apology.* Ithaca, N.Y.: Cornell University Press. Part 1 considers issues connected with supererogation and imperfect duty in Kant's system, while part 2 deals with matters concerning Kant's conception of virtuous disposition and acting from duty.

————. 1997. "Kantian Ethics." In *Three Methods of Ethics,* by Marcia W. Baron, Philip Pettit, and Michael Slote. Oxford: Blackwell. A relatively short and useful overview of Kant's moral theory in which it is contrasted with, and defended in relation to, consequentialism and virtue ethics.

Guyer, Paul, ed. 1998. *Kant's* Groundwork of the Metaphysics of Morals: *Critical Essays.* Lanham, Md.: Rowman & Littlefield. Essays by leading Kant's ethics scholars covering the main doctrines in Kant's *Groundwork.* Also included is a useful bibliography.

Herman, Barbara. 1993. *The Practice of Moral Judgment.* Cambridge: Harvard University Press. A collection of Herman's essays that are particularly suggestive in relation to Kant's views on moral worth and the application of the Categorical Imperative.

Hill, Thomas E., Jr. 1992. *Dignity and Practical Reason.* Ithaca, N.Y.: Cornell University Press. A collection of some of Hill's essays on Kant's ethics. Of particular interest is his attempt to make sense of and defend the Kingdom of Ends formulation of the Categorical Imperative, which was not discussed in this chapter.

Korsgaard, Christine. 1996. *Creating the Kingdom of Ends.* Cambridge: Cambridge University Press. Essays that deal with themes from both the *Groundwork* and *The Metaphysics of Morals.*

O'Neill, Onora. 1989. *Constructions of Reason.* Cambridge: Cambridge University Press. Essays on Kant's ethics including important work on maxims and the tests associated with Kant's UL formulation.

Timmons, Mark, ed. 2002. *Kant's* Metaphysics of Morals: *Interpretative Essays.* Oxford: Oxford University Press. Essays by different scholars on various aspects of Kant's more mature moral philosophy.

Wood, Allen. 1999. *Kant's Ethical Thought.* Cambridge: Cambridge University Press. A detailed interpretation of Kant's moral theory.

Notes

1. I will continue to refer to Kant's supreme moral principle using capital letters.

2. I have used the Mary Gregor translations of Kant's moral writings (see references section), and I will cite Kant's works using the following abbreviations: G for *Groundwork of the Metaphysics of Morals;* CPR for *Critique of Practical Reason;* and MM for *The Metaphysics of Morals.* References include the page number from the translated edition followed by the page number from the Akademie edition of Kant's works (so that readers using translations other than Gregor will be able to locate quoted passages by referring to the Akademie page numbers included in most translations).

3. In chap. 4, sec. 4, we encountered the distinction between practical and theoretical reason in connection with Aquinas's moral theory.

4. That is, all of its instances that correctly specify the necessary means to some end.

5. As we shall see in connection with categorical imperatives, Kant imposes constraints on the sorts of ends a fully rational agent would adopt.

6. Kant denies that we can determine with any degree of reliability which ends will, if achieved, contribute to our own happiness. He thus denies that we can formulate hypothetical imperatives that specify the means we must take in order to achieve our own happiness. Instead, he says we must make do with "counsels of prudence," which recommend certain courses of action with no guarantee that following them will in fact result in happiness. See G, 29/419.

7. It would be incorrect to say that all actions whose performance or nonperformance would fail to promote humanity *violate* imperfect duty since, normally, actions that count as fulfilling imperfect duties are not morally required (owing to the latitude in fulfilling them), and so failing to perform them is not necessarily a violation of such duties. However, there are cases in which failing to promote humanity constitutes a violation of imperfect duty. Arguably, in cases where some stranger is in desperate need of one's help (no one else is around) and one can help them at little or no cost to oneself, it would be a violation of the duty of beneficence to refrain (for no good reason) from helping. Kant's doctrine of imperfect duty is complex, and I have not discussed it in any detail. For a useful discussion of such duties, see Baron 1995, chap. 3.

8. I defend this interpretation of the different roles of the HEI and UL formulations in Timmons 1997.

9. I am following Kant in not making explicit what further end this person might have, since the argument Kant uses to show that this maxim would fail one of his tests does not depend on such information.

10. This is a version of an example by Feldman (1978, 116).

11. I am assuming that the maxim would also pass the CW test. But even if it does not, it is a defect in Kant's universalization test if this maxim does not fail the CC test.

12. This problem is often called *the problem of relevant descriptions* because maxims contain descriptions of one's action and circumstances.

13. This is not to say that such facts could never be relevant; facts of this sort might be relevant, but only if they have a bearing on treating humanity as an end in itself. In the false-promising case I am imagining, such facts have no such bearing and so are morally irrelevant.

14. Of course, we may misuse this capacity in immoral ways and when we do, the *use* of our autonomy is bad or evil. Still, as a capacity, our autonomy has, according to Kant, unconditional worth.

15. In chap. 9, the topic of virtue and vice will be discussed in some detail.

16. Happiness, then, unlike autonomy, is a *conditional* nonmoral good—its goodness as part of the highest good depends on being morally deserved.

17. A well-known contemporary defense of this view is by Philippa Foot (1972).

18. For a recent and advanced discussion of this matter, see the papers in Cullity and Gaut 1997.

19. This example is like the one featured in Stocker 1976.

20. See, e.g., Johnson 1997 and Engstrom 2001.

21. See Marcia Baron's essay in Baron, Pettit, and Slote 1997.

22. Moral absolutism was discussed in chap. 4 in connection with the natural law theory. Kant himself encourages this interpretation of his theory in a short essay he published toward the end of his life, "On the Right to Lie from Beneficent Motives," in which he claims that lying, even to save an innocent life, is always morally wrong. However, as I hope my presentation of Kant's moral theory makes clear, moral absolutism of this sort is not implied by either of the formulations of the Categorical Imperative we have examined. Hence, I reject absolutist interpretations of Kant's moral theory.

8

Moral Pluralism

Jean-Paul Sartre, a twentieth-century French existentialist philosopher, describes the case of a young man who is torn between staying with his mother and joining the French Free Forces in resisting Germany during World War II.[1] On the one hand, he has a great deal of concern for his mother, who will be alone if he leaves, and feels he ought to stay with her. But, on the other hand, he feels an obligation to his country in this time of war. He can't satisfy both obligations. What should he do?

This is a conflict of duty situation. In the last chapter, the case involving someone hiding an intended murder victim and lying to the would-be killers is another instance of this type of situation. Moral theories featuring a supreme moral principle, such as classical utilitarianism, imply a resolution of such conflicts. For the utilitarian, the young man's true obligation is to perform whichever action would maximize utility. Granted, deciding on the basis of utilitarian calculation what he ought to do will involve educated guesswork, and there is no assurance that the young man (or anyone else) would come to the correct (utilitarian) moral conclusion about what should be done. Nevertheless, the utilitarian can claim that there is a correct answer to the young man's quandary. It is the answer dictated by the principle of utility.

But suppose there is no single moral principle expressing some one general feature upon which the deontic status of all actions depends? This is what Sartre thought. He was skeptical of there being any such principle that one could apply to the case of the young man that would determine which of the courses of action open to him is morally right. Nor did Sartre think that there was some other rigorous method by which the man's dilemma could be resolved. Suppose Sartre is right about this matter. What then for moral theory?

One reaction is to give up on certain pretensions of moral theory, particularly those associated with monistic moral theories, and embrace some form of moral pluralism. To see what this involves, let us consider the contrast between monism and pluralism in ethics.

1. Moral Pluralism

Regarding the morality of actions, *moral monism* is the view that there is a single basic feature of actions that determines their deontic status. Hedonistic utilitarianism represents a version of monism since, on this view, an action is morally right if and only if it would produce at least as much overall utility (measured in terms of increase of pleasure and reduction of pain) as any other alternative action one might perform instead.

One criticism of hedonistic utilitarianism and other forms of moral monism is that they are overly reductive: they attempt to boil all morally relevant considerations down to a single, fundamental feature possessed of moral relevance. The result, according to the critics, is that such views distort moral reality, making it appear much more unified and simpler than it really is.

Instead, one might hold that there is a plurality of equally basic morally relevant features and thus a plurality of moral principles or rules.[2] The idea would be that each such rule expresses a basic morally relevant feature that, when present, bears on the overall deontic status of actions. So, for example, suppose that being an instance of lying is a basic morally relevant feature an action might possess, and suppose the same is true of being an instance of giving aid to someone in need. If so, we would have at least two basic moral rules, and, being *basic*, they could not be derived from some further, even more basic moral principle. Morality might be too complex to be captured in a single principle specifying some one underlying feature that determines the deontic status of any action.

One can be a pluralist about the nature of right action, about the nature of intrinsic value, or about both. If we focus for the time being on the nature of right action, *moral pluralism* involves two main claims:

1. There is a plurality of basic moral rules.

2. There is no underlying moral principle that serves to justify these moral rules.

Although there are various ways in which moral pluralism might be developed, the version we find in the writings of twentieth-century philosopher W. D. Ross (1877–1971) is one of the most influential versions in current moral theorizing. This chapter will focus on the rudiments of Ross's moral theory.

2. Moral Pluralism and Conflict of Duty Situations

In recognizing a plurality of basic moral rules, moral pluralism must come to grips with conflict of duty situations. Suppose that the list of basic moral rules recognized by the pluralist includes:

P1 You ought to keep your promises.

P2 You ought to render aid to those in need.

Consider the situation in which you must choose between keeping a promise to meet a friend at some particular time and stopping to render aid to an accident victim. In this particular situation, you can't fulfill both obligations. Moreover, application of these two rules yields contradictory moral verdicts. P1 implies that you ought to keep your promise and thus that it would be wrong to stop and give aid. P2 implies the reverse: you ought to stop and give aid (so it would not be wrong) and thus it would be wrong (and thus not obligatory) to keep your promise.

How might the moral pluralist handle such cases? One way would be to come up with some strict lexical ranking of the rules according to their relative importance. Rules higher up on the list would outrank, and hence take precedence over, those lower on the list. Call this brand of pluralism *lexical moral pluralism.*

Lexical moral pluralism can neatly handle cases of moral conflict. If, for example, we place the rule requiring that we render aid to others higher on the list than the rule requiring us to keep promises, then in the sort of case envisioned, we have a way to resolve the moral quandary in which P1 and P2 come into conflict.

The obvious problem with this prioritizing strategy is simply that it does not seem possible to rank order the moral rules featured in the pluralist's theory. For example, it is pretty clear that there are going to be cases in which the obligation to keep one's promises outweighs in moral importance the obligation to render aid to others. Suppose you are counting on me to pick you up to take you to an important job interview and on the way I see that I could stop to help someone struggling with his groceries. In this situation, unlike the previous one involving an accident victim, I really ought to keep my promise.

Of course, we may be able to form some generalizations about the relative importance of various types of obligations. Perhaps by and large the obligation to keep one's promises outweighs the obligation of helping others. But the point is that it is not possible to come up with a fixed, once-and-for-all ranking that would tell us how, in every possible circumstance, we are to decide between competing moral obligations.

Then it might seem that the moral pluralist is in a serious bind. There are conflict of duty situations in which we have competing obligations, yet there does not seem to be a way to adjudicate such conflicting obligations. There are actually two problems facing the pluralist. First, if the pluralist is going to avoid having rules that yield contradictory moral verdicts, she must somehow formulate her rules or otherwise organize them so that contradiction is avoided. This is a matter of satisfying the consistency standard for evaluating moral theories, so call this the *consistency problem* for the pluralist. Second, the pluralist needs to explain how we can adjudicate conflicts among moral rules in circumstances where they conflict and thereby arrive at justified verdicts about the rightness and wrongness of actions. Call this the *adjudication problem.*[3]

3. Prima Facie Duties

Ross's theory of right conduct involves a solution to this conflict problem. But to understand it, we must examine his particular version of moral pluralism, which features the notion of a *prima facie duty.*

To explain this notion, let us consider a very familiar sort of situation that does not involve having to make a moral decision. Suppose that you very much want to spend this evening with a certain friend, someone you are quite fond of. Your friend is dead set on going to see a particular film this evening and, in fact, has invited you to go. So, given your desire to spend time with her, you have a reason for going to the film in question. Moreover, if there are no other considerations that affect your choice, then not only do you have *a* reason to go to the film with your friend, you have a sufficient, *all-things-considered* reason to go.

However, suppose things are more complicated and it turns out that the film is one that you have recently seen and did not like, and you are quite sure that you would dislike having to sit through it again. So, you clearly have some reason for not going to the film with your friend. Since you have some reason for going and some reason for not going, you have to decide what to do by balancing your competing reasons. In balancing these competing reasons, you are trying to decide which of them is, in this situation at least, most important. Suppose you decide that spending time with your friend is more important in this situation than avoiding the film. All things considered, you decide that you should go.

Let us turn now to Ross. He distinguishes between what he calls a prima facie duty and a duty proper. His distinction here is basically the same as the one we just noted between what you have some reason to do and what you should do all things considered, only here we are concerned with what you have moral reasons to do.

Here is how Ross explains the idea of a prima facie duty:

I suggest 'prima facie duty' or 'conditional duty' as a brief way of referring to the characteristic (quite distinct from that of being a duty proper) which an act has, in virtue of being of a certain kind (e.g., the keeping of a promise), of being an act which would be a duty proper were it not at the same time of another kind which is morally significant. (Ross 1930, 19–20)

Let us illustrate the idea of a prima facie duty using Ross's own example of keeping a promise. Suppose that I have promised to meet you at a specific time and place in order to help you with a writing assignment. My act of meeting you at the specific time and place has a certain feature or characteristic; namely, it is an instance of keeping a promise. This fact about my act is morally relevant (significant) and provides a moral reason in favor of my doing the act. Ross would say that because of this fact about my act, the act is a prima facie duty. To say that the action in question is a prima facie duty is to say that (1) it possesses some morally relevant feature that counts in favor of my doing the act and (2) this feature is such that were it the only morally relevant feature of my situation, then the act in question would be my duty proper.

Unfortunately, Ross's term "prima facie" is misleading, as he himself points out. It suggests that what he has in mind is some action that *at first glance* seems to be one's duty but which, upon closer inspection, is not. But this isn't what he means. Some action is a prima facie duty if it does in fact possess some morally relevant feature that counts in favor of doing the action. Perhaps a way of seeing what Ross has in mind is to notice that calling an action a prima facie duty is to consider it under a single description—a description that picks out a morally relevant feature of the action. Thus, to classify an action as a prima facie duty is to zero in on one aspect or feature of the action that has a bearing on its rightness or wrongness. As we shall see below in section 5, whether an action is what Ross calls a duty proper (and thus something that we are morally required to do) depends on all of its morally relevant features. But first, let us focus on Ross's list of basic prima facie duties.

4. Basic Prima Facie Duties

According to Ross, there are seven basic prima facie duties, each of which is featured in a moral rule. Here is a brief characterization of each.

- *Duties of fidelity.* Some duties of fidelity depend on our having made an explicit promise to some party, which grounds a prima facie duty to keep one's promise. But Ross also recognizes an implicit promise to be truthful that we all can normally be assumed to make when we engage in conversation with others. So this type of duty includes the duty to avoid lying and deception.

- *Duties of reparation.* These duties depend on our having in the past performed a wrongful act in regard to others. So the fact that an action would make up for a past wrong is a morally relevant feature of the act and is a reason for performing the action.

- *Duties of gratitude.* This category of duty concerns our being benefited by others. The fact that an action of mine would constitute paying back one of my beneficiaries is a fundamentally morally relevant feature and makes the action of gratitude a prima facie duty.

- *Duties of justice.* Duties of justice here concern distribution of benefits among persons according to merit. So, for example, if someone is getting more or less than that person deserves, then (assuming I can do something about it) this fact gives me a moral reason to rectify the situation.

- *Duties of beneficence.* We are often in a position to help others improve their character or their intelligence, or increase their pleasure and reduce their pain. That some action we could perform would result in such benefits to others is a fundamental morally relevant feature and grounds a prima facie duty of beneficence.

- *Duties of self-improvement.* Actions through which we would improve our own character or intelligence are actions we have a prima facie duty to perform.

- *Duties of nonmaleficence.* In addition to duties of beneficence, Ross recognizes a prima facie duty to avoid injuring others. The fact that an action of mine would in some way injure another person is a feature of an action that counts against doing it, and therefore I have a prima facie duty not to perform any such action.

Ross recognizes additional prima facie duties, but he claims that they can be understood as arising from a combination of the basic ones on his list. Such prima facie duties are nonbasic. For instance, according to Ross, the prime facie duty to obey the laws of one's country results from the three basic prima facie duties of gratitude, fidelity, and beneficence:

> The duty of obeying the laws of one's country arises partly . . . from the duty of gratitude for the benefits one has received from it; partly from the implicit promise to obey [those laws]; and partly (if we are fortunate in our country) from the fact that its laws are potent instruments for the general good. (Ross 1930, 27–28)

How does Ross attempt to justify this list of basic prima facie duties? In striking contrast to those moral philosophers who would attempt to prove moral principles or rules, Ross claims that because his seven basic rules of right conduct are self-evident, they need no proof:

> That an act, *qua* fulfilling a promise, or *qua* effecting a just distribution of goods, or *qua* returning services rendered, or *qua* promoting the good of others, or *qua* promoting the virtue or insight of the agent, is *prima facie* right, is self-evident; not in the sense that it is evident from the beginning of our lives, or as soon as we attend to the proposition for the first time, but in the sense that when we have reached sufficient mental maturity and have given sufficient attention to the proposition it is evident without any need of proof, or of evidence beyond itself. It is self-evident just as a mathematical axiom, or the validity of a form of inference, is evident.... In both cases we are dealing with propositions that cannot be proved, but that just as certainly need no proof. (Ross 1930, 29–30)

Intuitionism in epistemology is the view that there are propositions expressing truths that can be understood and seen to be true (or at least justifiably held) without relying on independent evidence; their truth can be grasped by an exercise of intuition.[4] Ross's own brand of intuitionism involves some important complexity that we cannot pause to consider here, though we will return to it briefly in section 11. Let us turn instead to a statement of his theory of right conduct.

5. Ross's Theory of Right Conduct

Just as there are features of certain actions that morally favor the doing of them, there are features of certain actions that count morally against the doing of them. Duties of nonmaleficence represent clear examples of features that count against a course of action. Ross thus distinguishes between *prima facie right-making features* and *prima facie wrong-making features*. As the labels suggest, the former refers to any feature of an action that makes it prima facie obligatory (a prima facie duty), while the latter refers to any feature of an action that makes it prima facie wrong. We have already noted that, according to Ross's view, one's actual duty (duty proper) depends upon *all* the morally relevant features present in the situation. Furthermore, in the following passage, he makes it clear that one's actual duty depends on a *comparison* of various alternative actions open to one in a given situation.

> [R]ight acts can be distinguished from wrong acts only as being those which, of all those possible for the agent in the circumstances, have the greatest balance of *prima facie* rightness, in those respects in which they are *prima facie* right, over their *prima facie* wrongness, in those respects in which they are prima facie wrong. . . . For the estimation of the comparative stringency of

these prima facie obligations no general rules can, so far as I can see, be laid down. (Ross 1930, 41)

The idea is that in situations in which there is but one prima facie duty, one's actual duty is solely determined by that lone prima facie duty. Suppose, for example, there is someone who needs help and I am in a position to help her. As already noted, this fact about my situation grounds a prima facie duty of beneficence to help. Now if, in the situation at hand, there are no other morally relevant features grounding any other prima facie duties, then my prima facie duty of beneficence is also my actual, all-things-considered duty. However, Ross thinks that most situations in life calling for a moral response are not this simple. Rather, he thinks that in most situations we will be confronted with conflicting prima facie duties, and what he refers to as the "most stringent" of these duties is one's actual duty. To say that one prima facie duty is more stringent than another, competing prima facie duty is not, however, to say that the latter prima facie duty is somehow canceled out or "silenced." Rather, the idea is that in such situations, one prima facie duty overrides other, competing prima facie duties. Consequently, in cases where one prima facie duty is present but overridden, this fact about the situation may generate a further prima facie duty. For instance, in the case where I ought to break my promise to meet you in order to help an accident victim, the fact that my prima facie duty to keep my promise is overridden (but not canceled) means that I now have a new prima facie duty of reparation—to do what is necessary to make it up to you.

Making use of the idea that in particular contexts some prima facie duties are more stringent than others, we can thus set forth the theory of right conduct associated with Ross's view as follows.

Theory of Right Conduct

An action A is *obligatory* (one's actual duty) if and only if one has a prima facie duty to do A that is more stringent than any other conflicting prima facie duty that may be present.

An action A is *wrong* if and only if there is some alternative action open to one in the situation that, compared to A, one has a more stringent prima facie duty to perform.

An action A is *optional* if and only if in the situation either (i) one has no prima facie duties, or (ii) A and at least one other alternative action are equally stringent and of greater stringency than any other action one may have a prima facie duty to perform.

According to Ross's theory of right action, then, what makes some particular action right or wrong depends on the presence of basic right-making and/or wrong-making features and their comparative stringency.

Now that we have the rudiments of Ross's theory of right conduct before us, let us return to conflict of duty situations, which seem to pose a problem for pluralists.

6. Conflict of Duty Situations Revisited

In section 2, we noted that any plausible version of moral pluralism must avoid both the consistency and the adjudication problems that concern conflict of duty situations. This section and the next explain how Ross handles them.

The consistency problem, recall, is that in cases of moral conflict, where two or more rules apply and together they yield inconsistent moral verdicts, nonlexical pluralism apparently fails to avoid contradiction. In the example we were using to illustrate this problem, the two moral rules

P1 You ought to keep your promises

P2 You ought to render aid to those in need

both apply and lead to contradictory moral verdicts about what one ought to do.

The problem obviously stems from the fact that, as stated, both rules express absolute, exceptionless requirements. Since the moral rules expressing prima facie duties are clearly not exceptionless—the fact that they allow exceptions is built right into them—Ross avoids the problem. So, on behalf of Ross, we can replace the original rules with these:

RP1 Prima facie you ought to keep your promises.

RP2 Prima facie you ought to render aid to those in need.

Obviously, softening the two original rules in this way allows that when a situation arises in which they both apply, but in which the agent cannot both keep a promise and render aid, one of the two prima facie duties is overridden and so gives way to the other. We don't end up with contradictory moral verdicts. Ross's theory, with its rules of prima facie duty, thus avoids the consistency problem.

But notice that resolving the consistency problem in this way does not tell us *how* we are to resolve moral conflicts. We are still left with the adjudication problem. Ross tells us (in the last passage quoted above) that there seem to be no rules that govern questions of comparative stringency in particular contexts, so how are we to make reasonable judgments about our all-things-considered duties?

7. The Role of Moral Judgment

It is Ross's view that coming to all-things-considered moral verdicts about a particular action in contexts where there are conflicting prima facie duties requires *moral judgment*. Such judgment is to be understood as a capacity for balancing and weighing competing moral considerations and determining which of them (if any) is most stringent—a capacity that is not simply a matter of following principles or rules. Moral judgment takes us beyond moral rules and involves a kind of "creative insight" into the situation under consideration in determining what ought or ought not to be done.[5] Ross points out that

> In this respect the judgment as to the rightness of a particular act is just like the judgment as to the beauty of a particular natural object or work of art. A poem is, for instance, in respect of certain qualities beautiful and in respect of certain others not beautiful; and our judgment as to the degree of beauty it possesses on the whole is never reached by logical reasoning from the apprehension of its particular beauties or particular defects. (Ross 1930, 31)

In making aesthetic judgments about the beauty of some particular object, there are no precise principles or rules whose application yields a determinate aesthetic verdict; rather, in arriving at an overall aesthetic assessment, one must rely on aesthetic judgment. Similarly, in judging the rightness of some particular concrete action, all one can do is to examine carefully the various morally relevant facts of the case, determine which prima facie duties one has in the situation, and use one's capacity for moral judgment in coming to a conclusion about one's all-things-considered duty. If one's capacity for moral judgment is sufficiently developed, one will be able to arrive at a correct judgment about one's actual, all-things-considered duty. Of course, many situations involve a good deal of moral complexity, and Ross cautions that we should not expect to be to able to judge our all-things-considered duties with certainty.

The role of moral judgment, then, in coming to all-things-considered moral verdicts in particular cases is Ross's way of handling the adjudication problem.

Let us now continue our survey of Ross's pluralism by turning to his theory of value.

8. Ross's Theory of Value

Just as Ross is a pluralist about right and wrong, he is also a pluralist about value. According to Ross, there are four basic kinds of intrinsic good: *virtue, pleasure, the state consisting of pleasure in proportion to virtue,* and *knowledge.*

Ross's manner of arguing for these goods involves having his readers engage in thought experiments comparing two states of the universe, one that
lacks some good under scrutiny and another state identical to the first but
containing the good in question. For instance, in arguing that virtue is intrinsically good, Ross remarks:

> It seems clear that we regard all such [virtuous] actions and dispositions as
> having value in themselves apart from any consequence. And if one is inclined
> to doubt this and to think that, say, pleasure alone is intrinsically good, it seems
> to me enough to ask the question whether, of two states of the universe hold-
> ing equal amounts of pleasure, we should really think no better of one in
> which the actions and dispositions of all persons in it were thoroughly virtu-
> ous than of one in which they were highly vicious. To this there can be but
> one answer. (Ross 1930, 134)

With regard to the completeness of his list, Ross makes two observations. First, he reports that he is not able to think of some other item that
is intrinsically good and not merely either a species of one or other of the
four intrinsic goods on his list or reducible to some combination of them.
Aesthetic enjoyment, for instance, seems to be a combination of pleasure
and insight into (and hence a kind of knowledge about) the object of enjoyment. Hence, such enjoyment is reducible to a combination of pleasure
and knowledge—no need to add it to the list of basic intrinsic goods.

The second observation in defense of his list is that it fits with a widely
recognized classification of basic elements of the mind or soul into the faculties of cognition, feeling, and conation. Knowledge is an ideal state of
cognition, pleasure is an ideal state of feeling, virtue (which has primarily
to do with desire) is an ideal state of conation, and pleasure in proportion
to virtue represents an ideal relation between the feeling and conative parts
of the mind.

Moral Value

Moral goodness has to do with one's having a virtuous disposition, and,
for Ross, being virtuous is a matter of having and acting on certain motives. Ross identifies motives with desires, so virtue is a matter of having
and acting on certain desires that themselves are morally good.

Like Kant, Ross holds that the motive of duty has intrinsic moral worth,
but he also recognizes two other motives possessing such worth.[6] First,
there is the direct desire to produce good, which includes the desire to improve the character of persons (ourselves included) and the desire to improve the intellectual condition of persons (again, ourselves included). Second, Ross recognizes the desire to produce some pleasure or prevent some
pain for other beings as having intrinsic moral worth.

In recognizing three irreducibly basic types of morally valuable motives,

Ross again proceeds by inviting his readers to consider "what we really think" about matters of value (which can be facilitated through the use of thought experiments) in coming to reasonable conclusions about what are the basic types of intrinsic goods and what kinds of motives are morally good.

Now that we have Ross's pluralist theories of right conduct and value before us, how are they related?

9. The Structure of Ross's Moral Theory

It turns out that Ross's theory exhibits an interesting and complex structure. Some of Ross's prima facie duties have to do with the effects of our actions on others and ourselves. The duty of justice concerns bringing about a proper proportion of pleasure (or happiness) and virtue—one of the four basic intrinsic goods. The duties of beneficence and self-improvement concern production of the goods of pleasure, knowledge, and virtue in others and of virtue and knowledge in ourselves. Thus, commenting on the prima facie duty of justice, Ross says that it, along "with beneficence and self-improvement, comes under the general principle that we should produce as much good as possible" (Ross 1930, 27).

The prima facie duty of nonmaleficence requires that we refrain from harming others in various ways and that we thus refrain, as much as possible, from producing bad consequences. So these four prima facie duties, resting on a conception of good and bad consequences, may be called "value-based" prima facie duties.

By contrast, duties of "special obligation" are related by the fact that they concern past actions of ourselves or others and include the prima facie duties of fidelity, gratitude, and reparation. So, on Ross's view, there are two main types of duty, some based on considerations of value, others not. Figure 8.1 summarizes these two groups. Thus, part of Ross's theory of right conduct depends on his theory of value; part of it does not.

Figure 8.1 Basic Prima Facie Duties in Ross's Moral System

VALUE-BASED DUTIES	DUTIES OF SPECIAL OBLIGATION
Beneficence	Fidelity
Self-Improvement	Gratitude
Justice	Reparation
Nonmaleficence	

10. Summary of Ross's Moral Pluralism

In section 1, we noted that pluralist theories of right make two central claims. Let us restate them to allow for pluralist theories of value and then add some items to the list to capture some distinctive aspects of Ross's pluralism.[7]

1. There is a plurality of basic moral rules and a plurality of basic intrinsic goods.

2. There is no underlying moral principle that serves to justify these moral rules, nor is there some intrinsic good underlying the plurality of basic intrinsic goods.

3. These different rules and values may conflict.

4. There is no fixed priority of rules or values that resolves such conflicts.

5. Moral judgment—a capacity for adjudicating conflicts that cannot be fully captured by principles or rules—is needed to reach determinate moral verdicts in certain cases.

Because there is no underlying superprinciple or value (tenet 2), and because there is no fixed priority among the plurality of basic moral rules or values (tenet 4), Ross's theory is a clear example of what I have been calling *limited* moral pluralism. The *theory*—composed of various rules and values—is limited in its power to yield determinate all-things-considered verdicts about the right and the good.

11. Evaluation of Ross's Theory

Ross's theory of right conduct has some notable advantages in being able to accommodate certain deep-seated features of commonsense morality. (Here, we are employing the standard of intuitive appeal.) First, it fits nicely with how ordinary folks reason about matters of morality. In contexts calling for moral deliberation we are normally confronted with competing moral demands and have to judge which demand, from among the competitors, has the greatest moral weight in the case at hand. Ross's view fairly accurately describes this very common manner of moral deliberation.

Second, Ross's theory accommodates the intuitively appealing idea that personal relationships have moral significance. The fact that we have made a promise to someone, and thus entered into a kind of relationship with some specific individual, counts, and counts directly in determining what we ought to do in response. Most forms of consequentialism do not attribute any direct significance to such facts. Rather, for a consequentialist view, a moral obligation to keep a promise directly depends on the values of the consequences of keeping it; the fact that one promised has no intrinsic moral significance as it does for Ross.

Third, as we have seen, Ross's view deals plausibly with conflict of duty situations. As we have seen, on Ross's view, rules of prima facie duty can, in cases of conflict, be overridden, and thus his theory avoids the kind of inconsistency that threatens whenever supposedly exceptionless moral rules come into conflict. Ross's theory apparently satisfies the standard of consistency.

Ross's theory of right conduct and his theory of value seem to fit well, and thus receive some support from, our considered moral beliefs. We have just noted that Ross's theory of right conduct nicely accommodates certain of our beliefs about the moral importance of personal relationships. This belief about morality is reflected in some of our considered moral beliefs as when, for example, we judge that even if a sum of money that I have reserved for my daughter's education could be given to a more promising and needy student, my prima facie obligation to support my daughter, because she is my daughter, is of greater stringency than any prima facie obligation I have toward the education of some other individual.

Again, Ross's pluralism about what sorts of things have intrinsic value and what sorts of motives have moral value fits better with commonsense views on these matters than does, for example, hedonism about intrinsic value and a rigoristic view of moral goodness that, following Kant, only recognizes the motive of duty as having genuine moral worth.

All in all, then, Ross's moral theory seems to satisfy the standard of internal support.[8] However, before turning to some objections to Ross's theory, we ought to take notice of something that was mentioned very briefly in chapter 1 (note 6) concerning the standard of internal support. As explained in chapter 1, the principles or rules of a moral theory are said to enjoy internal support when they (together with any relevant nonmoral factual information) entail our considered moral beliefs. By contrast, when moral theories feature principles or rules whose implications conflict with our considered moral beliefs, that counts against those principles or rules. In this way, our considered moral beliefs are taken to be a basis for testing moral principles and rules.[9] However, the principles or rules of a moral theory may be consistent with our considered moral beliefs but fail to entail them. This is the case with the rules of prima facie duty featured in Ross's theory, and it is worth pausing to explain this point in a bit more detail.

As we have seen, the rules of prima facie duty featured in Ross's theory of right conduct do not (together with relevant nonmoral factual information) entail determinate moral verdicts in a wide range of cases. Thus, they do not enjoy the kind of strong internal support that a principle or rule enjoys when it does entail our considered moral beliefs. But although the rules of prima facie duty do not entail determinate moral verdicts, they do seem to be at least largely consistent with our considered moral beliefs. Let us say that when the principles or rules of a moral theory are consistent with our considered moral beliefs, this fact provides *weak internal support* for those principles or rules. And when the principles or rules of some theory (together with relevant nonmoral factual information) entail our considered moral beliefs (or a wide range of them), then let us say that this fact provides *strong internal support* for those principles or rules.

Given the distinction between strong and weak internal support, we must conclude that Ross's theory of right conduct enjoys only weak internal support from our considered moral beliefs.

Despite its advantages, Ross's theory faces certain challenges that concern (1) the apparent unconnectedness of the various prima facie duties, (2) its apparent overdemandingness, (3) its indeterminacy, (4) the apparent arbitrariness of moral judgment, and (5) its intuitionist epistemology. I will take these up in order.

The Unconnected-Heap Problem

Ross's seven basic prima facie duties seem unconnected—a heap of duties with nothing that ties them together so that they can be clearly understood as representing *moral* requirements. Call this the *unconnected-heap problem*.

One plausible response to this problem has been proposed by Robert Audi. His idea is that we can make use of Kant's notion of treating humanity as an end in itself (and never merely as a means), or, more simply, the notion of respect for persons, and view Ross's basic prima facie duties as interconnected by this basic moral notion. Here is how Audi explains his proposal:

> Is it not plausible to hold that in lying, breaking promises, subjugating, torturing, and the like one is using people merely as a means? And in keeping faith with people, acting benevolently toward them, and extending them justice, is one not treating them as ends, roughly in the sense of beings with intrinsic value (or whose experiences have intrinsic value)? The point is not that Ross's principles can be deduced from the categorical imperative . . . rather, the intrinsic end formulation of the imperative expresses an ideal that renders the principles of duty intelligible or even expectable. (Audi 1997, 48)

In discussing critically Kant's Humanity formulation of the Categorical Imperative, I pointed out that the notion of treating persons as ends in themselves (respecting persons) is vague and there is reason to be dubious of Kant's attempt to use this formulation of his supreme principle for purposes of *deriving* a system of duties. One way to put Audi's proposal is that we can view Ross's moral rules as an interpretation of the vague notion of respect for persons and, in doing so, be able to view them as having a kind of interconnection that makes sense of the idea that they express moral requirements.

But aside from this way of answering the unconnected-heap complaint, Ross would no doubt remind us that in doing moral theory "it is more important that our theory fit the facts than that it be simple" (Ross 1930, 19). Given Audi's proposal and Ross's reminder, I don't think that this objection has much force against Ross's theory.

The Overdemandingness Problem

Ross claims that the value-based prima facie duties oblige us to "produce as much good as possible," or, in the case of nonmaleficence, to minimize the bad effects of our actions on others. So, he concludes that in almost all situations, we are confronted with some actual duty to discharge.

> It is obvious that any of the acts that we do has countless effects, directly or indirectly on countless people, and the probability is that any act, however right it may be, will have adverse effects (though these may be very trivial) on some innocent people. Similarly, any wrong act will probably have beneficial effects on some deserving people. Every act therefore, viewed in some aspects, will be prima facie right, and viewed in others prima facie wrong. (Ross 1930, 41)

So, on Ross's theory, we are obligated to maximize the good unless there is some prima facie duty, representing a special obligation like fidelity, that is, in the situation, more stringent. But if I am just lying around on some Sunday afternoon taking it easy, it seems implausible to suppose what I am doing is morally wrong (given that I could go help someone). Ross's moral theory seems overdemanding in its claim that on all or most occasions we have some duty or other to discharge. In this way, it suffers from the same sort of problem typically raised against maximizing versions of utilitarianism that we considered in section 2 of chapter 6; that is, it fails to fit with certain of our considered moral beliefs.

One response on behalf of Ross would be to distinguish between something's being a moral *consideration* that favors performing some action and something's counting as a ground for a prima facie duty. The sort of distinction at work here is described by David McNaughton:

> The view that moral *requirements* provide reasons for acting which override other kinds of reason must be distinguished from the view that moral *considerations* always override other reasons for acting. The latter view would commit us to saying that any moral reason, however weak, always outweighs any other reason, however strong. But there are situations where, although there

are moral reasons in favour of a certain action they are not decisive; they do not constitute a requirement that one acts in that way. (McNaughton 1988, 115)

Following McNaughton's proposal (modified to apply to Ross's view), we could say that the fact that in a situation there is some action I could perform that would benefit others is a moral *consideration* that favors acting accordingly, but this kind of consideration does not ground a prima facie *requirement.* On the other hand, the fact that some specific person has been injured and I am the only one around who can help her (and I realize this fact) is an example where such facts do ground a prima facie duty of beneficence. The upshot would be that only in some circumstances do facts about helping others ground a prima facie duty; in most other contexts, the fact that I could do something or other to help someone or other only gives me some moral reason to act accordingly but does not ground a prima facie duty to so act. Of course, one would have to say something about when one is in a context involving a prima facie obligation of beneficence and when one is only confronted with a moral consideration of beneficence. However, if this could be done, then this is one way Ross's theory would avoid the problem of overdemandingness.

The Problem of Indeterminacy

I turn now to the charge of indeterminacy. A moral theory is indeterminate when, with respect to some moral issue or range of issues, it fails to yield moral verdicts about such cases—it fails to imply any unambiguous conclusion about the deontic status of the actions in question. Moral theories whose basic principles or rules rely on concepts that are excessively vague typically manifest indeterminacy. Although all or most moral theories can be expected to be somewhat indeterminate (owing to the fact that all concepts likely to be featured in the principles or rules of the theory will be somewhat vague), the more determinate the theory the better, according to the standard of determinacy for evaluating moral theories.

Ross's theory is guilty of being indeterminate when it comes to verdicts about one's actual duty since the rules of the theory fail to imply any determinate conclusions about such duties. But this is not because of excessive vagueness with respect to the various nonmoral concepts that pick out prima facie right-making and prima facie wrong-making features of actions. Concepts like promising, reparation, self-improvement, and the others featured in the rules of prima facie duty are reasonably clear. Indeed, at the level of judgments about one's prima facie duties, Ross's theory does not suffer from indeterminacy: in a wide range of cases it yields determinate verdicts about one's prima facie duties.

Moreover, the indeterminacy at the level of judgments of one's actual duties is perhaps not so worrisome since such indeterminacy is explicable as part of the very type of moral theory that Ross is defending. After all, Ross stresses the need for a moral theory that fits the complexity of moral phenomena, and such complexity (so he might plead) imposes a limit on how determinate a set of moral principles or rules that compose a moral theory can be. So, in the end, I would argue that the fact that Ross's theory is indeterminate when it comes to judgments about our actual duties is not a troublesome objection to his theory.

Moral Judgment and the Problem of Arbitrariness

Moral judgment of the sort involved in balancing and weighing competing prima facie duties and coming to a conclusion about one's all-things-considered duty has struck some philosophers as suspect. By definition, such judgment is not simply a matter of applying principles or rules that then yield a correct moral conclusion about some particular case. But then, why suppose the deliverances of moral judgment are anything but arbitrary from the point of view of rationality? To sharpen the objection, let us work with an example.

Consider a case in which the issue is whether it is morally permissible for a physician to engage in euthanasia in a particular case. Suppose that the individual is experiencing very severe pain (about which little can be done), is going to die in a matter of days, and is asking to be given a life-ending drug. In such a case, consideration of the patient's medical situation arguably grounds a prima facie duty to honor the request. On the other hand, the fact that bringing about the patient's death in this way would be a matter of knowingly and intentionally bringing about the death of an innocent person arguably grounds a prima facie duty to refrain from administering the drug. Now consider a thoughtful, well-educated individual contemplating this case whose moral sensibility (when it comes to matters of life and death) involves a deep feeling for the sanctity of human life. Such a person might, upon due consideration, conclude that the prima facie duty not to intentionally take an innocent human life is more stringent than the duty to alleviate the patient's pain. But no doubt there are thoughtful, well-educated individuals who, upon considering the case carefully, would judge that the prima facie duty to alleviate pain, at least in this case, overrides the opposing prima facie duty. People seem to vary quite a lot in their moral sensibilities, and thus one can expect quite a bit of variation in the all-things-considered judgments that thoughtful people will make in contemplating the very same cases. Thus, isn't the overall Rossian account of moral decision making unacceptably arbitrary?

Notice that this complaint is not saying that Ross's theory allows people to judge their actual duties without having any reasons to back up their judgments. Quite the contrary: thoughtful, well-educated people will be able to advance reasons (at least in principle) for the moral conclusions they draw in cases involving conflicts of duties. Rather, the complaint here is that the conclusion about actual duties that one arrives at will depend on one's moral sensibility, and since thoughtful people's moral sensibilities often differ, and since Ross gives us no clue for determining which from among conflicting sensibilities might be correct, there is a kind of arbitrariness in coming to conclusions about actual duties on the basis of moral judgment.

Although a full response to this objection is not possible here, three points are worth stressing. First, philosophers who are suspicious of moral judgment often point to natural science as a model of rational inquiry, assume that such inquiry is completely rule governed, and draw the conclusion that a view like Ross's that relies on moral judgment is defective. But recently some philosophers of science have argued that scientific rationality must make room for scientific judgment—a capacity for evaluating evidence and coming to reasonable scientific conclusions that goes beyond following rules.[10] If judgment is involved in scientific inquiry and if scientific inquiry is our very model of nonarbritrary, rational inquiry, then reaching moral verdicts by the use of the moral judgment need not be an arbitrary matter.

Second, we have been focusing on judgment that is involved in adjudicating conflicts among prima facie duties. But even moral theories that do not explicitly recognize a role for this adjudicative kind of moral judgment must admit that judgment is involved in the application of principles or rules to particular cases. In order to apply a rule against lying to a particular case, one must be able to determine that the act in question is an instance of lying. Now suppose that such a determination is a matter of applying some rule—a rule for applying moral rules. Then won't there have to be some further rule for applying the rule for applying moral rules? And then won't there have to be yet another rule for applying this further rule? Clearly, to avoid an infinite series of rules and rules for applying rules, we must recognize that applying a rule involves a capacity for what we are calling judgment. And if judgment is involved in the application of rules and principles, and if the process is not unacceptably arbitrary, then why suppose that judgment involved in adjudicating moral conflicts is unacceptably arbitrary?

Finally, in response to the arbitrariness objection we should allow that "moral ties" are possible. Perhaps in some cases, like the euthanasia case described above, the correct moral conclusion to draw is that both refraining from the act of euthanasia and engaging in it are morally permissible. This possibility is allowed for, given how the deontic category of the morally optional was defined for Ross's theory. One situation in which an action is morally optional for Ross is when there are competing prima facie duties that are equally stringent.

These brief remarks are by no means enough to answer fully the arbitrariness charge that some have raised against moral judgment. But investigating such a matter further would take us well beyond our survey of moral theories.[11]

Intuitionism

Recall that intuitionism in ethics is the view that some moral claims are self-evident and can be known through an appropriate grasp of those claims. Throughout the last half of the twentieth century, intuitionism (as an account of the justification of moral judgments) was largely dismissed by most moral philosophers. Recently, the situation has changed, and this view has been revived and ably defended.[12] Space does not permit us to examine the various philosophical issues raised by intuitionism. Instead, it should be noted that even if one rejects an intuitionist moral epistemology, this does not mean that one is thereby entitled to reject Ross's moral pluralism. Far from it. If it turns out that Ross's theory does a better job than any of its competitors in explaining the nature of right and wrong action—if, that is, it more adequately satisfies the standard of explanatory power than does its competitors—his theory would enjoy a strong measure of justification. I will say a bit more about this in the conclusion.

12. Conclusion

I believe that Ross's limited moral pluralism can plausibly deal with the unconnected-heap and overdemandingness objections. The theory itself is significantly indeterminate, but fidelity to the complex nature of morality is important, and, arguably, we cannot get more determinacy from theory than we find in a theory like Ross's. Finally, I have noted that even if one rejects epistemological intuitionism, there are other ways to justify a moral theory. In particular, in evaluating Ross's theory in relation to the main theoretical aim of a moral theory, we ought to take seriously the idea that a plurality of basic moral features is needed to adequately explain what makes right actions right and wrong actions wrong. Although I have not mounted a philosophical defense of this kind of pluralism, I do think that some version of limited moral pluralism (Ross's theory being a prime example) ought to be a default position in ethics—a position that more unified theories must unseat.[13]

In the next chapter, we examine some varieties of virtue ethics—a type of moral theory that makes considerations of virtue central in providing an account of right action. As we shall see, what I take to be the most plausible version of this general type of theory is also an example of limited moral pluralism.

Further Reading

Audi, Robert. 1997. "Intuitionism, Pluralism, and the Foundations of Ethics." In *Moral Knowledge and Ethical Character.* New York: Oxford University Press. A defense of ethical intuitionism making use of Ross's moral theory.

Dancy, Jonathan. 1991. "An Ethic of Prima Facie Duties." In *A Companion to Ethics,* ed. Peter Singer. Oxford: Blackwell. A useful presentation and critique of Ross's theory of right conduct.

McNaughton, David. 1996. "An Unconnected Heap of Duties?" *Philosophical Quarterly* 46: 433–47. A defense of Ross's moral pluralism against the unconnected-heap and indeterminacy objections.

Rawls, John. 1971. *A Theory of Justice.* Cambridge: Harvard University Press. Section 7, pp. 34–40, includes a brief critique of moral pluralism (which Rawls calls intuitionism).

Ross, W. D. 1930. *The Right and the Good.* Oxford: Oxford University Press. A classic defense of limited moral pluralism.

———. 1939. *The Foundations of Ethics.* Oxford: Oxford University Press. Contains chapters that further elaborate and defend the moral theory presented in his 1930 book.

Notes

1. See Sartre 1965.

2. Recall from chap. 1 the distinction between moral principles and moral rules regarding right conduct. We are understanding a moral principle as a general moral statement that purports to specify conditions under which any action is right or wrong. A moral rule is less general than a principle and states that some specific type of action is right or wrong.

3. As we shall see later, solving the first problem does not automatically yield a solution to the second.

4. This term is also used to refer to moral pluralism. But pluralism and epistemological intuitionism are independent of one another; a commitment to one does not entail commitment to the other. To avoid confusion, I will only use the term in the epistemological sense explained here.

5. I borrow the term "creative insight" from Charles Larmore (1987, 19).

6. Though, of course, for Kant, the motive of duty is a not a desire.

7. Here, I am following Hooker's (2000, 105) useful summary of Ross-style pluralism.

8. However, see below the discussion of the overdemandingness problem.

9. Though, as pointed out in chap. 1, some philosophers dispute testing moral principles and rules in this way.

10. See, e.g., Brown 1988, chap. 4; and Putnam 1981, chap. 8.

11. See Larmore 1987, chap. 1, for a defense of moral judgment.

12. The work of Robert Audi (1997) has been particularly influential in reviving intuitionism in ethics.

13. For a recent attempt to do just this, see Hooker's (2000) defense of rule consequentialism.

9

Virtue Ethics

We often look to others as models for the type of person we would
like to be because we think they possess certain admirable character
traits. Suppose Kristin has just begun her career as a finance director for a
large company. She relies on directors from other branches within the company for information that she needs to be able to do her job. But she has a
problem with the director from marketing, who is rather difficult to get
along with and who has not been responsive to Kristin's requests for time-
ly information. The matter is delicate because for Kristin to do her job well,
she needs to have a good working relation with her peers from other de-
partments. During a meeting she sees how skillfully a company director,
Linda, is able to interact with combative associates in a manner that is respectful and friendly while at the same time she is able to stand her ground
and make her views known. Over a period of months it becomes clear to
Kristin that Linda is quite skilled at handling difficult interpersonal inter-
actions, and she comes to admire Linda for having an admirable character
trait (call it interpersonal diplomacy) that she would like to develop.

Just as Kristin looks to Linda as someone to be like in certain business
dealings, so in moral thought generally we might look to individuals as
models of the types of persons we would like to be. Jesus, Buddha, Socrates,
Martin Luther King are among the individuals who have been thought to
exemplify certain traits of character and who therefore serve as models of
what sort of person to be.

The main focus of the moral theories we have examined so far has been
on moral questions about what to do. Questions about what sort of person to
be and, in particular, questions about the morality of character have remained
in the background. However, there is a tradition in ethics, going back to Plato
and Aristotle, in which the primary focus of moral inquiry is on questions of
what sort of person to be: excellence of character rather than right conduct is
of primary concern here. Questions about what sort of person to be concern

what sorts of qualities of character it is morally praiseworthy to acquire and maintain. Such qualities are called virtues. In recent times moral theories that take virtue to be central for understanding morality have been called *virtue ethics*. These theories will be the focus of this chapter.

Our study of virtue ethics will begin with some remarks about the nature of virtue, and then we will turn to the moral philosophy of Aristotle, whose work on virtue and morality continues to influence contemporary work in virtue ethics. We will then be in a position to present and critically examine some representative examples of contemporary virtue ethics.

1. What Is a Virtue?

Let us begin with a general characterization of the concept of a virtue and then proceed to illustrate with an example.

A virtue can be roughly described as (1) a relatively fixed trait of character or mind (2) typically involving dispositions to think, feel, and act in certain ways in certain circumstances, and which furthermore (3) is a primary basis for judging the overall moral goodness or worth of persons.

Consider, for example, honesty. To call someone honest is (in part) to attribute to that person a relatively fixed character trait that we can describe in terms of the person's thinking (an intellectual component); feeling (an affective component); and motivation and action (a motivational-behavioral component). Let us focus on each of these elements in turn.

- *Intellectual component.* First, an honest person is someone who has correct beliefs about when it is appropriate to tell the truth, how much of the truth it is appropriate to reveal, and so forth.

- *Affective component.* Second, an honest person is disposed to feel and express approval toward those who tell the truth and feel and express disapproval toward those who lie. An honest person is also disposed to feel guilty, or in some way badly, about her own acts of dishonesty and is likewise disposed to feel good about acts that express her honesty.

- *Motivational-behavioral component.* Finally, the virtue of honesty involves being disposed to tell the truth and avoid telling lies, where one is motivated to do so by a direct concern for honesty. Moreover, a person with this virtue typically, if not always, succeeds in telling the truth on appropriate occasions and avoids lying.

This brief profile of honesty is not intended to express a fully adequate account of this complex trait; far from it. For instance, there is more to the motivational-behavioral component of honesty than truth-telling and the avoidance of lying to others; honesty has partly to do with how one views oneself. Avoiding self-deception is a form of honesty. Moreover, it may be possible to have and exemplify the virtue of honesty without all three components holding true of the honest person. That is, while I have described honesty partly in terms of having a direct concern for the truth, it is arguable whether honesty strictly requires this specific kind of concern and associated motivation. Henry Sidgwick (1838–1900), for instance, claimed that the virtue of veracity (roughly, honesty) centrally involves "a settled resolve to produce in the minds of others impressions exactly correspondent to the facts, whatever his motive may be for doing so" (Sidgwick [1907] 1966, 224). So he would disagree that the veracious person is necessarily motivated by a direct concern for the truth.

However, even if such motivation is not a strict requirement for being an honest or veracious person, it is still true that the honest person who is so motivated can be said to possess the virtue in a most desirable way. After all, such a person enjoys a kind of harmony among her feelings, motives, and behavior that is lacking in someone who, for example, is grudgingly, but nevertheless steadfastly, honest. The point to keep in mind is that virtues may differ among themselves with regard to whether possession of the trait requires some specific motive (or range of motives) and also with regard to how central certain emotional elements are in possessing this or that virtue.

Another important feature of a trait like honesty is that normally it is acquired as a result of confronting over time a number of situations that call on us to be honest. By performing acts of honesty (in those circumstances calling for such actions) one comes to have the relevant set of intellectual, emotional, and motivational components characteristic of this trait. Thus, honesty and, in general, many (if not all) virtues are to be distinguished from excellences that one might have by nature—like a perfect sense of musical pitch, or natural beauty, or good eyesight. We are responsible for the virtues we have, and thus their possession is worthy of praise.

Philosophers often sort virtues into different groups. Most important for our concerns are the moral virtues, a partial list of which would most likely include benevolence, conscientiousness, courage, generosity, gratitude, justice, honesty, loyalty, and temperance. In addition to moral virtues, there are also intellectual virtues, including such acquired traits as open-mindedness, intellectual courage, and perseverance. Other widely recognized virtues like wit, obedience, and thrift, to name just a few, do not clearly belong in either of these categories. I doubt that it is possible to distinguish sharply between the moral and the nonmoral virtues. However, all that is required for our purposes is that we keep in mind clear cases of moral virtues like the ones mentioned above.

Virtue theorists are also interested in hierarchical relationships among the virtues, where the assumption is that some virtues are more basic than others. What are called *cardinal virtues* are most basic in the sense that (1) their being virtues does not depend on their being forms of, or otherwise subordinate to, any other virtue; and (2) all other moral virtues are either forms of, or are subordinate to, them. For example, many ancient Greek philosophers thought there were four cardinal virtues: wisdom, courage, temperance, and justice. Having wisdom—roughly, the disposition to judge correctly about which ends to choose and the best means for obtaining them—requires (or at least is aided by) such virtues as carefulness (in deliberating about means and ends) and ingenuity (in figuring out how to best satisfy a number of ends). These latter two virtues are thus subordinate to wisdom. Christian thinkers like Aquinas identified seven cardinal virtues: the three theological virtues, faith, hope, and love; and the four human virtues of prudence, fortitude, temperance, and justice. William Frankena (1908–94) argued that justice and benevolence are the two cardinal moral virtues.[1] This issue of hierarchy will come up again when we turn to contemporary versions of virtue ethics.

What I have said about the nature of virtue is but the tip of a rather large iceberg. To further our understanding of virtue ethics, let us now consider some of the leading ideas about the role of virtue in the good life that we find in Aristotle's writings.

2. Aristotle on Virtue and the Good Life

Aristotle's *Nicomachean Ethics,* one of the great works of moral philosophy, treats many topics in ethics with insight and subtlety. Most relevant for our purposes is Aristotle's conception of the highest good for human beings and the role that virtue plays in a good life, the rudiments of which are presented in books 1 and 2.

The Highest Good and Eudaimonia

Aristotle begins book 1 by claiming that human activities, including crafts and various forms of investigation, all seem to aim at some end, or good, and hence the good for human beings is apparently some end (or set of ends) at which human activities aim. The highest good, then, would be that end (or set of ends) that is most choiceworthy among the various ends pursued by humans. Aristotle's idea here is that we pursue all sorts of ends, some of them because we think they are a means to, or will contribute to, our obtaining further ends. One aims to do well in, say, a history course one is taking partly because one aims to complete a history major. And one aims to complete the major in order to earn a university degree, which in turn one wants in order to pursue graduate study in that discipline, and so on. In this way, ends can be organized into a hierarchy where the ends lower in the system are pursued for how they contribute to those ends higher up in the system.

The highest good, then, would be some end (or set of ends) that meets the following conditions: it is an end (1) for which all other ends are ultimately pursued, (2) which is pursued for itself, and (3) which is never pursued as a means to any other end. Any such end, in Aristotle's terminology, is *unconditionally complete*. Being unconditionally complete is one mark of the highest good being sought. Another mark is *self-sufficiency*, which an end possesses when having it makes life choiceworthy.

If the highest good must be unconditionally complete and self-sufficient, then ends like wealth are obviously eliminated from consideration, and so are the ends of pleasure and honor. We may choose pleasure and honor for themselves, but they lack unconditional completeness because there is something further for which we choose such ends, namely, *eudaimonia* or, as the Greek is usually translated, happiness (though sometimes it is translated as flourishing). Happiness is unconditionally complete since we pursue happiness as an end for its own sake, never for some further end, and all other ends are pursued for the sake of happiness. Thus, it is supreme among ends. Moreover, a happy life is self-sufficient, since achieving it makes life worth living and lacking in nothing. Thus, for Aristotle, the highest good for humans is a life of eudaimonia, or happiness.

The Function Argument

Of course, equating the highest good for humans with happiness (or flourishing) is not particularly informative; we need to specify further just what a happy human life consists in. Certainly, if we are interested in human happiness, we need to consider the essential nature of human beings, since what will make for a happy life depends crucially on the sort of beings human beings are. What, then, is the essential nature of human beings?

Aristotle answers this question with his so-called function argument, the guiding ideas of which can be set forth in four main steps.

First, we understand the nature of something when we understand its proper function or purpose (its *telos*).[2] Consider an artifact like a paint brush. To understand the nature of a paint brush (what it is), one must understand its purpose or function, which is to apply paint. A similar point can be made with regard to the roles human beings may occupy and the occupations they may have. To occupy the role of a parent involves having and raising children, and if one's occupation is farming, one engages in those activities proper to farming (or a particular kind of farming). Of course, roles and occupations vary from one individual to another. But Aristotle's main idea is that apart from the various roles and occupations one may have, all human beings share a certain common nature in virtue of being human. Furthermore, this common nature can be specified in terms of the function of human beings—a function they have simply in virtue of being human. Step 1 of the argument, then, can be put this way:

1.   The highest good of human beings concerns their purpose or function.

The second step in the function argument is the claim that if we are interested in the highest good of human beings—which we have identified with eudaimonia—then we need to focus on those features of humans that are distinctive of humanity (at least compared to other terrestrial creatures with which we are familiar). Thus, step 2:

2.   The purpose or function of human beings concerns what is distinctive of such beings.

All terrestrial living things participate in life, and plants are capable of nutrition and reproduction, so such capacities are not the focus of human eudaimonia. Furthermore, lower animals are capable of sense perception and locomotion, so these capacities as well cannot be central to human eudaimonia. What is comparatively unique to humans is their rational capacity. In particular, human beings possess both theoretical reason, through which we are able to grasp truths, and practical reason, by means of which we are able to determine which ends to pursue and how best to pursue them. Thus, the third step of the function argument:

3.   Rationality (or the exercise of our rational mental capacities) is what is distinctive of humans and hence its exercise is central in understanding the function of human beings.

From these three steps, then, we can derive the intermediate conclusion:

4.   The highest good of human beings involves the rational exercise of the soul (mind).

Now certainly something having a function can fulfill that function better or worse. There is a difference between a paint brush that can be used to apply paint and one that not only can do this but also applies paint well or in an excellent manner. We distinguish as well between a parent and a truly good parent, a farmer and a good farmer. A similar point applies to humans and the use of their rationality. We can distinguish between someone's merely using their reason and someone's using it well. Now as we know from our previous discussion, a virtue is an acquired disposition whose exercise promotes excellence in feeling and action. Aristotle thus writes, "[T]he virtue of a human being will likewise be the state that makes a human being good and makes him perform his function well" (*NE*,

42/1106a).[3] So the fourth main step in the argument is:

5. The good of a thing is its performing its function well, which, for humans, involves rational activity in accordance with, or guided by, virtue.

Putting this point together with the intermediate conclusion, we can draw the final conclusion of the function argument:

6. The highest good (and hence eudaimonia) of human beings is a life of rational activity of the soul in accordance with virtue.

So Aristotle's function argument attempts to derive a conclusion about the highest good for humans on the basis of facts about the function of such creatures. This argument, as you might expect, is very controversial. But let us not pause here to consider the objections to the argument. Rather, it should be noted that some contemporary virtue ethicists attempt to follow Aristotle in basing a moral theory on claims about eudaimonia, even if they disagree with Aristotle about what constitutes eudaimonia for humans. Later in the chapter, we will return to this issue.

Aristotle's function argument concludes that virtue is central to leading a happy, or eudaimon, life; this conclusion leads him to discuss in some detail the nature of virtue and vice. Among the most interesting doctrines concerning virtue and vice in Aristotle's work are the doctrine of the mean and the reciprocity of the virtues. Let us briefly examine them.

The Doctrine of the Mean

The conclusion of the function argument gives us a somewhat clearer idea of human eudaimonia, but obviously more must be said about the nature of virtue and the specific virtues that are involved in the highest good for humans. Although Aristotle would agree with much of what we said earlier in characterizing virtue, an important ingredient in his definition of virtue is the idea that a moral virtue is, or expresses, a mean between two extremes. Thus, Aristotle writes:

> [V]irtue is concerned with feelings and action, in which excess and deficiency are in error and incur blame, while the intermediate condition is correct and wins praise, which are both proper features of virtue. Virtue, then, is a mean in so far as it aims at what is intermediate. (*NE*, 44/1106b)

This is Aristotle's famous doctrine of the mean. The easiest way to understand it is to work with some examples.

According to Aristotle, courage is a virtue concerned in particular with proper feelings of fear and confidence. Focusing on the emotion of fear, we can say that a person who possesses the virtue of courage is disposed to react to dangerous situations with a proper amount of fear. On appropriate occasions, then, the courageous person avoids the excess of reacting with too much fear, which is typical of the vice of cowardliness, but such a person also avoids the opposite defect of reacting with too little fear, which is typical of the overconfident, rash person. Both cowardly and overconfident individuals fail to respond in the right way to situations of danger, whereas the courageous person experiences the proper amount of fear given the circumstances.

Generosity is a virtue that, for Aristotle, primarily concerns the giving and taking of money. While the generous person gives the right amount to the right people or causes, the ungenerous person fails to give enough or to the right people or causes, while the extravagant person either gives too much or gives to the wrong people or causes. Again, the idea is that between these vices lies the intermediate state of generosity. The truly generous person, then, gives the right amount to the right people and causes. Figure 9.1 lists some of the virtues and associated vices of character recognized by Aristotle.

A further important aspect of Aristotle's conception of the virtues is that in order to possess them, one needs practical intelligence (phronesis).[4] Having the virtue of practical intelligence (intelligence, for short) involves having sound judgment about practical matters. In particular, it involves the capacity to determine the right manner of feeling and action in contexts that

Figure 9.1 Some Virtues and Associated Vices According to Aristotle

VICE (DEFECT)	VIRTUE (MEAN)	VICE (EXCESS)
Cowardliness	Courage	Rashness
Stinginess	Generosity	Extravagance
Insensibility	Temperance (in relation to bodily pleasures)	Intemperance
Self-Deprecation	Truthfulness (about oneself in social contexts)	Boastfulness
Boorishness	Wittiness	Buffoonery
Quarrelsomeness	Friendliness	Flattery

call for some sort of virtuous response. Such judgment cannot be captured by any system of rules; rather it represents a capacity to come to correct judgments about practical matters that cannot be fully captured or reduced simply to the application of rules to particular cases. Intelligence, then, is a higher-order, overarching virtue involved in having the more specific virtues such as generosity, honesty, and benevolence. The role of intelligence in the possession and exercise of the virtues brings us to another interesting thesis about the virtues.

The Reciprocity of the Virtues

Aristotle apparently embraced the idea that having any one virtue requires that one have them all. Although this thesis is often referred to as the unity of the virtues, let us call it the *reciprocity of the virtues thesis* in order to distinguish it from another unity thesis to be introduced below.

Although at first the reciprocity thesis may seem clearly mistaken—after all, can't one be a just person and yet fail to be temperate?—there is a line of reasoning that leads naturally to the thesis. Suppose, for instance, a person is on a military campaign where food and water must be rationed.[5] Justice requires that he take only his fair share of supplies. But unless this person is also temperate, he will not be disposed to take just his fair share. If he is intemperate, he will be disposed to take more than his fair share, thus disposing him to injustice. Thus, being a truly just person requires that one also be temperate.

Now we can engage in a similar line of reasoning beginning with possession of the virtue of temperance that will lead us to conclude that full possession of this virtue requires being a just person as well. Thus, the virtues of justice and temperance are reciprocal: having one requires having the other. If systematic examination of the conditions required for possession of the other moral virtues leads to the same result, we arrive at the reciprocity thesis. I will leave it to the reader to ponder the plausibility of this thesis.

There is another, even more controversial unity thesis associated with the virtues according to which there really is not a plurality of virtues, but a single virtue. According to this *single-virtue thesis*, when we talk about honesty, courage, temperance, justice, and the rest, we are really referring to a single psychological state. Although Aristotle rejects the single-virtue view, Socrates is often cited as one of its proponents. Specifically, the Socratic view is that all virtue is knowledge about what is good and bad for human beings. Thus, to speak of courage is to speak of that part of knowledge of good and bad that concerns proper actions and emotional reactions in circumstances of danger, while to speak of justice is to speak of that part of knowledge of good and bad that concerns such things as proper distribution of goods in society.

In light of what was just said about practical intelligence and the reciprocity of the virtues, one can see how one might be led to embrace this single-virtue thesis. We noted that, according to Aristotle, possession of a virtue requires possession of intelligence, which, in turn, requires possession of all other virtues. But then if intelligence is operative in all cases of virtuous action, shouldn't we conclude that there is just one virtue—intelligence? If so, then what appear to be different character traits are really just aspects of a single complex state of the virtuous individual. Thus, what we call bravery, generosity, honesty, and the rest involve the operation of the all-encompassing virtue of intelligence applied in different circumstances.

While the single-virtue thesis entails the reciprocity thesis (if all virtues are at bottom one, then having one requires having them all), one can hold the latter but reject the former, which seems to have been Aristotle's considered view.[6] Again, I will let the reader ponder the plausibility of the single-virtue thesis and not comment on it here.[7]

We have only scratched the surface of the rich and subtle thought of Aristotle on the virtues and their relation to human eudaimonia. But as I mentioned at the outset, Aristotle's moral views, and his views about practical matters in general, significantly inform contemporary discussions of virtue ethics. So having glanced at some of the main elements in Aristotle's treatment of the virtues and the good life for humans, let us now turn to developments in contemporary virtue ethics, beginning with some general remarks aimed at situating this general type of moral theory with respect to the views featured in the previous chapters.

3. Virtue Ethics: Some General Remarks

Virtue ethics is often distinguished from other moral theories by citing a number of related points of contrast. Thus it is claimed that virtue ethics is "agent-centered" rather than "act-centered," that it is concerned with "being rather than doing," and that it attempts to answer the question, "What sort of person should I be?" rather than "What should I do?"

Such contrasts can be misleading because they suggest that virtue ethics is simply not concerned with questions about right and wrong action and thus is not a rival to the moral theories we have been studying. However, as we shall see, virtue ethics does provide an account of right action that does rival the accounts featured in other moral theories. To see this more clearly, it will help to contrast the overall structure of virtue ethics with the structures characteristic of other, competing views.

As explained in chapter 1, a moral theory has two main components: a theory of right conduct and a theory of value. And within a theory of value, we distinguish accounts of moral and of nonmoral value. Figure 9.2 expands slightly upon the chart from chapter 1 representing these branches.

Figure 9.2 Components of Moral Theory

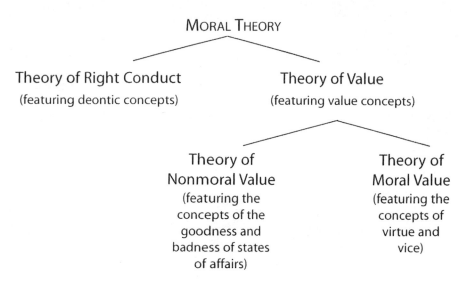

A moral theory is in the business of explaining the connections among the various batches of concepts. If one makes the deontic concepts (and associated categories to which they refer) featured in a theory of right conduct most basic in one's moral theory and then defines the value concepts in terms of the deontic concepts, one's overall moral theory is *duty based*. If, by contrast, one makes one of the two groups of value concepts most basic and defines the remaining two groups of concepts in terms of the most basic group, one's overall moral theory is *value based*. For instance, utilitarianism is a value-based theory featuring a welfarist conception of nonmoral value as most basic. Virtue ethics represents the other route for a value-based theory to go: make the concepts of virtue and vice basic and then use them to define right and wrong action and nonmoral value.

I have been putting the basic contrasts between types of moral theory in terms of concepts and how they are definitionally related. However, one can also express the main differences between types of moral theory in terms of talk about various sorts of facts. So, we can express the basic idea behind virtue ethics as follows:

VE Facts about virtuous agents and, in particular, facts about virtuous character traits possessed by such agents (1) are more basic than facts about right conduct and (2) are what explain why an action is right or wrong.

Notice that virtue ethics does not merely claim that focusing on what the virtuous agent would do can function as a decision procedure in helping us come to conclusions about the morality of actions. This point is worth stressing.

It might be the case that one way of coming to know whether an action is right or wrong in some circumstance is by appealing to what a virtuous agent would do. If, in the circumstance in question, a virtuous agent would refrain from doing A, then that is a reliable sign that A is wrong. But this way of *coming to know* whether an action is right or wrong is compatible with various possible explanations of what *makes* an action right or wrong. Even if one way (perhaps the best way) of coming to know what is right and wrong is by appealing to the choices of a virtuous agent, it might still be the case that what makes an action right or wrong is that it maximizes welfare, and if so, then a utilitarian moral theory provides a correct moral criterion of right conduct. Or, again granting that the best way to determine what one ought to do is by consulting a virtuous agent, it might nevertheless be the case that what makes an action right or wrong is to be explained in terms of how such actions bear on respecting persons, in which case a Kantian moral theory provides a correct moral criterion of right conduct.

What makes virtue ethics distinctive as a moral theory and thus a competitor to utilitarianism, Kant's moral theory, and other theories is the fact that it specifies a moral criterion that differs from these other views. It thus offers us an explanation of right and wrong action in terms of facts about a virtuous agent: an act is right *because* it is what a virtuous person does or would do. This claim about explanatory priority is expressed in VE.

Now in setting forth a theory of right conduct, any version of virtue ethics must accomplish two main tasks. First, it must begin with an account of a virtuous agent since, according to this type of theory, it is facts about the virtuous agent that make an action right or wrong. Accomplishing this first task involves in turn giving an account of a virtuous agent, by (1) specifying those character traits possessed by the agent that are virtues and (2) explaining what makes some character trait a virtue.

Suppose, then, that we are given an account of a virtuous agent, including an account of those character traits that are the virtues. With an account of a virtuous agent in hand, the second main task for virtue ethics is to characterize or define right and wrong action in terms of facts about a virtuous agent. In some circumstances, there are actions that a virtuous agent, guided by her virtuous character traits, would not fail to do. Such actions are obligatory. In other circumstances, there are actions that a virtuous agent would not do because they would express a vice. Such actions are wrong. So, for example, a wrongful act of telling a lie in some circumstance is wrong, according to virtue ethics, because a virtuous person would not tell the lie. And a virtuous person would not tell the lie because doing so would be dishonest, and dishonesty is a vice. And again, in still other circumstances, there are actions that a virtuous agent might (or might not) do, and this fact about them is what makes them optional. Here, then, are the principles of right conduct according to virtue ethics.

Theory of Right Conduct

An action A (performed in certain circumstances) is *obligatory* if and only if A is an action that a virtuous person (acting in character) would perform in the circumstances in question.

An action A (performed in certain circumstances) is *wrong* if and only if A is an action that a virtuous person (acting in character) would not perform in the circumstances in question.

An action A (performed in certain circumstances) is *optional* if and only if A is an action a virtuous person (acting in character) might perform in the circumstances.

Notice that there is an element of idealization built into these definitions. Since we are defining the notions of objective rightness and wrongness, we are to suppose that a model virtuous agent (whose choices and actions are the basis of right and wrong action) is aware of all of the morally relevant features of the circumstances pertaining to the act under evaluation and that the virtuous person (in the circumstances) acts (or refrains from acting) in ways that express the relevant set of virtues. This is why our model virtuous agent is described as "acting in character." We make these stipulations because we recognize that actual virtuous individuals may fail on occasion to exercise some virtue and so may, for example, fail to do the act that is obligatory. The virtuous agent featured in our definitions, then, is free from the kinds of defects that might interfere with an actual virtuous person's acting from virtue.

Much of the focus in the recent literature on virtue ethics concerns the relation between right conduct and virtue. A moral theory counts as a version of virtue ethics if right and wrong action is explained in terms of what a virtuous agent would or would not do. This is expressed above in VE. But VE says nothing about how the category of virtue (moral goodness) is related to the category of nonmoral goodness. There are two main possibilities here.

One might take the notion of nonmoral good as basic and use it to define or explain the virtues. In this case the concept of virtue is derivative or at least not fundamental in one's overall moral theory. For instance, one might take the notion of a happy or flourishing life as fundamental and characterize the virtues as traits that contribute to living a happy life. The

Figure 9.3 Two Main Structures for Virtue Ethics

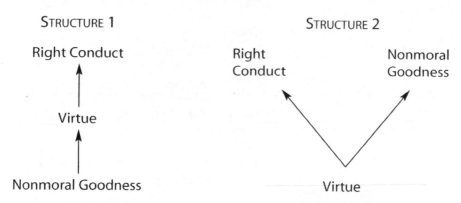

resulting moral theory will have the following structure: (1) a notion of goodness such as eudaimonia is fundamental, (2) virtue is understood in terms of eudaimonia, and (3) right action is in turn characterized in terms of virtue.

The second possibility is to treat virtue as morally fundamental and use it to define or explain both rightness and nonmoral goodness. The idea would be that certain character traits (or aspects of them) are intrinsically valuable—their goodness does not derive from being related to some other good. Moreover, facts about virtue and the life of a virtuous agent can be used to explain what makes a life a good one—a life worth living—and what makes right actions right.

Figure 9.3 shows these two possible structures a virtue ethic might take.[8] Any version of what we are calling virtue ethics features a *virtue-based account of right action*, although those versions conforming to the first structure are not (as a whole) virtue-based moral theories.

Let us now consider some examples of contemporary virtue ethics.

4. An Ethics of Care

One of the most important developments in recent moral theory has been the emergence of what has come to be called *care ethics*, which, as the label indicates, treats care as central for understanding the nature of morality. The development of care ethics was largely sparked by the psychologist Carol Gilligan's 1982 book, *In a Different Voice*. Gilligan's book is concerned to describe a "different moral voice" that she detected in various studies in which women subjects were asked to describe and react to various moral dilemmas. For instance, one study involved twenty-nine pregnant women, ranging in age from fifteen to twenty-three, who were facing the decision of whether to have an abortion. The moral voice of many of these woman represents a moral perspective that Gilligan calls a *care perspective*, which she contrasts with a familiar *justice perspective*.[9] Here is how Gilligan explains some basic points of contrast between these perspectives:

> From a justice perspective, the self as moral agent stands as the figure against a ground of social relationships, judging the conflicting claims of self and others against a standard of equality or equal respect (the Categorical Imperative, the Golden Rule). From a care perspective, the relationship becomes the figure, defining self and others. Within the context of relationship, the self as moral agent perceives and responds to the perception of need. The shift in moral perspective is manifest by a change in the moral question from "What is just?" to "How to respond?" (Gilligan 1987, 23)

Both moral perspectives, then, involve contrasting conceptions of (1) the image of self and its relation to other members of the moral community, (2) the nature of moral problems that arise for members of this community, and (3) how such problems can be rationally resolved. Figure 9.4 summarizes the differences between the justice and care perspectives with respect to these three points of contrast.

In her book, Gilligan argues that although many of her subjects were able to organize and think about a moral issue from either perspective, females tended to approach moral issues from the care perspective, while males tended to employ the justice perspective. Because psychological studies of moral development as well as moral theories have traditionally focused almost exclusively on the justice perspective, part of the importance of Gilligan's work is to bring into focus a moral orientation centered around care.

Inspired by Gilligan's work, some moral philosophers have attempted to develop and defend an ethic of care. The basic idea is that care is fundamental for understanding moral phenomena. Focusing on care as a virtue allows one to develop care ethics as a version of virtue ethics.[10] Let us begin by clarifying the notion of care, and then we will be in a position to present and evaluate an ethic of care understood as a version of virtue ethics.

What Is Care?

It is important to distinguish three senses of the term "care" in English, and hence three types of care.[11] Here is a brief description of each type.

- *Caring for.* To care for something (like ice cream) or some person involves liking and being attracted to the thing or person in question. You might not care for Thai cuisine; I do. I might not care for someone

Figure 9.4 Justice and Care Perspectives Contrasted

POINTS OF CONTRAST	JUSTICE	CARE
Conception of Self	The self as an individual, one among others. Individuality is primary.	The self as a member of various relationships. Relatedness to others is primary.
Nature of Moral Problems	To protect individual interests in a way that preserves equal respect for all. Moral problems in need of resolution center around questions of inequality.	To maintain and foster connections with others. Moral problems in need of resolution center around questions of disconnection and abandonment.
Moral Reasoning	Proper moral reasoning involves viewing matters impartially and appealing to principles in order to resolve moral conflicts.	Proper moral reasoning involves a sensitivity to the particularities of a moral issue. Principles may be of some use but cannot always be used to resolve moral conflicts.

(perhaps because he makes me feel uncomfortable) whereas you do care for him.

- *Having care of.* If something or someone is entrusted to me, I have care of the thing or person in question. Someone may have care of her sick daughter, in the sense of having the responsibility for her well-being. I may have care of your plants and cats while you are away; they are in my charge. Clearly, one may have care of without liking or being attracted to what one has care of, and so one may have care of something without caring for it.

- *Caring about.* To care about something or someone involves "being invested" in that thing or person; it involves regarding that thing or person as important to oneself.[12] Caring about something differs from caring for that thing. A father may not care for his teenage son but care about him. In caring about him, the father's own well-being is tied to his son's. He is delighted when his son excels in sports, is unhappy when he finds that his son has taken up smoking. One can also care for someone in that one likes and is attracted to the person in question, but one may not care about that person because one is rather indifferent toward her well-being.

It is this notion of caring about that is featured in care ethics and so let us focus on it.

Some Dimensions of Caring About

The notion of caring about is complex, and it will help in our understanding of care ethics if we make explicit some of its dimensions.

First, one can care about all sorts of things: persons, ideas, material objects, cultures, and so on. We are particularly interested in caring about persons—both ourselves and others—and in regard to such caring, it is important to distinguish *personal* and *impersonal* care, particularly in relation to caring about others. My caring about someone is personal when it is the particular person in question who is cared about. I care about my daughter because Emily is the person she is. By contrast, I care about someone impersonally when, for example, in a context of helping them, it is not the particular person in question who sparks my care, but the fact that this person is *someone who needs my help*. The identity of the person I help through my impersonal care is irrelevant to my caring; I care about them because they satisfy the description "someone in need" and I care about helping those in need (whoever they are). This distinction will be important later on.

Some other dimensions of caring about involve *breadth* and *degree*. Regarding breadth, one may only care about a small number of people and be indifferent to the rest of humanity; or, at the limit, one may care about all of humanity. But even if one's care extends to everyone, it is likely that there will be differences in one's degrees of caring about. Loving one's family members and friends involves caring about them very deeply. Normally, one's level of care directed toward casual acquaintances is of a lower degree than the sort one has for loved ones, though higher in degree than the level of care one has toward strangers.

We are particularly interested in care as a virtue, where the relevant notion of care is caring about and where, in particular, we are interested in caring about persons. Here, then, is a partial profile of caring about as a virtue:

- *Intellectual component.* Caring about persons (including oneself) involves the capacity to recognize when those cared about are in need, as well as knowing in general what is good for individuals in certain circumstances.

- *Affective component.* Caring about other persons involves being disposed to feel pleasure in response to their successes, pain in response to their failures. The intensity of such pleasures and pains will normally vary in relation to the closeness of the other. In caring about oneself, one is disposed to feel joy at one's successes, unhappiness and perhaps depression over one's failures.

- *Motivational-behavioral component.* Caring about others typically involves a non-self-interested desire to help them—one is disposed to act on someone's behalf out of a direct regard for that person's welfare. Caring about oneself involves wanting to do those things that will best promote one's well-being and wanting to avoid what will be detrimental to one's well-being.

Being a caring person—having the virtue of caring about—is far more complex than is indicated in the above profile. But I trust that enough has been said about the concept of caring about so that we can proceed to examine a version of virtue ethics that takes this concept as central.

A Version of Virtue Ethics Featuring Care

If we let care be the fundamental or cardinal moral virtue, then we can reformulate our generic statement of the principles of right conduct to capture the idea that the virtue of care is central in determining the rightness and wrongness of actions. In doing so, we simply specify that our hypothetical virtuous agent is one with the virtue of caring about—a caring agent.

Theory of Right Conduct: Ethics of Care

An action A (performed in some circumstance) is *obligatory* if and only if A is an action that a caring agent (acting in character) would perform in the circumstances in question.

An action A (performed in some circumstance) is *wrong* if and only if A is an action that a caring agent (acting in character) would not perform in the circumstances in question.

An action A (performed in some circumstance) is *optional* if and only if A is an action that a caring agent (acting in character) might perform in the circumstances in question.

We shall consider the advantages of virtue ethics, as a general type of moral theory, later on in the chapter. What many find especially attractive about an ethics of care is the fact that it can accommodate our sense that special moral significance attaches to those closest to us. This is not, of course, to say that considerations of caring for strangers cannot be more important in some situations than caring for loved ones and friends. But in general we suppose that relationships one has with family and friends have a special moral significance that is not plausibly captured by impartialist views like utilitarianism. Granted, the utilitarian can claim that we are more likely to maximize utility by giving special attention to family and friends, but this sort of indirect explanation of the moral significance of such relations seems less plausible than the account on offer by an ethics of care.

Objections to the Ethics of Care

One objection to the ethics of care is that not all instances of caring about are morally good. This point is developed by Jeffrey Blustein:

> One might care about another person in such a way that one does not leave the other sufficient scope for the expression and development of an independent personality. One might also care too much about x in the sense that x occupies too much of one's attention. My appraisal of x itself might be sound enough and x might not be something or someone that I wish I did not care about, but I might be so preoccupied or obsessed with x that I am prevented from leading a happy and productive life. (Blustein 1991, 40)

Other problematic cases include caring about someone in a way that involves injustice. To help someone in their plan to rob a bank simply to help them accomplish their goals is clearly wrong. Certainly, caring about someone or something is not morally admirable unless such caring is tempered by other moral considerations. The point of these observations is that in developing a care ethic, it is not enough to appeal to the notion of caring about since, as the examples, illustrate, there can be bad forms of such care.

Now in response to this worry, the defender of care ethics has a ready reply. *Genuine* care, according to the care ethicist—the sort of care that exemplifies the *virtue* of caring about—does not, for example, stifle the development of the person who is cared about, because having this virtue normally involves knowing what is in the genuine interests of self and others and being disposed to act accordingly. Since the virtue of caring about normally involves knowledge of what is genuinely good for objects of one's care, and since stifling someone's individuality and autonomy is not good for them, a person who acts as a caring person will care in ways that allow for the expression and development of an independent personality.

Again, in caring, one must understand the impact of one's caring efforts on the immediate recipient of the care and on others who may be affected.

Blindly helping the would-be robber carry out her plan—even if one is motivated by the desire to help—obviously ignores the impact on others and society generally of giving such help. So having the *virtue* of caring about involves having the sort of understanding that guides one's caring activities in ways that avoid bad forms of "care."

This kind of response seems entirely appropriate, but notice what is happening. The virtuous caring person who would avoid helping a criminal carry out some devious plan because of how it would affect the welfare of others is someone whose care is tempered by justice. It would be an act of injustice to help the would-be robber. In other words, the sort of caring about that is good and worthy of admiration is tempered by other virtues like justice. And this observation leads us to the next objection.

Critics of care ethics have argued that the virtue of care (even if the theory features the broad notion of caring about) is not an adequate basis for understanding the entirety of morality.[13] As we have just noticed, justice is required if we are to properly understand certain duties and obligations, and a case can be made for the importance of other virtues as well.

There are two ways in which a care ethicist might attempt to accommodate justice and other virtues. First, she might appeal to the reciprocity thesis and claim that to properly and fully possess a virtue like care requires that one possess certain other virtues. Perhaps one need not suppose that in having one virtue, one must possess *all* the rest. It might be that there is a core set of moral virtues whose possession is a package deal. But then what began as a monistic virtue ethic based on the sole virtue of caring about is now transformed into a pluralist version of virtue ethics featuring a number of basic virtues along with care. But this is to give up a care-*based* virtue ethic.

The second way in which a defender of a care-based virtue ethic might deal with the objection under discussion is to argue that the virtue of care is the most fundamental virtue and all other moral virtues are forms of, or subordinate to, care. Consider, for example, the virtue of honesty. One might argue that honesty is a form of caring about oneself and others. In caring about oneself and others, one cares about a person's capacity for making rational decisions—one cares about their autonomy. And in so caring, one must possess the virtue of honesty since deceiving oneself and others hinders autonomy. In a similar manner, one might claim that temperance is involved in properly caring about oneself.

Now if the care ethicist can incorporate a range of moral virtues in the way just explained, then one seemingly has a way of accommodating our duties and obligations that involves being just, honest, brave, and so forth while retaining a monistic virtue ethic based on care.

But now notice this. If honesty, temperance, justice, courage, and the other moral virtues are understood to be forms of care, then one suspects the notion of care being invoked is so abstract and "thin" that we might as well admit that there is a handful of specific virtues, none of which is more basic than the others. And once we admit this, we end up with a moral theory involving a very abstract moral ideal—the agent who cares about others—and instead of thinking that this ideal can be used to derive more specific virtues, it is more plausible to suppose that it functions as a way of connecting all of the more specific virtues that are the basis of moral evaluation. Let me explain this point a bit further by relating it to some observations we made in connection with Kant's concept of respecting humanity and in connection with Ross's moral pluralism.

In chapter 7 we noted that the idea of respecting humanity (treating someone as an end in themselves) is best understood as a very abstract moral ideal. It is too abstract (so it was suggested) to be the basis of a moral principle that one could use to derive a system of specific moral duties. Rather, as was suggested in chapter 8 in connection with Ross's theory, this ideal serves to connect the various rules of prima facie duty and help us understand why those rules having to do with fidelity, reparation, gratitude, justice, beneficence, self-improvement, and nonmaleficence express *moral* requirements. I am making a similar suggestion about the notion of care.

Once we notice that the broad notion of care featured in care ethics involves other virtues as forms of caring about, then the role of care in a moral theory is analogous to the role of respecting humanity in the theories of Kant and Ross. This means that like Ross's theory (as well as my interpretation of Kant's theory) an ethic of care is best understood as embracing a kind of pluralism, in this case, virtue pluralism. The suggestion, then, is that there is a plurality of equally basic moral virtues that determine moral goodness of persons as well as the basis of the rightness and wrongness of actions. What makes them *moral* virtues is that they can be seen as forms of care.

I am not suggesting that there are no essential differences between, for example, Kant's moral theory and an ethic of care. A care ethic recognizes the moral importance of the sort of care present in relationships of love and friendship—what I have been calling personal care—and this may be missing (and certainly is not emphasized) in Kant's theory. According to Kant's moral theory, one of the two major categories of duties of virtue concerns the happiness and well-being of others. Kant does allow that we can show differential concern and care for those who are close to us: "If one is closer to me than another (in the duty of benevolence) . . . I am therefore under an obligation to greater benevolence to one than to the other."[14] However, this sort of caring about—an impersonal form of caring—involves caring about loved ones and friends *as persons possessing dignity* and not as persons with the particular identities involved in personal care. (You may recall that we noted a similar point about how a utilitarian might account for the value of caring about particular others.)

Even if a care-*based* version of virtue ethics is problematic for the reasons mentioned, we can nevertheless incorporate into a pluralistic version of virtue ethics the idea that moral significance attaches to personal caring. So let us now consider a pluralist version of virtue ethics.

5. Pluralist Virtue Ethics

Pluralist versions of virtue ethics recognize a plurality of basic or cardinal virtues (at least two) that are central in characterizing the notion of a virtuous agent. And for the virtue ethicist, as we have seen, the notion of a virtuous agent is central in explaining the nature of right action. To illustrate, let us work with a version of virtue ethics that recognizes benevolence, courage, generosity, gratitude, justice, honesty, loyalty, and temperance as basic moral virtues. Thus, recalling the principle concerning obligatory actions featured in the virtue ethics theory of right conduct:

> An action A (performed in certain circumstances) is *obligatory* if and only if A is an action that a virtuous person (acting in character) would perform in the circumstances in question.

If we now define a virtuous agent as one who possesses the set of virtues just mentioned, we end up with a more precise principle of obligation:

> An action A (performed in certain circumstances) is *obligatory* if and only if A is an action that a person having the virtues of benevolence, courage, generosity, gratitude, justice, honesty, loyalty, and temperance would perform in the circumstances.

The principles for the categories of the optional and the wrong are specified in a similar manner.

A pluralistic virtue ethic must involve some account of how conflicts among the virtues are to be resolved. Suppose, for example, one of your family members is wanted by the police, and since you know of his whereabouts, you are torn between being truthful and being loyal.[15] In cases where two or more virtue considerations are relevant and indicate incompatible courses of action, what should one do?

I am sympathetic to those virtue ethicists who propose that conflicts among the virtues be understood in a way analogous to how Ross understands conflicts of duty.[16] Ross, you may recall, denies that there is any fixed rank ordering of the basic prima facie duties to which one can appeal in adjudicating conflicts among them. Nor, according to Ross, is there any moral superprinciple or rule that determines how such conflicts are to be adjudicated. Rather, coming to correct moral verdicts in these cases of conflict is a matter of having and using good moral judgment, or *phronesis*.

I believe the most plausible form of pluralist virtue ethics will be similar to Ross's theory in denying that there is any fixed rank ordering of basic virtues to which one can appeal in adjudicating cases where the virtues conflict. That is, in circumstances where considerations involving one virtue favor the performance of an action while considerations involving another virtue favor refraining from that same action, a virtuous agent must use sound moral judgment in coming to a correct verdict about what ought to be done. Of course, this means that the most plausible version of virtue ethics is going to be a version of limited moral pluralism.

Let us now turn from presentation to evaluation of virtue ethics.

6. Evaluation of Virtue Ethics

The recent revival of virtue ethics has been spurred largely by dissatisfaction with other moral theories, particularly Kantian and utilitarian theories. The dissatisfaction centers around the accounts of right action and virtue offered by rivals to virtue ethics.

The main complaint about non-virtue-based accounts of right action is that they attempt to identify abstract moral principles and rules that are then supposed to be applied to particular cases in order to arrive at justified moral judgments about the particular case at hand. Three related criticisms are often raised here. Let us examine them.

First, critics contend that the sorts of principles and rules featured in Kantian and utilitarian moral theories are too abstract to be very helpful in particular cases. This seems particularly true in connection with the Humanity formulation of Kant's Categorical Imperative, which requires that we treat ourselves and others never as mere means but always as ends in ourselves. Because this principle is so abstract, it seems to be useless for purposes of deciding what one ought to do in a wide range of particular cases. Does the practice of capital punishment involve using the one executed as a *mere* means? One finds advocates of this practice claiming that it respects the dignity of those executed and so does not amount to treating them as mere means, but one also finds opponents of capital punishment who claim that the dignity of the executed is violated and so the practice does treat some persons as mere means.

Virtue ethics avoids this problem because, although its account of right action does involve an appeal to abstract principles that make reference to what an ideal virtuous agent would do in certain circumstances, the principles are made more concrete when a specification of the virtues is added to the account.

A second related complaint is that non-virtue-based accounts of right conduct tend to be too reductive, in the sense that they attempt to account for our obligations in terms of some one fundamental morally relevant feature. Kant's theory attempts to account for obligation in terms of whether or not an action treats someone as a mere means, while utilitarianism attempts to account for obligation in terms of whether or not an action maximizes utility. The problem with such accounts of right action, according to the critics, is that they cannot plausibly account for various areas of moral life. In particular, a utilitarian moral theory is not able to account plausibly for special relationships involving family and friends. A pluralist version of virtue ethics, which can and should allow for considerations of caring about particular others, obviously avoids this problem and, in general, does not suffer from trying to account for right and wrong in terms of utility maximization or in terms of any single feature of actions.

Finally, critics often contend that non-virtue-based accounts of right action are unacceptably algorithmic in the way they attempt to deal with concrete moral problems. That is, such accounts seem to involve the idea that anyone who understands the principle of utility or the Universal Law formulation of the Categorical Imperative can mechanically apply it to some concrete situation calling for a moral response and derive a correct moral verdict about what one ought or ought not do. But, according to the critics, such a mechanical approach to moral decision making ignores the important role of moral judgment or phronesis in proper moral judgment and decision making. And, as we have seen, moral judgment plays a crucial role in a virtue-based account of right action.

I hope that it is fairly obvious to the reader that these objections to non-virtue-based approaches to accounts of right action do not favor a virtue-based account over certain non-virtue-based approaches. For example, Ross's non-virtue-based account of right action (1) does not involve overly abstract moral principles that determine the deontic status of individual actions; (2) is not overly reductive; and (3) rejects any algorithmic approach in the process of reaching correct moral verdicts about particular cases by recognizing an important role for moral judgment in this process. I have also argued that other moral theories, including natural law theory, utilitarianism, and Kant's moral theory, when suitably refined, are much like Ross's view in these respects.

So although the features of virtue ethics just mentioned are advantages of the theory over theories that lack them, they do not single out this type of moral theory as superior to all rival moral theories.

Turning from accounts of right action to accounts of virtue, defenders of virtue ethics make a dual complaint about how the virtues are treated by utilitarianism and Kantian approaches. First, the very notion of a virtue is often defined by such theories in terms of motivation, that is, as a matter of simply being disposed to do what is right. Thus, for example, the virtue of honesty is defined simply as the character trait that disposes one to tell the truth and avoid lies on appropriate occasions. One problem with such definitions, according to the critics, is that a virtue-based account of right action is obviously ruled out from the start. Clearly, an account of right action cannot be truly virtue based unless right and wrong action can be explained in terms of virtue or the activities of the virtuous agent without appealing to the concept of a right action in understanding what a virtue is. And defenders of virtue ethics think that the virtues can be understood independently of the notion of right action (and related deontic notions).

The second complaint is that defining a virtue merely as a disposition to do what is right does not do justice to the rich complexity of virtuous character traits. As we have seen, a virtue is a complex state involving not only a motivational-behavioral component but also intellectual and affective components.

Again, these complaints do not show that a virtue ethic is necessarily superior to rival moral theories, since it is open to a non-virtue-based theory to reject definitions of the virtues in terms of right action and recognize the complexity of virtuous character traits.

So far, then, we have not found any reasons for preferring a virtue ethic to at least some of its rivals. If a virtue-based ethic is superior to its non-virtue-based rivals, it will have to be because grounding a theory of right conduct on considerations of virtue provides a more plausible account of right action than does any competing view. But there are reasons for doubt about this matter, as we shall see.

Objections to Virtue Ethics

I want to consider three main objections to virtue ethics having to do with its account of right action. The first has to do with the fact that the theory fails to provide real guidance in concrete situations calling for a moral decision; the second has to do with how the theory explains right action; and the third raises a skeptical worry about the threat of relativism. Let us take these up in order.

Indeterminacy. The standard of right conduct set forth by virtue ethics tells us that an action's rightness or wrongness depends on what a virtuous agent (acting in character) would do in some specific situation. A virtuous agent possesses a range of virtues, and in cases where the relevant virtues conflict, there is no superrule or rank ordering of the virtues that determines what the virtuous agent would do. Rather, as we have explained, in such cases, the virtuous agent, who, we assume, has practical intelligence, is able to discern which virtue consideration in the situation at hand is most important and acts accordingly. Such intelligence or phronesis is not something that can be fully characterized in terms of rules or principles. Thus, according to the objection, the theory fails to yield real guidance in a great many cases.

Earlier, the fact that the principles of virtue ethics (at least the kind of pluralist version presented in section 5) do not represent a moral algorithm for making moral decisions and are thus significantly indeterminate was put forth as an advantage of the theory—an advantage because it looks as if we cannot plausibly expect more determinacy from the principles of a plausible moral theory. Here, this very same fact about the theory is being used to criticize it.

The best response to this objection is simply to admit that virtue ethics is limited in this way and then go on to explain that such limits are to be expected given the complexity of moral phenomena. Since we have already encountered this theme of limited determinacy and will briefly return to it again in the concluding chapter, let us move on to other objections.

Virtue Explanations of Right Conduct. The second and third objections are not so easily answered. Although I do not think they count decisively against this type of theory, they do present serious challenges to any virtue-based account of right conduct and at least call for the advocate of virtue ethics to work out certain details of the theory. The first of these has to do with the account of right action in terms of the virtuous agent, which is distinctive of virtue ethics. The challenge I have in mind can be posed in the form of a dilemma. Let me explain.

According to the theory of right conduct in question, an action's rightness or wrongness depends on what a virtuous agent (acting in character) would do in some situation. The idea is that facts about our hypothetical virtuous agent—facts about her character traits—are what explain why certain actions are right and others are wrong. Let us take an example.

Suppose that in a situation in which some particular individual needs help, our hypothetical virtuous agent would perform an act of beneficence. According to the theory of right conduct, such an action is right (indeed, obligatory). What on this account *makes* it right? Presumably, the fact that such an action would flow from, and hence express the character trait of, benevolence. But, we may ask, why does this character trait bestow upon actions flowing from it the property of rightness? The obvious thing to say is that this character trait is good. The goodness of the character trait, then, bestows upon the action flowing from it the property of rightness.

Of course, we can now ask why this character trait is good. There would seem to be two possible responses. First, one might claim that its goodness cannot be explained but rather is just an unexplained fact about the trait in question. But this response seems unsatisfying since there does seem to be a way of plausibly explaining why a trait like benevolence is good. Here is one such explanation. The goodness of benevolence is due to the fact that it involves certain attitudes and motives directed toward the well-being of others—others who have a dignity and worth. It is thus the fact that others have a dignity and worth that explains why certain attitudes and motivation characteristic of benevolence are good.

But notice what has happened. If we explain the goodness of benevolence in the way just proposed, then it seems we can explain the rightness of an act of beneficence directly in terms of how such an act affects creatures having dignity and worth. In other words, when we follow through and try to understand what it is, according to virtue ethics, that makes right actions right and wrong actions wrong, we are led by a series of plausible steps to a view that makes rightness and wrongness depend on facts about whether the action treats others in a manner that respects their dignity and worth.[17]

So the dilemma is this. In explaining right conduct in terms of character traits, we can ask what it is about those traits that confers rightness or wrongness on an action. Traits that confer rightness do so in virtue of their being good. Now, either the goodness of such traits is an unexplained brute fact or it isn't. On the one hand, to claim that it is an unexplained brute fact seems implausible in light of the fact that we can offer explanations of the goodness of such traits. On the other hand, the sorts of explanations we are inclined to offer allow us to explain the rightness of an action without appealing to character traits themselves.

There are two possible responses to this dilemma. First, an advocate of virtue ethics might claim that certain character traits just are intrinsically good and that their goodness need not be further explained. In coming to know which character traits are good and hence count as virtues, one might claim that there are self-evident truths about the virtues that, given sufficient maturity, one can come to grasp through intuition.[18] Or, if one rejects intuitionism, one can perhaps appeal to the standard of internal support and argue that because claims about the goodness of certain traits are supported by the body of our considered moral beliefs, we have good reason to suppose that the traits in question are intrinsically good.

Another response to the dilemma is to attempt to explain the goodness of certain character traits in terms of their contribution to human eudaimonia or flourishing.[19] The prospects for accomplishing this Aristotelian project are featured in the third challenge, to be taken up shortly. However, for the time being, let us suppose that the goodness of a character trait (and hence its status as a virtue) is to be explained by appeal to some notion of human flourishing. In particular, one can attempt to show that possession of certain traits contributes to the flourishing of the individual who possesses them or that they contribute to the flourishing of people in general. And, of course, one might attempt to show both claims. But if one can explain the goodness of a character trait in terms of its contribution to human flourishing, why can't one explain the rightness of an action (or perhaps a type of action) directly in terms of its contribution to human flourishing? If we can, then we don't need to first explain the goodness of traits in terms of flourishing and then explain the rightness of actions in terms of the goodness of traits; we can explain both the goodness of traits and the rightness of actions directly in terms of flourishing.

These worries go to the heart of virtue ethics because if virtue considerations do not serve to properly *explain* the deontic status of actions, then the principles of virtue ethics fail to satisfy the standard of explanatory power, which means that they do not express correct moral criteria for right action. But instead of pursuing this further, let us turn to questions about the attempt to account for the virtues in terms of human flourishing.

Virtues and Human Flourishing. A final challenge to virtue ethics has to do with a skeptical worry about the virtues. There has been some dispute among philosophers about what character traits are virtues. Is compassion a virtue? The nineteenth-century German philosopher Friedrich Nietzsche denied it. What about modesty? The seventeenth-century Scottish philosopher David Hume did not think so. Humility? Not according to Aristotle.[20] So how can we determine which character traits really are the virtues and which ones really are the vices? We need some account of why a character trait is a virtue.[21] One might claim that what counts as a virtue fully depends on the values of one's culture and that, consequently, there is no objective backing to what is and is not a virtue; rather it is all relative to culture. But it has been the aim of those advocating virtue ethics to avoid this kind of relativism.

So the challenge to the virtue ethicist is to provide an account of the virtues that explains why certain character traits are virtues and others are vices, and to do so in a way that avoids relativism.

Some contemporary virtue ethicists have taken on this challenge by attempting to follow Aristotle's lead and ground the virtues in an account of eudaimonia (happiness, flourishing). As we have seen, the basic idea behind this sort of neo-Aristotelian approach is to argue that certain character traits are virtues because they contribute to eudaimonia (either of the individual who possesses them or of people generally). The two-part strategy associated with this idea is, first, to provide an account of human flourishing and, second, to show that certain character traits, because they importantly contribute to such flourishing, are for that reason good and hence count as virtues.

What account, then, can be given of human flourishing? Presumably, we base an account of the flourishing of something on that thing's internal nature; in particular, we base it on the characteristic activities of the thing in question. Were there a single, relatively specific characteristic human activity—such as contemplation—then one could go on to specify those character traits that contribute importantly to this activity, and they would be the virtues. Human beings are capable of intellectual contemplation, but it seems arbitrary to pick this specific form of human activity and claim that a contemplative life alone is what true human flourishing is all about. The problem is that humans, unlike other animals, are quite diverse in their goals and activities. We thus recognize human lives given over to projects other than contemplation as flourishing lives. Can one specify which projects are truly characteristic of human beings in order to come up with some specific form of characteristic activity that constitutes human flourishing?

Certainly, it won't help the project of grounding some set of virtues to appeal to the *actual* goals and projects of individuals in giving an account of flourishing, because doing so will lead very quickly to relativism. Some individuals place a high premium on competitive activity where certain character traits serve the person well. Others shun competition and aim to lead a simple, conflict-free life; for them a different set of character traits contributes to their flourishing. And so on. If we appeal to the actual goals and projects of individuals, we end up making what counts as a virtue relative to a person's value system. As we have noted, the virtue ethicist hopes to avoid relativism.[22]

The hope is to find some characteristic feature of human beings that such beings have quite apart from their specific goals and projects and whose realization in humans could plausibly be understood to constitute human flourishing. One suggestion is that flourishing for humans consists in the development of a cohesive sense of self and the activities that express one's self.[23] To develop such a sense of one's self will require, for instance, that one form a coherent, integrated plan for living so that one's goals and projects can be achieved. Certain character traits like prudence will be needed for success in pursuing the development of a unified sense of self. However, the problem with appealing to a very general notion of flourishing like the one in question is that it is not specific enough to be of use in determining which, from among a great many character traits, are virtues and which are vices.

A nice illustration of this point can be found in an article by Sarah Conly where she persuasively argues that traits like courage and justice cannot be shown to be virtues by appealing to this very general conception of flourishing. Here is her example of how one might flourish (in the sense of having a developed and unified sense of self) without being a just person.

> Take Lorenzo the Magnificent. If Florence in the Renaissance was great it is largely Lorenzo who made it so. Astute and ambitious, he navigated the labyrinthine difficulties of fifteenth-century Italian politics with dexterity, establishing himself securely as tyrant. Under his rule, industry, commerce, and public works made enormous progress, leading Florence to unequaled prosperity. At the same time, Lorenzo was not only a great patron and appreciator of the arts, but extremely creative himself. . . . He seems, indeed, to have done everything well. And while we are not privy to Lorenzo's personal experience, there seems to be good reason to believe that, successful in all he undertook, he was happy. Yet there is no doubt that Lorenzo was an extremely

unjust person. He trampled the liberty of Florence underfoot, he lied, he spied, and he assassinated his enemies with abandon. Yet, while incontrovertibly unjust, he seems to have flourished. (Conly 1988, 92)

A similar point can be made about the other character traits that typically show up on lists of virtues. Conly concludes that no account of flourishing is going to be able to serve as a plausible justification of what we ordinarily take to be virtues. And while I would not draw such a strong conclusion on the basis of the problems we have just considered, the challenge to the virtue ethicist to provide an account of the virtues remains.[24]

The challenge now under consideration, like the previous one, can be expressed as a dilemma. On the one hand, if an account of eudaimonia is going to be of some use in specifying some traits as virtues and others as vices, it will likely be too narrow in its conception of flourishing, thus implausibly restricting the kinds of lives that can count as flourishing. On the other hand, if one attempts to work with some conception of flourishing that is wide enough to allow for various recognizable types of human flourishing, the conception in question will be too vague and general to be of use in specifying certain traits as virtues and others as vices and do so in a way that captures what we normally think about virtue and vice.

One apparent way out of this dilemma is to grant that one can flourish through a variety of types of lives. This pluralistic conception of human flourishing is nicely described by Hilary Putnam.

> If today we differ with Aristotle it is in being much more pluralistic than Aristotle was. Aristotle recognized that different ideas of Eudaimonia, different conceptions of human flourishing, might be appropriate for different individuals on account of the difference in their constitution. But he seemed to think that ideally there was some sort of constitution that every one ought to have; that in an ideal world (overlooking the mundane question of who would grow the crops and who would bake the bread) everyone would be a philosopher. We agree with Aristotle that different ideas of human flourishing are appropriate for individuals with different constitutions, but we go further and believe that even in the ideal world there would be different constitutions, that diversity is part of the ideal. And we see some degree of tragic tension between ideals, that the fulfillment of some ideals always excludes the fulfillment of others. But to emphasize the point again, belief in a pluralistic ideal is not the same thing as belief that every ideal of human flourishing is as good as every other. We reject ideals of human flourishing as wrong, as infantile, as sick, as one-sided. (Putnam 1981, 148)

Being a pluralist about human flourishing would avoid the narrowness that results if we try to claim that only one way of life constitutes genuine flourishing. This form of pluralism would presumably allow us to derive sets of virtues pertaining to each of the types of human flourishing. And, as Putnam points out, this sort of pluralism about human flourishing avoids a kind of "anything goes" relativism.[25]

It seems to me that the kind of pluralism about flourishing Putnam advocates is the most promising route for the virtue ethicist to take. But pursuing this project in detail is not something we can tackle here.

7. Conclusion

Virtue ethics represents an alternative to the other moral theories surveyed in this book. Because of its recent emergence as a contender, philosophers sympathetic to virtue ethics are in the process of working out what such a theory is all about, particularly with respect to right action. I have suggested that the most plausible version of virtue ethics will be a version of limited moral pluralism.

The three challenges I have raised for virtue ethics are just that—challenges—and as the virtue ethics approach develops, we may find that there are convincing ways of dealing with them. (I have explained why I think the first of the challenges can plausibly be met.) In the meantime, the recent flurry of interest in virtue ethics has sparked the development of an important rival to Kantian, utilitarian, and other moral theories and has served to bring matters of character, virtue, and vice into clearer focus in moral theory.

Further Reading

Anscombe, Elizabeth. 1958. "Modern Moral Philosophy." *Philosophy* 33: 1–19. Reprinted in *Collected Philosophical Papers*. Minneapolis: University of Minnesota Press, 1981. An important paper challenging the notion of duty featured in moral theory and advocating a revival of interest in the virtues for doing moral philosophy. Reprinted in Crisp and Slote 1997.

Crisp, Roger, ed. 1996. *How Should One Live? Essays on the Virtues*. New York: Oxford University Press. Contains essays on virtue ethics written for this volume by various scholars.

Crisp, Roger, and Michael Slote, eds. 1997. *Virtue Ethics*. New York: Oxford University Press. Contains classic essays on virtue ethics.

Gilligan, Carol. 1982. *A Different Voice*. Cambridge: Harvard University Press. Groundbreaking work in moral psychology that has inspired the development of care ethics.

Held, Virginia, ed. 1995. *Justice and Care: Essential Readings in Feminist Ethics*. Boulder, Colo.: Westview Press. A collection of essays by various authors exploring the relations between justice and care.

Hurka, Thomas. 2001. *Virtue, Vice, and Value*. New York: Oxford University Press. An exploration of the nature of virtue and vice. Chapter 8 raises objections to recent versions of virtue ethics.

Hursthouse, Rosalind. 1999. *On Virtue Ethics.* New York: Oxford University Press. A defense of a neo-Aristotelian version of virtue ethics.

MacIntyre, Alasdair. 1981. *After Virtue.* Notre Dame, Ind.: University of Notre Dame Press. An important book in helping to revive interest among philosophers in the virtues and virtue ethics.

Noddings, Nel. 1984. *Caring: A Feminine Approach to Ethics and Moral Education.* Berkeley and Los Angeles: University of California Press. A defense of a care ethic with particular attention paid to moral education.

Paul, Ellen F., Fred D. Miller, and Jeffrey Paul, eds. 1998. *Virtue and Vice.* Cambridge: Cambridge University Press. A wide-ranging collection of essays by leading scholars.

Pincoffs, Edmund. 1986. *Quandaries and Virtues: Against Reductivism in Ethics.* Lawrence: University of Kansas Press. A defense of a pluralistic version of virtue ethics.

Slote, Michael. 1992. *From Morality to Virtue.* Oxford: Oxford University Press. Systematic defense of virtue ethics as being superior to Kantian and utilitarian rivals.

Statman, Daniel, ed. 1997. *Virtue Ethics: A Critical Reader.* Washington, D.C.: Georgetown University Press. Contains important essays on virtue ethics and includes a useful introductory essay by the editor.

Zagzebski, Linda. 1996. *Virtues of the Mind.* Cambridge: Cambridge University Press. Part 2 contains an extended account of the virtues as well as a version of virtue ethics.

Notes

1. See Frankena 1973, 63–65.

2. The ideas that follow are familiar from our chap. 4 study of Aquinas's natural law moral theory, which, as we noted, was influenced by the work of Aristotle.

3. All references to Terence Irwin's 1985 translation of Aristotle's *Nicomachean Ethics,* hereafter abbreviated *NE;* the first page number refers to the Irwin translation, the second to the standard form of reference (Bekker page and column) to Aristotle's works.

4. In chap. 8, we saw that an important element in W. D. Ross's moral theory is the role played by what he calls "moral judgment," which I understand to be identical to what Aristotle calls "phronesis."

5. This example was suggested to me by Tim Roche.

6. See *NE,* 169–71/1144b–45a.

7. For an illuminating discussion of these theses in Aristotle and the works of other ancient philosophers, see Annas 1993, chap. 2.

8. Obviously, when one thinks about it, there are other possible structural views compatible with the basic virtue ethic claim expressed in VE. For instance, having characterized right action in terms of virtue, one might either characterize nonmoral value in terms of right action or simply characterize nonmoral value independently of the notions of virtue and right action.

9. The justice perspective is to be understood broadly and so is meant to in-

clude the moral points of view expressed not only in Kant's moral theory (which the following quote makes clear) but also in utilitarianism, natural law theory, and Ross's moral pluralism.

10. Although one need not develop the view as a version of virtue ethics.

11. The following distinctions are drawn in Blustein 1991, chap. 2. See also Tronto 1989 for a discussion of the distinction between caring for and caring about.

12. This is how Frankfurt (1999) describes caring about.

13. See Friedman 1987 for a discussion of this point.

14. Kant 1797, 200–201.

15. You may recall the case of Ted Kaczynski, the Unabomber, whose brother eventually notified authorities with information leading to the arrest of Kaczynski.

16. Hursthouse (1999, chap. 3) and Pincoffs (1986, chap. 6, esp. 103–4) advance this sort of view.

17. I am not claiming that all other virtues can be explained in just this way— by appealing to dignity and worth. The example of beneficence is meant to challenge the claim that we can best explain moral rightness and wrongness in all cases by appealing to character traits.

18. This kind of epistemological intuitionism was explained in chap. 8.

19. I mentioned earlier that Aristotle's use of "eudaimonia" is often translated as "happiness." However, contemporary philosophers working out moral theories inspired by Aristotle prefer talking about human flourishing, perhaps because talk of happiness in ethics is associated with hedonistic theories of the good featured in classical utilitarianism.

20. This particular list I take from Hursthouse 1999, 32.

21. In section 3 of this chapter, we noted that one main task for virtue ethics is to give an account of the virtuous agent, which in turn requires an explanation of what makes a character trait a virtue.

22. Harman (1983) makes this point.

23. Attributed by Conly (1988, 89) to Alasdair MacIntyre (1981).

24. For an intriguing attempt to carry out the neo-Aristotelian project, see Hursthouse 1999, part 3.

25. Conly (1988, 88–89) briefly considers, and finds reasons to reject, a pluralist approach—what she calls "collective notions of flourishing." She suspects that appealing to a plurality of ideals of flourishing involves a kind of circularity that undermines the project of justifying a set of virtues by appealing to a conception (or conceptions) of flourishing.

10

Moral Particularism

The moral theories that we have surveyed in the previous chapters provide moral principles and rules that purport to specify those features of an action in virtue of which it is right or wrong. These theories all agree that in correctly applying moral principles of right conduct to concrete circumstances, one must attend to the morally relevant details of each context or circumstance. In the third chapter, devoted to moral relativism, we expressed this widely shared assumption as the *context sensitivity thesis:* the rightness or wrongness of a concrete action, performed in some context, depends in part on nonmoral facts that hold in the context—facts concerning agents and their circumstances.

Moral particularism, like traditional moral theories, emphasizes the importance of the details of concrete situations in determining the morality of actions. But this view is far more radical in its claims about how the morality of an action depends on such details. Indeed, the moral particularist challenges the idea that it is possible to specify once and for all those features that are always going to be relevant in determining the rightness or wrongness of an action. This means that there can't be the sorts of principles and rules featured in traditional moral theories of the kind we have been examining and that therefore the project of traditional moral theory is deeply mistaken. The particularist claims that the moral relevance of any feature depends entirely on context.

To understand moral particularism, we must step back and reflect on some common ingredients in the traditional moral theories we have been examining.

1. The Project of Traditional Moral Theory

Let us begin by recalling some of the remarks about moral theory that were mentioned in chapter 1 and which have been illustrated in subsequent chapters.

As we have seen, a moral theory involves the attempt to explain the nature of morality. More precisely, that part of a moral theory concerned with right and wrong action—its theory of right conduct—attempts to *explain* the nature of right and wrong action by locating those features of actions, persons, and situations that *make* an act right or wrong. Similarly, that part of a moral theory concerned with the nature of goodness and badness—its theory of value—attempts to *explain* the nature of good and bad by locating those features that *make* something good or bad. This dual explanatory project of moral theory is its main *theoretical aim*.

But moral theory also has been understood as having a *practical aim*—the aim of explaining how one can come to correct moral conclusions about the morality of actions and the value of persons, things, experiences, and states of affairs.

Traditional moral theories have attempted to accomplish these two aims by formulating moral principles and rules that (1) represent *moral criteria* specifying what makes actions right or wrong, or something intrinsically good or bad, and (2) can serve as a *decision procedure* for arriving at correct moral verdicts about what to do. A moral theory, then, is primarily in the business of presenting and defending moral principles and rules that accomplish these aims.

To understand the main claims of moral particularists and why they are against moral theory so understood, we need to dig a bit deeper into the nature of traditional moral theory and make explicit certain very basic assumptions—assumptions that are reflected in the sorts of principles and rules central in these theories.

Let us focus for the time being on moral principles of right conduct, just to keep things as simple as possible. A principle of right conduct, in its theoretical role, purports to specify some *nonmoral features* of actions in virtue of which an action is either right or wrong. A nonmoral feature is one that can be understood without reference to a moral concept. For instance, according to the divine command theory (which we examined in chapter 2), what *makes* an act right or wrong are facts about what God commands. Because we can understand the concept of a command, including a command issued by God, without appealing to moral concepts, the concept of a command is a nonmoral concept. Thus, the fact that some action has been commanded is a nonmoral feature of that action. But this feature is of fundamental moral relevance, according to this theory, because it is that *in virtue of which* an action is right or wrong.

Again, consider classical utilitarianism, according to which the rightness of an action depends on how much intrinsic value it would bring about (if performed) compared to how much intrinsic value would be brought about by performing various alternative actions. On this theory, the rightness of an action depends on considerations of intrinsic value. However, according to classical versions of utilitarianism, episodes of pleasure and pain

are the only bearers of intrinsic value (that are relevant to moral evaluation). So, according to classical utilitarianism, facts about how much overall
pleasure and pain would be brought about by an action are what make an
action right or wrong. Since the concepts of pleasure and pain are nonmoral concepts, facts about how much pleasure and pain an action would
produce represent, according to this theory, the most basic or fundamental
nonmoral but morally relevant features of actions that bear on their rightness and wrongness.

Similar remarks apply to the other moral theories we have examined.
Each of them sets forth moral principles of right conduct that purport to
express the underlying nature of right and wrong conduct in terms of what
are taken to be fundamental nonmoral but morally relevant features of actions.[1]

Let us now make some observations about the moral principles and rules
featured in all of these theories. As I shall explain, there are three important
theses characteristic of moral theories—and the principles and rules they
feature—that are the focus of criticism by moral particularists: (1) the unity
thesis, (2) the thesis of universal relevance, and (3) the polarity thesis. Let us
examine them in order.

The Unity Thesis

Moral theories represent moral phenomena as more or less strongly unified—as exhibiting some underlying pattern. Think of it this way. There are
many types of actions that we commonly recognize as being wrong: lying,
theft, killing, rape, malicious gossip, and so on. One natural question to ask
about these types of wrong actions is whether there is any underlying feature that they all share *in virtue of which* they are wrong. We might discover
that there is some one underlying feature of wrong actions that makes them
all wrong. If so, then some version of moral monism would be true. Alternatively, we might discover that although there is no one such underlying
feature, there is a small set of features that together can be used to explain
the wrongness of a wide range of actions. If so, then some form of moral
pluralism would be true. In either case, if there are such underlying features,
then the moral phenomenon of wrong action is unified: there is an underlying pattern that connects all wrong actions and serves to explain their
wrongness. Here, then, is the unity thesis:

U   There is a small fixed set of nonmoral features of actions (persons,
    institutions, and so forth) that are fundamental in explaining the
    deontic status of any action. Call them *fundamental morally relevant
    nonmoral features.*

Sometimes the claim made by this thesis is expressed by saying that morality has fixed and definite nonmoral contours—that there is a fixed pattern of underlying right-and wrong-making features of actions—that shape the moral status of actions.

So one basic assumption of the moral theories we have studied is the claim expressed by the unity thesis. However, it is important to notice that the sorts of features mentioned in the unity thesis are *fundamental* morally relevant features. We should further distinguish between fundamental and nonfundamental morally relevant features.

There are a great many features of actions, persons, and their situations that may or may not be morally relevant depending on context. Suppose for the moment that the classical version of utilitarianism is true. Then the fact that some action is a lie is not of fundamental moral relevance. As noted above, what is fundamentally morally relevant regarding actions for the classical utilitarian are facts about the production of pleasure and pain. So the fact that an action is a lie might or might not be relevant, depending on whether this fact about the action has any bearing on the production of either pleasure or pain. In contexts where this fact about an action would have no bearing on the production of pleasure or pain, it is not a morally relevant feature. So, if one is a classical utilitarian, the relevance of the fact that an action is a lie is to be explained by fundamental morally relevant facts about the production of pleasure and pain.

The point being illustrated here is simply that for any moral theory many features of a situation or facts about an action or a person might or might not be morally relevant, depending on context. But a moral theory attempts to discover those features whose relevance is fundamental. And, according to the thesis of unity, there is a small set of fundamental morally relevant features. According to monistic moral theories of right conduct, there is but one fundamental morally relevant feature, while according to pluralist moral theories of right conduct, there is a small handful of such features.

What makes such fundamental morally relevant features especially interesting is the fact that they are understood by traditional moral theory to have two important characteristics: universal relevance and polarity.

The Universal Relevance Thesis

According to the universal relevance thesis,

UR If a feature is a fundamental morally relevant nonmoral feature, then it is morally relevant in any context in which it is present.

Thus, for the classical utilitarian, the fact that an action would produce some amount of pleasure (or pain) is always a morally relevant fact. For Ross, the fact that an action is an instance of breaking a promise is always a morally relevant feature of the action.

The Polarity Thesis

Again, for Ross, the fact that an action is an instance of promise break-ing is a prima facie wrong-making feature of the action. Such wrong-making features have what we might call a negative polarity: they count against doing the act. By contrast, other fundamental nonmoral features mentioned in some of Ross's moral rules have a positive polarity: they count in favor of doing the act. For instance, the fact that an action would benefit someone else is a prima facie right-making feature of the action and so has a positive polarity. In addition to assuming that a fundamental morally relevant nonmoral feature is universally relevant, traditional moral theory assumes that all such features, whenever present, have the same po-larity. Here, then, is the polarity thesis:

P   A fundamental morally relevant nonmoral feature always possesses
      the same polarity in any context in which it is present.

For the classical utilitarian, the fact that an action would bring about some episodes of pleasure always has a positive polarity and counts in favor of doing the act. The fact that an action would produce some episodes of pain has a negative polarity and counts against performing the act. Of course, for the utilitarian, whether an action ought or ought not to be done depends on the net balance of pleasure and pain the action would bring about if performed compared to other alternative actions. But the point here is that considerations of pleasure and pain always count, and count in the same way, in determining the morality of actions.

We can summarize the universal relevance and polarity theses by saying that according to traditional moral theory, there are some nonmoral fea-tures of actions that are universally relevant and relevant in the same way (have the same polarity) whenever they are present. These are supposed to be the features of fundamental moral relevance that explain and unify moral phenomena.

2. Particularism versus Generalism

The theses of universal relevance and polarity make explicit some impor-tant characteristics of the sorts of fundamental nonmoral features that are mentioned in the unity thesis. Let us refer to this battery of assumptions as *moral generalism,* since these assumptions add up to the idea that there is a fixed set of nonmoral features of actions whose relevance and polarity never change and thus hold universally.[2]

Moral particularism is opposed to moral generalism. Moral particularists reject the three theses just presented, and in thus rejecting moral generalism, they attack the main theoretical aim of moral theory, the aim of discovering fundamental morally relevant nonmoral features of actions, persons, and situations that would serve to unify morality. Since the moral principles and rules featured in standard moral theories purport to express such fundamental unifying features, moral particularists deny that there are such principles and rules. Particularists thus reject the theoretical aim of traditional moral theory, the aim of providing moral criteria for right action and value. One implication of the rejection of such principles and rules is that they cannot serve the practical function of reliably guiding us to correct moral verdicts about particular cases. Thus, moral particularists also reject the main practical aim of a moral theory, the aim of providing a decision procedure, based on principles and rules, for determining the morality of actions. Because traditional moral theories involve both of these aims—theoretical and practical—moral particularism is often thought of as an antitheory stance in ethics (though, as we shall see, one can view moral particularism as advocating a nontraditional way of doing moral theory).

However, rejecting moral generalism does not mean that moral particularists are skeptics about morality itself. What makes the label "particularism" apt for the view under examination is that particularists propose to understand the nature of right conduct and value (as well as how proper moral reasoning should proceed) without appeal to the sorts of moral principles and rules (and the generalist assumptions that they carry with them) that are characteristic of traditional moral theory. Their idea is that the moral relevance of the nonmoral features of a particular situation depend crucially on the details of the situation and so cannot be read off from some principle or rule. Furthermore, proper moral thinking and reasoning about particular cases is understood to be a matter of attending to the details of particular situations rather than a matter of applying principles and rules to situations. Thus, in addition to its negative appraisal of the ambitions of traditional moral theory, moral particularism has its positive side as well. To begin our examination of the particularists' outlook, let us first examine the negative side of their view and then turn to their positive proposals.

3. Against Generalism

As I've mentioned, the particularist's case against traditional moral theory (and the sorts of principles and rules featured in such theory) involves a rejection of the three theses presented above. Against the polarity and universal relevance theses, particularists have argued by example. That is, for any nonmoral feature that allegedly is both universally relevant and always has the same polarity, the particularist describes situations in which the feature either fails to be relevant at all or reverses its polarity. In short, the particularist denies that there are any nonmoral features that are fundamental in the way that traditional moral theory takes for granted. And if there are no such features, then the unity thesis is false. Since the main part of particularists' attack on moral theory concerns the theses of polarity and universal relevance, let us examine their case against each one.

Reversal

The fact that an action would bring about pleasurable consequences is taken by classical utilitarians as a nonmoral feature that is always morally relevant (whenever present) and relevant in the same way in that it counts in favor of the action's rightness. But consider this case as described by David McNaughton:

> A government is considering reintroducing hanging, drawing, and quartering in public for terrorist murders. If reactions to public hangings in the past are anything to go by a lot of people may enjoy the spectacle. Does that constitute a reason in favor of reintroduction? Is the fact that people would enjoy it here a reason for its being right? It would be perfectly possible to take just the opposite view. The fact that spectators might get a sadistic thrill from the brutal spectacle could be thought to constitute an objection to reintroduction. Whether the fact that an action causes pleasure is a reason for or against doing it is not something that can be settled in isolation from other features of the action. It is only when we know the context in which the pleasure will occur that we are in a position to judge. (McNaughton 1988, 193)

Perhaps in most contexts the fact that an action would bring about pleasure has a positive polarity and thus counts in favor of the action being right. However, as the example illustrates, in other contexts the pleasure brought about by some action reverses its polarity and counts against the action being right and in favor of the action being morally wrong. Here is another example of reversal, offered by Jonathan Dancy, who has us consider

> a family game called 'Contraband', in which players are smugglers trying to get contraband material past a Customs Officer. The game requires them to lie; if one doesn't do plenty of lying, it spoils the game. That an action is a lie is commonly a reason not to do it; here it is a reason in favour. (Dancy 1993, 61)

Of course, a few examples like these do not suffice to disprove the polarity thesis. Even if the particularist is correct in claiming that such features as causing pleasure and being a lie can reverse polarity, there may be other nonmoral features whose polarity remains constant from context to context. But such examples serve as the basis of a challenge to the generalist: the particularist challenges the generalist to come up with nonmoral features whose polarity cannot be reversed. The particularist doubts that there are any such features.

Silencing

Even if nonmoral features can reverse their polarity, it still may be the case that there is a set of such features that are morally relevant whenever they are present. That is, even if the polarity thesis is false, the universal relevance thesis might still be true. But, again, particularists offer examples that call into question the universal relevance thesis. For instance, the fact that I borrowed something from you would appear to be a morally relevant consideration and gives me a reason for returning it to you. But suppose that I find out that you stole the book. One way to look at the case is to suppose that my borrowing the book from you is morally relevant and gives me some reason to return it to you, although the fact that you stole the book is also relevant and gives me an even stronger reason to return it to its owner. But another way to look at the case is to deny that in the context in question the fact that I borrowed the book from you gives me any reason at all to return it to you. According to this second way of looking at the case, my having borrowed the book from you is simply not morally relevant in this context. The particularist claims that this latter way of viewing the matter is more plausible and illustrates how features that are typically morally relevant may have their relevance silenced in certain contexts.

Again, working from examples is not enough to decisively disprove the universal relevance thesis, but examples do ground a challenge to the generalist: the particularist challenges the generalist to identify any nonmoral features that maintain their moral relevance in all contexts. The particularist thinks there are no such features.

Shapelessness

According to the unity thesis (U), there is a small fixed set of morally relevant nonmoral features that are fundamental in explaining the rightness and wrongness of actions. Such features are understood by the generalist to be universally relevant and always to have the same polarity. So if there are no nonmoral features that are universally relevant and whose polarity remains the same, then the unity thesis is false. The point is often put in terms of morality being shapeless. The claim is that there is no fixed set of nonmoral features that determine and hence "shape" the moral landscape.

4. Atomism versus Holism

We can crystallize the basic difference between moral generalists and their particularist opponents by distinguishing two accounts of the nature of morally relevant features. A generalist is committed to what we may call *relevance atomism* (also called *reasons atomism*):

RA There are some morally relevant nonmoral features of actions whose relevance (including polarity) in a context is unaffected by other features that may be present in that context. Such features thus possess their relevance atomistically and in effect carry it with them from context to context.

Moral particularists reject atomism and offer in its place an account of the nature of moral relevance that we may call *relevance holism* (reasons holism):

RH The relevance (including polarity) of any nonmoral feature in a context can be affected by the other features that are present in that context. Thus, no nonmoral feature possesses relevance atomistically; rather its relevance—whether and how it is relevant—is a holistic matter.

So the dispute between generalists and particularists depends on which party is right about the nature of moral relevance.

Having now examined the negative strand of the particularist's outlook about morality, let us examine its positive side.

5. The Particularist's Proposal

Despite its negative thrust, moral particularism does offer positive proposals about right and wrong action and about value. It also has something to say about proper moral reasoning. Moreover, the particularist can recognize the importance of moral rules, at least when they are properly understood. Let us begin, then, with the particularist's proposals regarding right conduct and value.

Right Conduct

The moral particularist agrees with the generalist that the rightness or wrongness of some concrete action depends on the morally relevant nonmoral features of the action in question. But the particularist denies the atomistic idea that certain nonmoral features must always be morally relevant and relevant in the same way. Rather, the relevance and polarity of a feature are determined holistically in a particular context. Within a particular context of action, then, certain features are going to be relevant, and we may suppose that in many, if not most, such situations, there will be morally relevant features that favor doing some action A, and there will also be morally relevant features that favor refraining from A. Moreover, we may also assume that in such cases, certain of these features are likely to override other, competing features and thus hold a position of moral dominance with respect to the overall rightness or wrongness of the action.

Here is a very simple case to illustrate. Suppose that an action I might perform in some circumstance would benefit someone in need of help and that this feature of the action is a morally relevant feature in the circumstances in question and counts in favor of that action. Reminiscent of Ross, we can say that in the context, this feature is a *right-making* feature, meaning that if it were the only relevant feature in the context, it would make the action obligatory; however, if it is not the only relevant feature, it may be overridden. To continue, suppose also that my action of benefiting the person in need would require that I break a promise, a feature of the action that counts against doing it (counts as a *wrong-making* feature). If, in the particular situation in question, it is morally more important that I aid the one in need than that I keep my promise, the former feature of my action is morally dominant and determines what I ought to do.

We can make use of the idea of a moral feature (or set of features) being dominant in a particular situation or context in order to set forth, on behalf of the particularist, moral principles of right conduct.

Principles of Right Conduct

A concrete action A (performed in a particular context) is *obligatory* if and only if the dominant morally relevant features in the context favor doing A.

A concrete action A (performed in a particular context) is *wrong* if and only if the morally dominant relevant features in the context favor not doing A.

A concrete action A (performed in a particular context) is *optional* if and only if either (i) there are no morally relevant features that obtain in the context, or (ii) there are competing sets of features none of which are dominant.

It is important to notice that presenting the particularist's positive proposal about the rightness and wrongness of concrete actions in terms of moral principles does not conflict with the rejection of traditional moral theory and the principles featured in such theories. The principles of right conduct just presented do not purport to do what the sorts of moral principles featured in traditional moral theory attempt to do. That is, the above principles do not purport to set forth fundamental nonmoral features of actions that are always relevant and relevant in the same way. Rather, together they simply enunciate a set of trivial truths about right and wrong action—which is all, according to the particularist, that can be said in general about right and wrong conduct. It is trivially true that the rightness or wrongness of some concrete action depends on those morally relevant features that, in the context, have the greatest moral weight. What else could be the basis for an action's being right or wrong? Because they are trivial, it is perhaps misleading to think of them as moral *principles*. However, it would definitely be misleading to think of these principles as giving us a deep theoretical account of, and hence a unifying theory about, the underlying nature of all right and wrong action. There is no such deep account to give, according to the particularist.

Although the focus so far in this chapter has been on matters of right conduct, one can easily infer from what has been said the basic idea behind a particularist approach to value. The goodness or badness of something for the particularist will depend on nonmoral features that are morally relevant. However, the particularist claims that whether some feature is morally relevant (and in what way) will depend on context. So, for instance, the fact that some experience would be one of pleasure may not always be relevant in determining its overall value; there can be cases in which this feature is either silenced or its polarity reversed. That a sadist would experience pleasure from performing acts of sadism does not count as tending to make the experience a good one. Indeed, arguably, it is part of what contributes to the badness of the experience.

Moral Rules

Although particularism rejects moral rules as traditionally understood, rules have a place in the particularist's scheme. In the previous chapters, we have encountered two important sorts of moral rules: rules of absolute duty and rules of prima facie duty. Rules of absolute duty (absolute moral rules), you may recall, specify types of action, like killing an innocent human being or lying, that one is never permitted to perform. Such rules are exceptionless. By contrast, rules of prima facie duty of the sort featured in Ross's moral theory (see chapter 8) specify types of action that we have a duty to perform or refrain from performing (depending on the duty) unless we have a stronger moral reason to act otherwise. But rules of both sorts assume atomism and thus purport to specify features of actions that are always morally relevant and relevant in the same way. As we have seen, the moral particularist rejects relevance atomism and so rejects both sorts of rules.

However, there are moral rules that the particularist can allow. I will call them *rules of prima facie relevance*. These rules differ from Ross's in that they only purport to specify those features of actions, persons, and their circumstances that are likely to be morally relevant in the sorts of circumstances in which human beings typically find themselves. That is, even if the fact that an action would involve breaking a promise is not always morally relevant and relevant in the same way, we can still generalize from past experience and claim that this sort of fact is very likely to be morally relevant

Figure 10.1 Types of Moral Rules

Generalist Rules		Particularist Rules
Exceptionless rules	Rules allowing exceptions	Rules of prima facie relevance
e.g.	e.g.	e.g.
Absolute duties "Lying is wrong."	Prima facie duties "Lying is prima facie wrong."	"Lying is prima facie relevant and prima facie has a negative polarity."

whenever present and is very likely going to count against performing the action. Granted, in unusual circumstances, this feature may be silenced or reversed. However, from past experience we can assume that this feature is very likely going to be negatively relevant in almost all circumstances in which it is present. Such rules of prima facie relevance, then, represent inductive generalizations.

Figure 10.1 summarizes the types of moral rules.

Moral Reasoning and Moral Knowledge

It should be clear that the particularist can allow rules of prima facie relevance to play a role in moral reasoning about the morality of particular, concrete actions. In most cases we are likely to encounter, if we have good inductive evidence for thinking that the fact that an action is a lie is a morally relevant feature of the action, we can appeal to the relevant rule about lying and come to justified moral conclusions about the likely relevance of lying in some newly encountered case. Of course, we may find that the case is an unusual one and that, contrary to what one normally expects, the fact that some action would be a lie does not count morally at all or, as in Dancy's example of the Contraband game, it counts in favor of telling lies.

However, in the end, coming to know whether some concrete action is right or wrong depends on being able to discern all of the morally relevant features in the circumstance in question as well as being able to determine which of them are dominant. To be able to do this with any degree of reliability, one must possess what Aristotle called phronesis (practical intelligence), or what we have also been calling moral judgment.

The role of phronesis in coming to all-things-considered moral verdicts about specific cases is emphasized by generalists like Ross and by advocates of virtue ethics. I have also suggested that other moral theories need to recognize its importance. But whereas Ross thinks that phronesis is needed to adjudicate conflicts when the prima facie duties conflict, the particularist thinks that phronesis is needed in determining what is going to count as a relevant feature of a situation and how it counts, as well as being crucial for adjudicating any conflicts between relevant features that compete for dominance.

6. Antitheory?

We have seen the ways in which moral particularism is opposed to the generalism that is characteristic of traditional moral theory. If one defines normative moral theory as the search for features that are universally relevant, relevant in the same way, and which thus give morality a fixed and definite shape, then the main negative thrust of particularism is against normative moral theory. According to this definition, particularism represents an antitheory position in ethics.

However, the particularist does have a theory to offer about the nature of morally relevant features; it is encapsulated in the thesis of relevance holism (RH). This metaethical theory (metaethical, because it is a theory about the nature of morally relevant properties) does have implications about how, in a particular context, right conduct and value are determined. It thus addresses the theoretical aim of moral theory—the aim of providing an explanation of the nature of right and wrong, good and bad. Of course, it does not provide an *account* of their nature in the sense of identifying a set of underlying nonmoral features that could be used to unify morality.

Again, moral particularism does address the practical aim of moral theory—the aim of explaining how one can come to correct moral verdicts about the rightness and wrongness of concrete actions and about the value of concrete items—although it does not provide any sort of decision procedure of the sort featured in traditional moral theories involving the application of principles or rules to particular cases.

In the end, I don't think it matters much whether or not we think of moral particularism as an antitheory stance in ethics. It is clearly opposed to the generalist project characteristic of traditional moral theory, but it does make positive proposals about the nature of right conduct and value.

7. Evaluation of Particularism

If the moral particularist's rejection of generalism is correct, then, as we have noted, the main project of traditional moral theory is undermined. The search for moral principles and rules that express the underlying nature of morality (claims the particularist) is like the search for a fountain of youth—completely hopeless. The particularist thinks that this situation is not as bad as it might at first appear and, as we have seen, has some positive proposals to make about the proper form of moral rules and about proper moral reasoning and knowledge. In evaluating moral particularism, I want to make two observations about the debate between generalists and particularists and then consider an argument to the effect that rejecting generalism and embracing particularism would not be a good thing for society.

Has Generalism Been Refuted?

The particularist claims that the thesis of relevance atomism is false and that therefore so is generalism. But are there any nonmoral features whose moral relevance and polarity cannot be affected by the presence of other features and thus (contrary to the claims of the particularist) remain constant from context to context in which they are present? Furthermore, how can we resolve the dispute between generalists and particularists over this matter? Let us take these questions up in order.

The particularist, as we have seen, is fond of working with examples of features that are allegedly always relevant and relevant in the same way and then explaining how, in certain contexts, the relevance of such features is either silenced or reversed. But perhaps the particularist has not attended to the right features. This is, in fact, what defenders of generalism maintain. Let us explore further.

To think clearly about whether there are any nonmoral features whose relevance and polarity are invariant across all contexts, it is important to distinguish between nonmoral features—features that can be understood without appealing to moral concepts—and features that are "morally loaded." The particularist can allow that there are morally loaded features that are always relevant and relevant in the same way.

Consider the feature an act may have of being a *murder.* Is the fact that an action is an instance of murder always morally relevant? It would seem so. Does this feature always have a negative polarity? Again, it would seem so. But these facts about murder are easily explained by noting that "murder" just means *wrongful* killing, and so by definition the fact that an act is one of murder always counts against it. So, it seems reasonably clear that the feature of being an act of murder is always morally relevant and relevant in the same way. This kind of morally loaded feature is not the kind of feature under consideration in the dispute over generalism. As explained earlier, generalism claims that there are *nonmoral* features (hence features that are not morally loaded) that are universally relevant and relevant in the same way.

To understand more fully the significance of the point being made, let us consider some possible candidate features to which a generalist might be tempted to point as being always relevant and relevant in the same way:[3]

- killing an innocent human being

- causing sadistic pleasure

- harming others

- keeping a morally permissible promise that was elicited without coercion or deception.

For each of these features, the particularist is going to claim either that the feature is morally loaded and so does not count in favor of generalism, or that the feature is not morally loaded, in which case it will be possible to describe contexts in which it is either silenced or reversed. Certainly, the notion of *innocence* seems to morally load the first entry on the list. To say that a human being is innocent is to say that she or he is *not morally deserving* of such treatment. So even if this feature is always relevant and relevant in the same way whenever it is present, it will not help the generalist's cause.

How about causing sadistic pleasure? In *Webster's New Collegiate Dictionary,* "sadism" is defined as "a sexual perversion in which gratification is obtained by the infliction of physical or mental pain on others."[4] In this same dictionary, the word "perverse" is defined as "turned away from what is right or good," and "perversion" is defined as "the action of perverting" or "the condition of being perverted." It would seem, then, that reference to sexual *perversion* is morally loaded, so the second feature on the list does not count in favor of generalism.

What about the feature an act may have of *harming others?* Let's suppose that the concept of harm is not morally loaded. Are there contexts in which harming someone—in the sense of causing them physical or mental pain— is either silenced or reversed? Consider a case in which the recipient of the pain is a masochist and welcomes the painful experience. Or consider a case not involving masochism in which a physician, in treating a patient's arthritis, uses bee stings at the relevant place on the patient's body to accelerate the production of certain chemicals that will reduce the arthritic inflammation.[5] Shouldn't we say that in this case (and the masochist case) harming another counts in favor of such action?[6] If so, this feature can be reversed—again, no help to the generalist.

Finally, the fourth candidate on the list explicitly mentions promises that are morally permissible, and so it is obviously a morally loaded feature.

So, we return to our main question: are there any nonmoral features that are always morally relevant and relevant in the same way? Brad Hooker, a defender of generalism, offers this one: intentionally killing someone against that person's will. The main concepts involved in the characterization of this feature are intentionally doing something, killing, and acting against someone's will. Now I suspect that it is possible to understand each of these three concepts without having to make use of moral concepts. And, of course, this kind of feature is morally relevant in at least most cases in which it is present. So the question is whether it possible to think of a context in which this feature is either silenced or reversed.

Here is one possibility. Suppose that a known serial killer has a number of hostages whom he plans to murder just for fun, and soon. As the story goes, I am in a position to save the intended victims, but only if I kill the maniac. I just happen to be off hunting by myself and approach an apparently abandoned shack where the killer (whom I recognize from the media publicity) is holding the hostages. I overhear the killer explaining to his hapless captives how he is about to kill them all, so I take aim and kill him just in time. I have just intentionally killed a human being against his will. (I didn't confer with him before killing him about his desire to live, but it is not part of his plot to kill himself. So we may presume that killing him is against his will.) Should we say, along with the generalist, that the feature "intentionally killing a human being against his will" is morally relevant and counts against the act of killing but is overridden in the circumstances? Or should we say instead that in the circumstances this fact about my action does not at all count against my killing—that it is a consideration that must be overridden?

Speaking for myself, I can well understand the outlook of someone who would deny the relevance of the feature in the context I just described. But I can equally well understand the generalist, who is obviously going to claim that intentionally killing someone against his will in the case at hand is morally relevant yet greatly overridden by other relevant considerations. So the dispute between the generalist and the particularist over this case (and many others) turns crucially on whether it is correct to say that a feature that is generally relevant in a certain way is overridden or whether it is silenced.[7] This point brings us to the second critical observation I wish to make about particularism.

The point I wish to make is about the very dispute between the generalist and the particularist. Some readers may have gotten the impression that there is not much substance to the dispute between the two camps. With respect to cases in which the relevance of some feature is being disputed, one side—the generalists—says that the feature in question is relevant but overridden, while the other side—the particularists—says that it is silenced. In either case, the feature is not dominant in determining the all-things-considered moral verdict in the case. The question I wish to raise is methodological: how can the dispute between the two camps be resolved? So far, the discussion has simply appealed to the reader's intuitions about the relevance of features in various contexts. The particularist has been keen to give examples of contexts in which features that are normally relevant in a certain way either are not relevant or reverse their polarity. And the examples are supposed to "grab" the reader and strike her in the way they strike the particularist. But readers may well differ in their reactions to the cases that are presented for their consideration. What strikes one reader as a case of some feature being silenced may strike another as a case of that feature being overridden. So appealing to the reader's intuitions about moral relevance only goes so far, and not far enough in deciding between relevance atomism and relevance holism.

Some defenders of particularism have attempted to show that evidence for particularism is available in the form of a certain psychological response of agents who confront complex moral situations like the ones being cited in the examples of silencing and reversal. The response in question is *regret*.

The idea is that in determining whether a feature is overridden or instead silenced in some context, we can appeal to considerations of regret. Here is an illustration. Suppose that in the situation I am in, I must lie to save a life; furthermore, it is clear that I should (all things considered) tell the lie. If the fact that my action would be a lie is a feature that is relevant (rather than silenced), then its presence as a relevant consideration counting against telling the lie is still in force and its influence felt, so to speak. Since I cannot both save the life and avoid lying, and so cannot fulfill my prima facie duty of fidelity (as Ross would say), it makes sense for me to feel some degree of regret at having told the lie. I regret that I had to lie in order to save a life and do the all-things-considered right action.

But now consider a different context, in which the fact that my action is a lie is silenced. For some consideration to be silenced in a context means that it doesn't figure into the moral mix at all in determining the all-things-considered right action. So if the fact that my action would be a lie isn't even morally relevant, then it does not make sense to feel regret at having told the lie.

Perhaps, then, there is a way in which we might adjudicate a dispute over whether a feature in some context is overridden or silenced. The proposal is to appeal to considerations of *rational regret*—whether it *makes sense* to have an attitude of regret with respect to the feature in question. If it does, then that is evidence that the feature is relevant but overridden. If it does not, then that is evidence that the feature is silenced.

Now it is clear that there are cases in which features that are normally morally relevant are overridden. The question is whether there are any cases in which such normally relevant features are silenced. Are there any clear cases involving a feature that is normally relevant and favors doing A but where it would not make sense to experience regret for not having done A?[8] We were just considering the maniacal killer case as one possibility. Should the person who kills the maniac feel regret upon contemplating what he did? It is not clear to me. A large part of my hesitation comes from the suspicion that judgments about whether it makes sense (is rational) to experience regret in relation to some feature that is not dominant (or not

among the ones that are dominant) in some context depend on one's judgment about whether the feature is overridden or silenced. That is, I suspect
that one will think that regret makes sense—is rational to experience—in
relation to some feature if and only if one judges that this feature is morally relevant. If this suspicion is correct, then appealing to considerations of
rational regret won't help in trying to decide questions about being overridden versus being silenced.

Before moving on, let us return to the first issue taken up in this section,
the issue of whether generalism has been defeated. We examined a few features offered by generalists as being immune to silencing and reversal and
found them to be unconvincing. But perhaps we have thus far simply failed
to fix on nonmoral features that really are always relevant and never switch
polarity. Here is one candidate:[9]

> killing a human being against his or her will when this individual has
> not killed or threatened to kill or seriously injure any other human

Notice that my maniacal killer example can't be used to cast particularist
doubt on this feature since the maniac is, of course, someone who has killed
humans and is threatening to kill more. So assuming this description is not
morally loaded, are there cases in which actions fitting it are either silenced
or reversed? Suppose the generalist is right and this feature can't be silenced
or reversed. How many such features are there? If there are only a very few,
then perhaps as Dancy quips, the particularist "will have lost a battle but
won the war" (Dancy 2000, 131).

Is Particularism Bad for Society?

What would a society of dedicated particularists be like? How would
such a society compare to one of dedicated Rossians? Brad Hooker argues
that a society of particularists would in general be less trustworthy than a
society of Rossian generalists.

> You know of generalists that they take a limited number of certain general
> features to count morally in the same way every time they occur. You know
> of generalists that they believe that any of these features can be outweighed
> only by one or more [of this] limited number of features. Neither of these
> things is true of particularists. In so far as they reject general moral principles,
> particularists leave us unable to form confident expectations about what they
> will do. (Hooker 2000a, 22)

How persuasive is this sort of argument? And what bearing does it have on
the question of whether generalism or particularism is true?

As for the first question, let us take Hooker's example of Patty the par-

ticularist and Gerry the Rossian generalist. As the story goes, you find yourself approached by Patty, who asks that you help her bring in her crop now
in return for promising to help you with yours when the time comes. Both
of you need help; without it, financial ruin is certain. Compare your level
of trust in Patty with the level of trust you would have in Gerry if he approached you with the same proposal. In comparing our levels of trust, we
are to assume that both Patty and Gerry are committed to behaving morally, Patty according to her particularist outlook, and Gerry according to his
Rossian outlook. Hooker thinks we will agree that if all we know about
Patty and Gerry is that one is a committed particularist and the other is a
committed generalist, we will have greater trust in Gerry keeping his end
of the bargain when the time comes than we will have in Patty. The point
is supposed to generalize. With respect to the practical issue of fostering
greater trust, particularism loses to Rossian generalism in that "collective
public commitment to Rossian generalism would lead to considerably
more trust amongst strangers than would collective public commitment to
particularism" (Hooker 2000a, 21).

Why does Hooker think that a society of particularists will foster less
trust than a society of Rossian generalists? He claims that you have less to
worry about regarding Gerry than Patty, since Gerry necessarily attaches
some moral significance to the fact that he has made a promise to you, and
there are only a limited number of considerations that might interfere with
his deciding to keep his promise. "But for Patty, any fact can become piv-
otal to whether she will take her having promised as any moral reason at
all for her to do what she promised" (Hooker 2000a, 20).

I am less certain than Hooker seems to be about there being any very
significant difference in levels of trust that it makes sense to have in relation
to Patty and Gerry. Let me make just two observations. First, once we distinguish (as we did earlier in this chapter) between features that, for the
generalist, are of fundamental moral relevance and those that are of nonfundamental, derived relevance, any fact might become relevant for the
generalist just as it might for the particularist. For the generalist, any fact
that is not among the fundamental morally relevant features but that becomes relevant in some context will have its relevance explained by appealing to those features of fundamental relevance that are present in the
context. For the particularist, we can suppose that any fact that is not relevant normally but is in the context in question will have its relevance explained by the presence of other features. If facts about the weather become
morally relevant in relation to keeping one's promise, it will be because this
feature of the situation bears on such considerations as, for example, one's
safety in being outside that are present in the circumstances.

My second observation is that I don't see why one should worry that
much about the trustworthiness of Patty (and committed particularists
generally) in matters of keeping promises, avoiding lies, avoiding harming

others, and other matters of perennial moral concern. As a serious and committed particularist, Patty is going to approach her having promised to help you with a strong presumption that her having promised will be morally relevant and is likely to be the dominant consideration once the time comes to help you. Granted, things come up, and she may find herself having to choose between keeping the promise and doing something else that is of greater moral significance. If the circumstances are dire enough, she may find that her having promised to help you is completely silenced. Suppose it turns out that you killed the real owner of the property now under your control and that you are impersonating him in order to hoodwink some unwitting distant relations into thinking that you are the real McCoy so that you can come into a sizable inheritance. (I believe I saw an episode of *Alfred Hitchcock Presents* with roughly this plot line.)

My point is that Patty, as a conscientious particularist, is going to approach each situation calling for a moral decision with a battery of considerations that she has good reason to suppose will be relevant. (These considerations can be encapsulated, as we saw, by rules of prima facie relevance.) Furthermore, she will realize that a situation has to be quite bizarre before considerations having to do with promising, lying, killing, and so forth fail to be relevant (or switch their typical polarity). Won't a society of Pattys be as trustworthy as a society of Gerrys? Remember, it's not that Gerry can be counted on to keep his promise no matter what. He is a Rossian generalist—he believes that considerations might crop up that would override his prima facie duty to help you with your crop.

So I am not convinced by Hooker's attempt to show that a society of Rossian generalists is more trustworthy when it comes to keeping promises, refraining from harming others, lying, and so forth, than would be a society of particularists. But what if Hooker is correct in his speculations about comparative trustworthiness? Does this have any bearing on the truth or falsity of particularism?

As Hooker is well aware, in many instances it is a mistake to infer that some theory or claim is false because of what would happen were people to believe in that theory or accept that claim. If it turned out to be true that general belief in the theory of evolution would be bad for society, this fact about the effect of a general belief in that theory has nothing whatever to do with the question of whether or not it is true. Can't one make the same point in connection with Hooker's claim about the social effects of acceptance of particularism? He thinks that when it comes to moral theories (as compared to scientific theories), the consequences of their acceptance on human well-being can count either for or against their truth.

Getting to the bottom of this issue about the relation between the truth of a moral theory or doctrine and its acceptance value would take us into certain metaethical questions that cannot be dealt with here.[10] Here is yet another place where things must be left for the reader to think about.

8. Conclusion

I have not tried to resolve the dispute between generalists and particularists. Indeed, I have suggested that there may be no non-question-begging way of resolving it, in which case, we end up in stalemate. I am not convinced, however, that this much matters, at least from a practical standpoint. After all, both parties to the dispute agree on the importance of phronesis in contexts of moral deliberation, and both parties can, in principle, agree on a list of moral rules that may guide such deliberation, whether generalist rules indicating features that are always relevant and relevant in the same way, or particularist rules indicating features that are likely to be relevant in a certain way.

Further Reading

Dancy, Jonathan. 1983. "Ethical Particularism and Morally Relevant Properties." *Mind* 92: 530–47. Contains an analysis and criticism of Ross's moral generalism and an initial statement of particularism.

———. 1993. *Moral Reasons.* Oxford: Blackwell. Chapters 4–7 present a sustained defense of particularism against various versions of generalism.

———. 2000. "A Particularist's Progress." In *Moral Particularism,* ed. Brad Hooker and Margaret Little. Oxford: Oxford University Press. Further development of the particularist's view.

Hooker, Brad. 2000. "Moral Particularism—Wrong and Bad." In *Moral Particularism,* ed. Brad Hooker and Margaret Little. Oxford: Oxford University Press. An attempt to argue just what the title indicates.

Hooker, Brad, and Margaret Little, eds. 2000. *Moral Particularism.* Oxford: Oxford University Press. A collection of essays written for this volume debating moral particularism.

Little, Margaret. 2000. "Moral Generalities Revisited." In *Moral Particularism,* ed. Brad Hooker and Margaret Little. Oxford: Oxford University Press. A defense of particularism that attempts to explain how a particularist can allow moral generalizations to play a role in justifying and explaining moral phenomena.

McNaughton, David. 1988. *Moral Vision.* Oxford: Blackwell. Chapter 13 is a very readable presentation and defense of particularism.

Notes

1. What about Ross's theory? Some of his prima facie duties rest on moral features of actions. E.g., the prima facie duty to promote justice has to do with considerations of happiness in relation to *merit,* and, arguably, the concept of merit concerns what one morally deserves. Similar remarks apply to the duties of reparation (involving past *wrongs*), self-improvement and beneficence (involving *virtue),* and gratitude (in response to *morally legitimate* favors from others). For purposes of

this chapter, I will assume that it is possible to specify the bases of Ross's prima facie duties in nonmoral terms. On this point, see Jackson, Pettit, and Smith 2000. (I thank Brad Hooker for raising this issue.)

2. Although the term "moral generalism" has come into use to refer to the set of assumptions in question, "moral universalism" is a better term here because the idea is not that certain nonmoral features are generally (but perhaps not always) morally relevant and relevant in the same way, but that they maintain their relevance universally, without exception.

3. These are taken from Hooker 2000, 7–11.

4. *Webster's New Collegiate Dictionary,* s.v. "sadism," "perverse," "perversion."

5. This case was suggested to me by Mitch Haney.

6. The generalist may want to insist that harming someone is not just a matter of causing them mental or physical pain but also involves *injuring* them or thwarting their *interests,* which mere infliction of pain need not do. The generalist may be right about this matter, but then to determine whether harming others, in the relevant sense of harm, is morally loaded would require that we investigate the notions of injury and interest being employed.

7. Here, for the sake of simplicity, I am just focusing on the alleged phenomenon of silencing.

8. We must also assume that there is no other feature that in the context favors doing A and is relevant.

9. Suggested to me by Brad Hooker.

10. For some discussion of this issue, see Timmons 1999, chap. 3.

11

Conclusion

In the previous chapters, we have surveyed a variety of moral theories, including the divine command theory, moral relativism, the natural law theory, utilitarianism, Kant's moral theory, moral pluralism, virtue ethics, and moral particularism. My primary aim has been to explain and then critically evaluate these theories. I have not attempted to defend some one theory as ultimately correct or superior to all of its rivals. But I have argued that a plausible moral theory is likely going to be a version of limited moral pluralism.[1] In concluding, I want to reinforce this claim by explaining why this should not be surprising. I will then close with a few observations about the project of moral theory.

1. Why Limited Moral Pluralism?

To say that a theory of right conduct is pluralist is to say that it features a plurality of fundamental morally relevant features that are the basis for rightness and wrongness of actions. Similar remarks apply to pluralist theories of intrinsic value. To say that a moral theory is limited is to say that the moral principles or rules of the theory do not (together with relevant factual information) yield determinate moral verdicts about a large range of specific cases.[2] What would explain the fact (if it is a fact) that any plausible moral theory is likely to be a version of limited moral pluralism?

The most obvious response (and one suggested throughout the book) concerns the complexity of ordinary moral thought and discourse. Here is how Bernard Williams makes the point:

[O]ur ethical ideas consist of a very complex historical deposit. When we consider this fact, and the relations that this deposit has to our public discourse and our private lives, there seems no reason at all to expect it to take, in any considerable measure, the shape of a [strongly unified] theory. (Williams 1995, 189)

As Williams goes on to point out, if one thinks that a proper starting place in developing a moral theory is with the various moral convictions with which we find ourselves, then in attempting to capture moral considerations that are part of a "complex historical deposit," we are going to be driven toward moral pluralism.

This same complexity also supports the idea that no plausible moral theory is going to be able to produce some method for adjudicating conflicts among the values, virtues, or prima facie duties that make up the plurality of basic morally relevant features. So the complexity of the various moral considerations that play an important role in our thinking helps explain why any plausible moral theory is likely to be a limited moral pluralism.

We come to the same conclusion about the likely shape of any plausible moral theory by reflecting on the importance of moral judgment (phronesis) in practical thinking in general and moral reflection in particular. Again, the point is made by Williams in connection with making judgments about what is morally important:

> Judgments of importance are ubiquitous, and are central to practical life and to reflection at a more general level about the considerations that go into practical decision. Moreover, judgments of importance indeed require judgment. There are certainly reasons why some considerations are more important than others . . . but judgment is still needed to determine how far those reasons can take you. It may be obvious that one kind of consideration is more important than another (for instance, one kind of ethical consideration is more important than another), but it is a matter of judgment whether in a particular set of circumstances that priority is preserved: other factors alter the balance, or it may be a very weak example of the consideration that generally wins. (Williams 1995, 190)

The idea that judgment is required to decide which moral considerations in certain contexts are overriding (most important) is an idea we have seen in Ross. What Williams goes on to point out about judgment is that there is no reason to suppose that there is some one measure or fixed principle by which one can decide matters of relative importance. In other words, the sort of judgment in question that is so crucial to moral thinking cannot be fully captured in some set of principles or rules—a claim emphasized by Ross, virtue ethicists, and other moral pluralists.

Thus, the complexity of ordinary moral thought and the urge to have one's moral theory cohere with our considered moral beliefs push moral theory in the direction of limited moral pluralism. The importance of moral judgment reinforces this verdict. We have seen how the natural law theory,

Kant's moral theory, utilitarianism, and virtue ethics can take this form. Of course, Ross's theory is a prime example of limited moral pluralism. What I am here pointing out is simply that some form of limited moral pluralism is to be expected given the complexity of moral life and the apparent ineliminable role of moral judgment.

2. The Project of Moral Theory Once Again

Suppose I am right and any plausible moral theory is going to be a form of limited moral pluralism. Now (1) if versions of many of the moral theories we have studied (if not all of them) can take this form, and (2) if, because they are limited in power, they are likely to be consistent with our considered moral beliefs, then they are going to have pretty much the same (limited) implications about which actions are right and what sorts of things (including people) are good. And if they do, then do they all collapse into a single theory? What is left of the differences between, and conflicts among, such theories, assuming that they basically agree in what they imply about right, wrong, good, and bad?

The answer is that these theories still differ in two important ways. First, they differ in overall structure. John Rawls, in an often quoted passage, remarked that "Moral theory is the study of substantive moral conceptions, that is, the study of how the basic notions of the right, the good, and moral worth [the morally good] may be arranged to form different structures" (Rawls 1975, 286). Given that there are three kinds of basic moral notions, there would seem to be the following kinds of possible structures that a moral theory might take. (1) One kind of notion is most basic and can be used to characterize the other two. (2) Of the three types of basic notions, two are equally basic, while the third is to be understood in terms of one or both of the others. (3) All three types of notions are equally basic—each can be understood without appeal to the other two. (4) None of the three types of notions is basic—to understand any one of them, we must appeal to the other two.

The moral theories we have examined differ in their structures. For instance, utilitarianism and virtue ethics are value-based theories, but while utilitarianism typically understands the concept of (nonmoral) good to be most basic, many versions of virtue ethics take the concept of moral worth (moral goodness) to be most basic. Thus one important difference among the moral theories concerns matters of structure, which are significant for at least two reasons.

First, for purposes of understanding morality, philosophers are interested in relations among concepts. Questions about structure expressed by Rawls have to do with relations among the basic concepts in ethics and the categories they represent.

Second, the issue of structure has implications for theoretical questions about what makes something right or wrong, good or bad, as well as for practical questions about how to proceed in coming to have justified moral beliefs. If some type of value-based moral theory is correct—say, a theory that makes the rightness and wrongness of actions depend on some relation between actions and what is of intrinsic value—then this fact would give us insight into the nature of rightness and wrongness. Again, knowing what makes an action right or wrong should be useful in our practices of justifying moral beliefs. If, for example, we knew that some version of utilitarianism were true, then we would know that to justify a moral belief about the rightness of an action would require that we bring considerations of welfare to bear on the matter.

In addition to differences over structure, moral theories differ in content. For instance, both the natural law theory and utilitarianism are value-based theories that make considerations of nonmoral value basic in morality. However, natural law theorists embrace a perfectionistic account of intrinsic value; utilitarians reject perfectionism in favor of a welfarist account of intrinsic value.

So, even if we should expect a correct moral theory to take the form of limited moral pluralism, this does not settle questions about the structure or content of the theory. There is still much interesting work to be done in arriving at a philosophically justified view about which form of limited moral pluralism is best. Indeed, given my remarks about judging the plausibility of a moral theory, there is work to be done in metaethics on the issue of how (if at all) it is possible to arrive at a philosophically justified moral theory. Such issues are matters of lively contemporary debate in ethics.

Notes

1. If we allow moral particularism to count as a nongeneralist version of moral pluralism, then my remarks apply to this nontraditional type of moral theory as well.

2. We can be more specific by distinguishing *theoretical limits* and *practical limits*. I have been most interested in the former. But the moral principles featured in a theory might be difficult or impossible to use as a decision procedure and thus be practically limited without also being theoretically limited. This is the case with utilitarianism. See chap. 5.

Appendix

Standards for Evaluating Moral Theories

The following standards are explained in chapter 1, section 6.

Consistency. A moral theory should be consistent in the sense that its principles, together with relevant factual information, yield consistent moral verdicts about the morality of actions, persons, and other objects of moral evaluation.

Determinacy. A moral theory should feature principles that, together with relevant factual information, yield determinate moral verdicts about the morality of actions, persons, and other objects of evaluation in a wide range of cases.

Intuitive Appeal. A moral theory should develop and make sense of various intuitively appealing beliefs and ideas about morality.

Internal Support. A moral theory whose principles, together with relevant factual information, logically imply our considered moral beliefs receives support—internal support—from those beliefs. On the other hand, if the principles of a theory have implications that conflict with our considered moral beliefs, this is evidence against the correctness of the theory.

Explanatory Power. A moral theory should feature principles that explain our more specific considered moral beliefs, thus helping us understand *why* actions, persons, and other objects of moral evaluation are right or wrong, good or bad.

External Support. The fact that the principles of a moral theory are supported by nonmoral beliefs and assumptions, including well-established beliefs and assumptions from various areas of nonmoral inquiry, is some

evidence in its favor. On the other hand, the fact that the principles conflict with established nonmoral beliefs and assumptions is evidence against
the theory.

Glossary

Entries are followed by chapter and section numbers where these terms are introduced.

absolutism (moral). The view that there are certain types of actions (e.g., intentionally killing innocent humans) that are always wrong regardless of the consequences of such actions. (chap. 4, sec. 2)

acceptance utility. The net value that would result were a given rule to be accepted by a significant proportion of the members of some group. (chap. 6, sec. 4)

actual consequence utilitarianism (ACU). A version of utilitarianism that states that an action A is right if and only if A has as high an *actual utility* as any alternative action that the agent could perform instead. (chap. 5, sec. 5)

actual utility. The utility that would (actually) result from an action were it to be performed. (chap. 5, sec. 5)

act utilitarianism (AU). A version of utilitarianism according to which the values of the consequences of concrete specific actions determine the deontic status of actions. (chap. 6, sec. 4)

all-things-considered duty. An action that, once all of the morally relevant considerations are brought to bear, is one's actual duty. (chap. 8, sec. 3) *See also* prima facie duty.

applicability standard. A standard for evaluating moral theories that states that in providing a decision procedure, a moral theory ought to specify a procedure that human beings, with their limitations, can actually use in moral deliberation. (chap. 5, sec. 5)

applied ethics. That branch of normative ethics that is concerned with specific moral issues, particularly controversial ones such as abortion, capital punishment, and treatment of animals. (chap. 1, sec. 7)

atomism. *See* relevance atomism.

care ethics. A type of moral theory that makes considerations of caring about individuals central in developing an overall theory of right conduct and value. (chap. 9, sec. 4)

273

caring about. Caring about someone or something involves "being invested" in that person or thing. (chap. 9, sec. 4)

casuistry. The art of applying principles to specific cases to reach justified moral conclusions about those cases. (chap. 7, sec. 5)

Categorical Imperative. Kant's supreme principle of morality. In the Humanity as an End in Itself formulation, it requires that we treat humanity, in ourselves and in others, always as an end in itself, never as a mere means. In the Universal Law formulation, it requires that we act only on those maxims that we can will to be universal laws. (chap. 7, sec. 4) *See also* hypothetical imperative (formal principle of).

categorical imperatives. In Kant's ethics, categorical imperatives express obligations that are valid for an agent simply because she is a free and rational agent and are thus valid independently of her desires. In Kant's moral theory, moral obligations are properly expressed as categorical imperatives. (chap. 7, sec. 2)

commensurability (of values). The idea that different values can be balanced, weighed, and thus compared according to a common scale. In cases where no such balancing and weighing is possible, values are said to be incommensurable. (chap. 4, sec. 6)

consequentialism. A type of moral theory that makes the deontic status of actions depend entirely on the values of the consequences of individual actions or rules associated with individual actions. (chap. 5, sec. 1)

considered moral beliefs. Those beliefs that are deeply held and widely shared and which one would continue to hold were one to reflect carefully on their correctness. (chap. 1, sec. 6)

consistency standard. A standard for evaluating a moral theory that requires that its principles (or rules) yield consistent moral verdicts about the morality of actions, persons, and other objects of moral evaluation. (chap. 1, sec. 6)

context sensitivity thesis (CS). A thesis that claims that the rightness or wrongness of an action (performed in some particular context) depends in part on nonmoral facts that hold in the context in question—facts concerning agents and their circumstances. (chap. 3, sec. 2)

deontic concepts (categories). Concepts such as obligation, duty, right, wrong, forbidden, permissible, impermissible, optional. In ethics, they are used primarily for the evaluation of actions. (chap. 1, sec. 4)

deontic status of actions. The rightness or wrongness of actions. (chap. 1, sec. 4)

descriptive relativism. *See* moral diversity thesis.

desire fulfillment utilitarianism (DFU). A version of utilitarianism that understands utility in terms of fulfillment of desires. (chap. 6, sec. 5) *See also* utility, utilitarianism.

determinacy standard. A standard for evaluating a moral theory that says that the principles (or rules) of a moral theory should yield determinate moral verdicts about the morality of actions, persons, and other objects of evaluation in a wide range of cases. (chap. 1, sec. 6)

direct violation (D). A violation of a basic value by an action in which (1) the action will bring about the hindrance or destruction of a basic value, and (2) that action cannot be justified by the principle of double effect. Such violations are part of the theory of right conduct for the natural law theory. (chap. 4, sec. 9)

divine command theory. A theory that holds that the nature of right and wrong, good and bad depends on God's commands. An action is obligatory, for example, because God commands that we do it. (chap. 2, sec. 1)

double effect. *See* principle of double effect.

ethical hedonism (EH). The view that experiences of pleasure are intrinsically good and experiences of pain are intrinsically bad, and they are the only items of nonmoral intrinsic value with which ethics is concerned. (chap. 5, sec. 2)

ethics. That branch of philosophy concerned with morality; it includes *normative ethics* and *metaethics* as its main branches. (chap. 1, sec. 7)

Euthyphro dilemma. For a theist, a dilemma that involves the issue of how God's commands are related to morality. On the one hand, if morality is dependent on God's commands (as claimed by the divine command theory), then one must reject certain basic claims about God's nature—for example, that God is perfectly morally good and fully rational. On the other hand, if morality is independent of God's commands, then one must reject the idea that God is creator of all things. (chap. 2, sec. 3)

expected utility. The utility of an action that will probably result (can be expected to result) if the action is performed. (chap. 5, sec. 5)

explanatory power standard. A standard for evaluating a moral theory that requires that the theory (its basic principles or rules) explain our more specific considered moral beliefs, thus helping us understand *why* actions, persons, and other objects of moral evaluation are right or wrong, good or bad. (chap. 1, sec. 6)

external support standard. A standard for evaluating a moral theory that asserts that the fact that the principles of a moral theory are supported by various nonmoral beliefs and assumptions—beliefs and assumptions that are "external to" morality—is some evidence in favor of the theory. (chap. 1, sec. 6)

extrinsic goodness (badness). Goodness (or badness) possessed by something in virtue of that thing being appropriately related to something that has intrinsic goodness (or badness). For example, the goodness of knowledge is extrinsic if such knowledge is a means to some intrinsic good such as happiness. Note that something can be both intrinsically and extrinsically good. (chap. 1, sec. 4)

fundamental morally relevant nonmoral feature. A nonmoral feature of some action or other object of evaluation that is fundamental in explaining the morality of the action or object. (chap. 10, sec. 1)

generalism (moral). The view that right and wrong, good and bad depend on certain nonmoral features of actions and other items of evaluation that are always morally relevant and relevant in the same way. (chap. 10, sec. 2) *See also* relevance atomism, relevance holism.

generic principle of utility (GPU). A principle that states that an action A is right if and only if A has as high a utility as any alternative action that the agent could perform instead. (chap. 5, sec. 1) *See also* utilitarianism.

hedonism. The view, with respect to value, according to which (1) only experiences of pleasure are intrinsically good and only experiences of pain are intrinsically bad, and (2) what makes such experiences good and bad respectively are features (their pleasantness and unpleasantness) possessed by those experiences. (chap. 5, sec. 2) *See also* ethical hedonism, hedonistic conception of utility.

hedonistic conception of utility (HU). A conception that claims that the utility of an action is equal to the overall balance of pleasure versus pain that would be produced were the action to be performed. (chap. 5, sec. 2) *See also* utility.

hedonistic utilitarianism (PHU). A principle that states that an action is right if and only if it produces at least as high an overall balance of pleasure versus pain as would any other alternative action. (chap. 5, sec. 2)

holism. *See* relevance holism.

humanity as an end itself (HEI). A formulation of the Categorical Imperative that states: so act that you use humanity, whether in your own person or in the person of any other, always as an end, never merely as a means. (chap. 7, sec. 4)

hypothetical imperative (formal principle of) (HI). As described in Kant's moral theory, a formal principle of rational choice and action that requires that we adopt the necessary means to our ends. (chap. 7, sec. 2)

impartialism. In ethics, the idea that everyone ought to be given equal consideration in matters of morality. (chap. 5, sec. 1)

internal support standard. A standard for evaluating a moral theory that requires that the theory (its basic principles or rules), together with relevant information, logically imply our considered moral beliefs. (chap. 1, sec. 6)

intrinsic goodness (badness). Goodness (or badness) possessed by something just in case the ground of the thing's goodness (or badness) is intrinsic to the thing. (chap. 1, sec. 4)

intuitive appeal standard. A standard for evaluating a moral theory that requires that the theory make sense of various beliefs about morality that are intuitively appealing. (chap. 1, sec. 6)

maxim. In Kant's moral theory, a "subjective principle of volition"—presumably an intention—upon which an agent acts. (chap. 7, sec. 7)

metaethics. That branch of ethics that concerns semantic, metaphysical, and epistemological questions about moral thought and discourse. (chap. 1, sec. 7) *See also* moral semantics, moral metaphysics, moral epistemology.

monism. In ethics, the view that there is some single basic feature of actions in virtue of which they are right or wrong. One can also be a monist about value. (chap. 8, sec. 1) *See also* pluralism.

moral disagreement. A disagreement that occurs when two or more parties disagree about the morality of some action or other object of evaluation. Such disagreement is fundamental when it stems from a disagreement over basic moral norms; otherwise it is nonfundamental. (chap. 3, sec. 5)

moral diversity thesis (MD). A thesis that claims that the moral codes of some cultures include basic moral norms that conflict with the basic moral norms that are part of the moral codes of other cultures. This thesis is often called descriptive relativism. (chap. 3, sec. 3)

moral epistemology. That branch of metaethics that is concerned with knowledge and justification of moral claims. (chap. 1, sec. 7)

moral judgment (phronesis). A developed capacity to arrive at moral verdicts about specific cases that cannot be fully explained in terms of the application of principles, rules, or any other rigorous method that would determine a correct verdict. (chap. 8, sec. 7)

moral metaphysics. That branch of metaethics that is concerned with questions about, e.g., the existence and nature of moral properties and facts. (chap. 1, sec. 7)

moral norms. General moral statements that specify some action as either required, prohibited, or permissible. (chap. 3, sec. 1)

moral principle. A general moral statement that purports to set forth conditions under which an action is right or wrong or something is good or bad. (chap. 1, sec. 3)

moral relativism (MR). A moral theory according to which the rightness and wrongness of actions (for a person living in a culture at some time) depend on the basic moral norms of that person's culture. A similar account is given about the nature of goodness and badness. (chap. 3, sec. 1)

moral rule. A general moral statement that specifies some type of action (or other object of evaluation) as having a certain moral quality. For example, "killing is wrong." (chap. 1, sec. 3)

moral semantics. The branch of metaethics that is concerned with questions about the meaning and truth of moral claims. (chap. 1, sec. 7)

moral theory. A branch of ethics that is primarily concerned with investigating the nature of the right and the good. (chap. 1, sec. 2)

moral value (worth). Value (or worth) that has to do with the goodness and badness of persons (as responsible agents) and, in particular, with the goodness and badness of those character traits and associated motives in virtue of which persons are morally good or bad. (chap. 1, sec. 4)

natural law theory. A type of moral theory that (on most versions) attempts to ground morality in facts about human nature. Also characteristic of the theory are perfectionism, moral absolutism, and the principle of double effect. (chap. 4, sec. 2)

natural law theory, Aquinas's basic principle of (NLT). Principle that states that life, procreation, knowledge, and sociability are to be preserved and promoted, their hindrance and destruction are to be avoided. (chap. 4, sec. 4)

nonmoral feature. A property of something that can be characterized without using moral terms. Such features are the basis for moral evaluation. (chap. 10, sec. 1)

nonmoral value. Value that has to do with the goodness and badness of things other than responsible agents. (chap. 1, sec. 4)

normative ethics. That branch of ethics that attempts to answer both general moral questions about what to do and how to be (the main concern of moral theory) and moral questions about specific moral issues such as abortion, euthanasia, capital punishment, and so forth (the main concern of applied ethics). (chap. 1, sec. 7)

obligatory action. In ethics, an action that is morally required; something one ought to do; an action that is one's duty. (chap. 1, sec. 4)

optional action. In ethics, an action that is neither morally obligatory nor morally wrong; it is merely permitted. (chap. 1, sec. 4)

particularism (moral). A view that denies that there are any nonmoral features of actions and other objects of evaluation that are always morally relevant and relevant in the same way. It thus denies atomism about relevance and instead affirms relevance holism. (chap. 10, sec. 2)

perfectionism. With respect to value, the view that the good of some kind of thing is a matter of its achieving perfection for things of that kind. *Moral perfectionism* refers to those moral theories that accept perfectionism about value in relation to human beings and make considerations of human perfection the basis for understanding right and wrong action. (chap. 4, sec. 3)

phronesis. From a Greek word meaning intelligence. In ethics phronesis refers to moral judgment. (chap. 9, sec. 2) *See also* moral judgment.

pluralism. In ethics, the view with respect to right conduct that there is a plurality of basic features that can make an action right or wrong. One can also be a pluralist about value. (chap. 8, sec. 1) *See also* monism.

polarity thesis (P). A thesis that claims that if a fundamental morally relevant nonmoral feature is ever a right-making or good-making feature, it is so in all cases in which it is present, and similarly for features that are wrong-making or bad-making. (chap. 10, sec. 1)

prima facie duty. An action that (1) possesses some morally relevant feature that counts in favor of one's doing the act and (2) is such that if it were the only morally relevant feature of one's situation, then the act in question would be one's all-things-considered duty. (chap. 8, sec. 3) *See also* all-things-considered duty.

principle (doctrine) of double effect (PDE). A principle that claims that one is permitted to perform an action that has at least one good and one bad effect if and only if the following conditions are met: (1) the action, apart from its consequences, must not be wrong; (2) the bad effect must not be intended by the agent; and (3) the bad effect must not be "out of proportion" to the good effect. (chap. 4, sec. 7)

probable consequence utilitarianism (PCU). A version of utilitarianism that states that an action A is right if and only if A has as high an expected utility as any alternative action that the agent could perform instead. (chap. 5, sec. 5) *See also* actual consequence utilitarianism.

relevance atomism (RA). A view that claims that there are nonmoral features of actions whose relevance (in determining the moral qualities of actions and other items of evaluation) in a context is unaffected by other features that may be present in that context. The denial of relevance holism. (chap. 10, sec. 4)

relevance holism (RH). A view that maintains that the moral relevance of any nonmoral feature in some context depends upon the other features present in that context. The denial of relevance atomism. (chap. 10, sec. 4)

right action. Broadly, any action that is not wrong. More narrowly, an action that is morally required and hence obligatory. (chap. 1, sec. 4)

right-making feature. A feature of an action that counts in favor of the action's rightness. Similarly for the notion of a good-making feature. (chap. 8, sec. 5)

rule utilitarianism (RU). A form of utilitarianism that makes the deontic status of an individual, concrete action depend on the utilities associated with the rules that apply to some situation. An action, on this view, is right if and only if it is allowed by a rule with as high a utility as any other alternative rule applying to the situation. (chap. 6, sec. 4)

theory of right conduct. The branch of moral theory concerned with the nature of right and wrong action. (chap. 1, sec. 5)

theory of value. The branch of moral theory concerned with the nature of goodness and badness. (chap. 1, sec. 4)

unity thesis (U). A thesis that claims that there is a small fixed set of nonmoral features of actions (persons, institutions, and so forth) that are fundamental in explaining the deontic status of any action. Such features serve to unify moral phenomena. (chap. 10, sec. 1)

universalism. In ethics, the idea that *all* individuals who will be affected by some decision or action count in matters of morality. (chap. 5, sec. 1)

universality thesis (UT). A thesis that states that there are moral norms whose correctness or validity is independent of the moral norms a culture does or might accept and thus express universally valid moral standards that apply to all cultures. (chap. 3, sec. 1)

universal law (UL). A formulation of the Categorical Imperative that states: act only in accordance with that maxim through which you can at the same time will that it become a universal law. (chap. 7, sec. 7)

universal relevance thesis (UR). A thesis that states that if a feature is a fundamental morally relevant nonmoral feature, then it is morally relevant in any context in which it is present. (chap. 10, sec. 1)

utilitarianism. A type of moral theory according to which the deontic status of actions depends entirely on considerations of utility. (chap. 5, sec. 1) *See also* utility, generic principle of utility, act utilitarianism, rule utilitarianism.

utility. A technical term within the utilitarianism tradition that refers to net intrinsic value associated with actions, rules, or other items of moral evaluation, where value has to do with welfare. (chap. 5, sec. 1)

value-based moral theory. A theory that takes considerations of value to be prior to considerations of right conduct. Considerations of value are therefore used in such theories to explain the nature of right conduct. (chap. 1, sec. 5)

value concepts (categories). Categories, including good, bad, and evil, that are used in ethics primarily in evaluating the moral status of persons (including their character traits and associated motives) as well as things, experiences, and states of affairs. (chap. 1, sec. 4)

vice. A trait of character or mind that typically involves dispositions to act, feel, and think in certain ways and is central in the negative evaluation of persons. The traits of dishonesty and disloyalty are examples. (chap. 9, sec. 2)

virtue. A trait of character or mind that typically involves dispositions to act, feel, and think in certain ways and is central in the positive evaluation of persons. The traits of honesty and loyalty are examples. (chap. 9, sec. 1)

welfare. The well-being of individuals. (chap. 5, sec. 1)

welfarism. The view that the only kind value that is of fundamental relevance for ethical evaluation is the welfare of individuals. (chap. 5, sec. 1)

wrong action. In ethics, an action that one ought not to do, an action that one is morally prohibited from doing, an action that one has a duty not to do. (chap. 1, sec. 4)

wrong–making feature. A feature of an action that counts toward an action's wrongness. Similarly for the notion of a bad–making feature. (chap. 8, sec. 5)

References

Adams, Robert M. 1973. "A Modified Divine Command Theory of Ethical Wrongness." In *Religion and Morality: A Collection of Essays*, ed. Gene Outka and John P. Reeder. New York: Doubleday. Reprinted in Paul Helm, ed., *Divine Commands and Morality* (Oxford: Oxford University Press, 1981).

————. 1979. "Divine Command Ethics Modified Again." *Journal of Religious Ethics* 7: 71–79. Reprinted in Paul Helm, ed., *Divine Commands and Morality* (Oxford: Oxford University Press, 1981).

Annas, Julia. 1993. *The Morality of Happiness.* Oxford: Oxford University Press.

Aquinas, Saint Thomas. 1988. *On Politics and Ethics.* Trans. Paul E. Sigmund. New York: W. W. Norton.

Aristotle. 1985. *Nicomachean Ethics.* Trans. Terence Irwin. Indianapolis: Hackett.

Audi, Robert. 1997. *Moral Knowledge and Ethical Character.* Oxford: Oxford University Press.

Baron, Marcia W. 1995. *Kantian Ethics Almost without Apology.* Ithaca, N.Y.: Cornell University Press.

Baron, Marcia W., Philip Pettit, and Michael Slote. 1997. *Three Methods of Ethics.* Oxford: Blackwell.

Benedict, Ruth. 1934. *Patterns of Culture.* Boston: Houghton Mifflin.

Bentham, Jeremy. [1789] 1948. *An Introduction to the Principles of Morals and Legislation.* New York: Hafner.

Blustein, Jeffrey. 1991. *Care and Commitment.* Oxford: Oxford University Press.

Brandt, Richard B. 1959. *Ethical Theory.* Englewood Cliffs, N.J.: Prentice-Hall.

————. 1979. *A Theory of the Good and the Right.* Oxford: Oxford University Press.

Brink, David O. 1989. *Moral Realism and the Foundations of Ethics.* Cambridge: Cambridge University Press.

Brown, H. I. 1988. *Rationality.* London: Routledge.

Buchanan, Allen. 1996. "Intending Death: The Structure of the Problem and Proposed Solutions." In *Intending Death*, ed. Tom L. Beauchamp. Upper Saddle River, N.J.: Prentice-Hall.

Conly, Sarah. 1988. "Flourishing and the Failure of the Ethics of Virtue." *Midwest Studies in Philosophy* 13: 83–96.

Crisp, Roger. 1997. *Mill on Utilitarianism.* London: Routledge.

Cullity, Garrett, and Berys Gaut, eds. 1997. *Ethics and Practical Reason*. Oxford: Oxford University Press.

Dancy, Jonathan. 1993. *Moral Reasons*. Oxford: Blackwell.

Davis, Nancy. 1984. "The Doctrine of Double Effect: Problems of Interpretation." *Pacific Philosophical Quarterly* 65: 107–23.

Donner, Wendy. 1998. "Mill's Utilitarianism." In *The Cambridge Companion to Mill*, ed. John Skorupski. Cambridge: Cambridge University Press.

Engstrom, Stephen. 2002. "The Inner Freedom of Virtue." In *Kant's* Metaphysics of Morals: *Interpretative Essays*, ed. Mark Timmons. Oxford: Oxford University Press.

Feldman, Fred. 1978. *Introductory Ethics*. Englewood Cliffs, N.J.: Prentice-Hall.

Finnis, John. 1980. *Natural Law and Natural Rights*. Oxford: Oxford University Press.

Foot, Philippa. 1972. "Morality as a System of Hypothetical Imperatives." *Philosophical Review* 81: 305–16. Reprinted in Philippa Foot, *Virtues and Vices* (Berkeley and Los Angeles: University of California Press, 1978).

Frankena, William. 1973. *Ethics*. 2d ed. Englewood Cliffs, N. J.: Prentice-Hall.

Frankfurt, Harry G. 1999. "On Caring." In *Necessity, Volition, and Love*.Cambridge: Cambridge University Press.

Friedman, Marilyn. 1987. "Beyond Caring: The De-Moralization of Gender." In *Justice and Care*, ed.Virginia Held. Boulder, Colo.: Westview Press.

Gilligan, Carol. 1982. *In a Different Voice*. Cambridge: Harvard University Press.

————. 1987. "Moral Orientation and Moral Development." In *Women and Moral Theory*, ed. Eva Feder Kittay and Diana T. Meyers.Totowa, N.J.: Rowman & Littlefield.

Griffin, James. 1986. *Well-Being*. Oxford: Oxford University Press.

Hare, R. M. 1981. *Moral Thinking*. Oxford: Oxford University Press.

Harman, Gilbert. 1975. "Moral Relativism Defended." *Philosophical Review* 84: 3–22.

————. 1983. "Human Flourishing, Ethics, and Liberty." *Philosophy and Public Affairs* 12: 307–22.

Harman, Gilbert, and Judith Thomson. 1996. *Moral Relativism and Moral Objectivity*. Oxford: Blackwell.

Helm, Paul, ed. 1981. *Divine Commands and Morality*. New York: Oxford University Press.

Himmelfarb, Gertrude. 1995. *The De-Moralization of Society*. New York: Alfred A. Knopf.

Hooker, Brad. 2000a. *Ideal Code, Real World*. Oxford: Oxford University Press.

————. 2000b. "Moral Particularism—Wrong and Bad." In *Moral Particularism*, ed. Brad Hooker and Margaret Little. Oxford: Oxford University Press.

Hume, David. [1739] 1978. *A Treatise of Human Nature*. 2d ed. rev. Ed. P. H. Nidditch. Oxford: Oxford University Press.

Hurka, Thomas. 1993. *Perfectionism*. Oxford: Oxford University Press.

Hursthouse, Rosalind. 1999. *On Virtue Ethics*. Oxford: Oxford University Press.

Jackson, Frank, Philip Pettit, and Michael Smith. 2000. "Ethical Particularism and Patterns." In *Moral Particularism*, ed. Brad Hooker and Margaret Little. Oxford: Oxford University Press.

Johnson, Robert. 1997. "Kant's Conception of Virtue." *Jahrbuch für Recht und Ethik* (*Annual Review of Law and Ethics*) 5: 365–87.

Kant, Immanuel. [1785] 1997. *Groundwork of the Metaphysics of Morals.* Trans. Mary Gregor. Cambridge: Cambridge University Press.

———. [1788] 1997. *Critique of Practical Reason.* Trans. Mary Gregor. Cambridge: Cambridge University Press.

———. [1788] 1996. *The Metaphysics of Morals.* Trans. Mary Gregor. Cambridge: Cambridge University Press.

Kitcher, Philip. 1999. "Essence and Perfection." *Ethics* 110: 59–83.

Kluckhohn, Clyde. 1955. "Ethical Relativity: Sic et Non." *Journal of Philosophy* 52: 663–77.

Larmore, Charles E. 1987. *Patterns of Moral Complexity.* Cambridge: Cambridge University Press.

Lisska, Anthony J. 1996. *Aquinas's Theory of Natural Law.* New York: Oxford University Press.

MacIntyre, Alasdair. 1981. *After Virtue.* Notre Dame, Ind.: University of Notre Dame Press.

Mackie, J. L. 1977. *Ethics: Inventing Right and Wrong.* Harmondsworth, England: Penguin Books.

Marquis, Donald B. 1991. "Four Versions of Double Effect." *Journal of Medicine and Philosophy* 16: 515–44.

McNaughton, David. 1988. *Moral Vision.* Oxford: Blackwell.

Mill, John Stuart. [1863] 1979. *Utilitarianism.* Indianapolis: Hackett.

Moody-Adams, Michele M. 1997. *Fieldwork in Familiar Places.* Cambridge: Harvard University Press.

Mortimer, Robert C. 1950. *Christian Ethics.* New York: Hutchinson's University Library.

Nozick, Robert. 1974. *Anarchy, State, and Utopia.* New York: Basic Books.

O'Connor, John. 1967. *Aquinas and Natural Law.* London: Macmillan.

Pincoffs, Edmund. 1986. *Quandaries and Virtues.* Lawrence: University of Kansas Press.

Plato. 1976. *Euthyphro, Apology, Crito.* Trans. F. J. Church. Indianapolis: Bobbs-Merrill.

Putnam, Hilary. 1981. *Reason, Truth, and History.* Cambridge: Cambridge University Press.

Rawls, John. 1971. *A Theory of Justice.* Cambridge: Harvard University Press.

———. 1975. "The Independence of Moral Theory." *Proceedings and Addresses of the American Philosophical Association* 48: 5–22. Reprinted in S. Freeman, ed., *John Rawls: Collected Papers* (Cambridge: Harvard University Press, 1999).

Ross, W. D. 1930. *The Right and the Good.* Oxford: Oxford University Press.

Sartre, Jean-Paul. 1965. *Essays in Existentialism.* New York: Philosophical Library.

Scheffler, Samuel. 1982. *The Rejection of Consequentialism.* Oxford: Oxford University Press.

Sidgwick, Henry. [1907] 1966. *The Methods of Ethics.* 7th ed. New York: Dover.

Singer, Peter. 1994. *Rethinking Life and Death.* New York: St. Martin's.

Stocker, Michael. 1976. "The Schizophrenia of Modern Moral Theories." *Journal of Philosophy* 73: 453–66.

Sumner, L. W. 1996. *Welfare, Happiness, and Ethics.* Oxford: Oxford University Press.

Sumner, William G. [1906] 1959. *Folkways.* New York: Dover.

Swinburne, R. G. 1974. "Duty and the Will of God." *Canadian Journal of Philosophy* 4: 213–27. Reprinted in Paul Helm, ed., *Divine Commands and Morality* (New York: Oxford University Press, 1981).

Timmons, Mark. 1997. "Decision Procedures, Moral Criteria, and the Problem of Relevant Descriptions in Kant's Ethics." *Jahrbuch für Recht und Ethik (Annual Review of Law and Ethics)* 5: 389–417.

————. 1999. *Morality without Foundations.* Oxford: Oxford University Press.

————, ed. 2002. *Kant's* Metaphysics of Morals: *Interpretative Essays.* Oxford: Oxford University Press.

Tronto, Joan C. 1989. "Women and Caring: What Can Feminists Learn about Morality from Caring?" In *Justice and Care,* ed. Virginia Held. Boulder, Colo.: Westview Press.

Williams, Bernard. 1995. "What Does Intuitionism Imply?" In *Making Sense of Humanity.* Cambridge: Cambridge University Press.

Williams, Bernard, and J. J. C. Smart. 1973. *Utilitarianism: For and Against.* Cambridge: Cambridge University Press.

Wong, David. 1984. *Moral Relativity.* Berkeley and Los Angeles: University of California Press.

Index

absolutism, moral, 62n4, 67, 80, 87–89, 181,187n22. *See also* moral rules
Adams, Robert M., 34n4
Annas, Julia, 242n7
anthropologist's arguments, 46–47, 51–52
antitheory (in ethics), 257
applicability standard, 122
applied ethics, 17–19
Aquinas, Saint Thomas, 33, 66–75, 80, 84–86, 93–96, 100n1, 100n5, 101n20, 186n3, 214, 242n2

arbitrariness objection, 206–7
Aristotle, 68, 71, 180, 211–12, 214–20, 238, 242n2, 242n4, 242n7, 256
atomism. *See* relevance, moral
Audi, Robert, 34n2, 203–4, 209n12
autonomy, 157, 175

bad, concept of, 8–10
Baron, Marcia, 186n7, 187n21
Benedict, Ruth, 59
Bentham, Jeremy, 103, 105–9, 111–13, 117, 121, 124, 128, 131, 137, 182
Bible, 25, 33
Bland, Tony, 65, 88
Blustein, Jeffrey, 229, 243n11
bold denial strategy, 137
Brandt, Richard, B., 50, 54
Brink, David O., 144–49, 150n6
Brown, H. I., 209n10

Buchanan, Alan, 101n14
Buddha, 211

care: caring about, 227–28; contrasted with justice, 225–26; personal versus impersonal, 227; types of, 225–26; virtue of, 227–28
care ethics, 224–32; objections to, 229–32; theory of right conduct, 228; as a version of moral pluralism, 231
casuistry, 162
Categorical Imperative,156–58; as a decision procedure, 164, 171, 181; Humanity formulation of, 157, 163, 171, 203, 233; justification of, 181; as a moral criterion, 164, 171, 181; tests associated with, 166–71; Universal Law formulation of, 163–75, 234. *See also* contradiction in conception test; contradiction in the will test
categorical imperatives, 153, 156
commensurability of values, 77, 108. *See also* incommensurability of values
conflict of duty situations, 74–75, 96–97, 183–84, 189, 191–92, 197. *See also* moral disagreements
Conly, Sarah, 243n23, 243n25
consequences, actual versus probable, 122–26. *See also* utilitarianism

promising case, 133–34
punishment case, 131–32
Putnam, Hilary, 209n10, 240–41

Rawls, John, 150n5, 150n7, 269
reason (rationality): practical, 71–72,
    152–55, 216; theoretical (specula-
    tive), 71–72, 152, 216
reciprocity of the virtues thesis,
    218–20
refraining from helping others case,
    169–70
regret, 261–62
relevance, moral: atomism, 252–53;
    holism, 253. *See also* morally rele-
    vant features
remote effects, 137–38
respect for persons (humanity),
    144–45, 149, 182, 203–4
reversal, 251
right, concept of, 8; objective versus
    subjective, 126
right conduct, theory of, 11–12
Roche, Tim, 242n5
Ross, W. D., 97, 146, 185, 231–34,
    242n4, 242n9, 248–49, 254–57,
    261, 265n1, 268–69. *See also* moral
    pluralism
rules. *See* moral rules

Sartre, Jean-Paul, 189, 209n1
Scheffler, Samuel, 101n16
self-defense cases, 74–76, 84–85,
    100n13
self-evident propositions, 71–72, 195
self-perfection, duties of, 159–60
separateness of persons objection,
    148–49
shape (and shapelessness), 248, 252
Sidgwick, Henry, 213
silencing, 252
Singer, Peter, 101n15
single-virtue thesis, 219–20
Smith, Michael, 266n1
sociability (as a basic value), 71–73
Socrates, 27–28, 211, 219
Stocker, Michael, 187n19

suicide, 1–3, 72, 100n5
Sumner, L. W., 98, 150n4
Sumner, William G., 40, 62n3
supererogation objection, 135–36
supererogatory, category of, 135
Swinburne, R. G., 35n7

Ten Commandments, 21n3, 25
Timmons, Mark, 21n7, 187n8, 266n10
tolerance. *See* moral relativism
Tronto, Joan, 243n11

unconnected-heap problem, 203–4
unity of the virtues thesis. *See* reci-
    procity of the virtues thesis; single-
    virtue thesis
unity thesis, 247–48, 252
universalist (moral theory), 104–5, 134
universality thesis, 41
universalizability, 166
universal law formulation of the Cate-
    gorical Imperative. *See* Categorical
    Imperative
universal relevance thesis, 248, 252
utilitarianism: actual consequence ver-
    sion of, 123–24, 128; act versus rule
    versions of, 138; characterized,
    104–5; contrasted with virtue
    ethics, 233–34; desire fulfillment
    versions of, 143–44; evaluation of,
    147–48; as a form of generalism,
    246–48; generic principle of, 106,
    143; hedonistic version of, 106–7;
    and limited moral pluralism,
    146–47; nonhedonistic versions of,
    142–44; pluralist version of,
    144–47; practical objections to,
    121–27; probable consequence ver-
    sion of, 123–24, 128; and rules,
    127–8, 138–42; rule versions of,
    138–42, 170; theoretical objections
    to, 131–36; theory of right con-
    duct, 105–6; and two levels of
    moral thinking, 126–28
utility: acceptance utility, 139; actual
    versus expected, 123–26; concep-
    tion of, 105; conformance utility,

About the Author

Mark Timmons is professor of philosophy at the University of Memphis. He has published extensively on topics in moral theory, metaethics, Kant's ethics, and epistemology. Along with Walter Sinnott-Armstrong, he is co-editor of *Moral Knowledge? New Essays in Moral Epistemology* (1996). He is author of *Morality without Foundations: A Defense of Ethical Contextualism* (1999) and editor of *Kant's* Metaphysics of Morals: *Interpretative Essays* (2002).